STUDIES IN ECONOMICS
Edited by Charles Carter
Vice Chancellor, University of Lancaster

12

Rich and Poor
Countries

STUDIES IN ECONOMICS

Rich and Poor Countries

BY

HANS W. SINGER

Institute of Development Studies, University of Sussex

AND

JAVED A. ANSARI

City University, London,
and Institute for the Study of International Organisation,
University of Sussex

London

GEORGE ALLEN & UNWIN LTD

RUSKIN HOUSE   MUSEUM STREET

First published in 1977

© George Allen & Unwin (Publishers) Ltd, 1977

ISBN 0 04 330274 2 hardback
0 04 330275 0 paperback

Printed in Great Britain
in 10pt Times Roman Type
by Biddles Ltd, Guildford, Surrey

To our parents
Dr Henrick and Antonia Singer
and
Humayun and Tahera Ansari

PREFACE

Events move fast these days as far as relations between rich and poor countries are concerned. Almost every day presents new developments in the clamour of the poor countries for a 'New International Economic Order', and in the more or less reluctant reaction of the rich countries in the face of such pressures. The dramatic success of the Organisation of Petroleum Exporting Countries (OPEC) has resulted in a major shift of economic power and has created an entirely new set of economic relations.

This book was largely drafted and written before the impact of these new developments was fully felt. While no book on this subject can be up-to-date in the light of a rapidly changing situation, this book deals with some of the fundamental aspects of the relationship between rich and poor countries as they will continue to govern economic relations with the poorer non-OPEC countries (which, after all, contain a very high proportion of the people of the old Third World and, indeed, of mankind as a whole).

Another limitation of this book which must be borne in mind is that it has been written specifically to be useful to the general reader as well as to second- and third-year undergraduates. For that reason no highly technical or theoretical discussions should be expected. We have tried in this book to combine a certain modest measure of elementary theory with some discussion of policy problems which are of importance in the actual empirical relations between rich and poor countries.

There are many people to whom we owe thanks for their advice and comments on various sections and drafts. Above all, we thank Professor Charles Carter, the editor of this series, and Mr C. Furth of Allen & Unwin, for the patience with which they acted as mid-wives at this difficult birth. Our thanks are also due to Professor C. D. Harbury of the City University, London, for constant help and encouragement. An important contribution was made by Caroline Miles in relation to the chapter on Adjustment Assistance, in which field her knowledge is well known. We are also grateful to Mr Frank Ellis and Miss Lyn Reynolds of the Institute of Development Studies, Mr John Salter of Queen Mary College, University of London, and Miss Elizabeth Westhead for valuable comments, and to Margot Cameron, Mary Keane, Marita Caffrey and Abdul Latif for their patient typing and retyping.

CONTENTS

11

PART ONE

PERSPECTIVES

CHAPTER 1

Introduction: The Current Economic Crisis and the Developing World

The current world economic crisis is a central concern of all students of economics today, and especially of those studying development problems. Theorists investigate the flaws in our approaches and institutions which gave birth to this present crisis. Policy makers query the institutions and the rules which governed and shaped economic life in the post-Second World War era. The common man seeks an insight into the working of the national and the international economy in order to understand the implications of this chaos.

An alarming aspect of this concern is the introversion and short-sightedness of many of the solutions and schemes which are now put forward to overcome the impending catastrophe. The crisis is con-ceived of as being precipitated by events regarded as external to the Western economic system – the rise in the prices of some primary commodities, exceptional droughts, the Arab-Israeli war of 1973, etc. – and solutions are devised which seek to insulate the Western world from such developments in the future. National energy policies are devised with the explicit objective of attaining national self-sufficiency. International economic organisations create elaborate mechanisms for the recycling of oil revenues back to the Western financial centres. 'Beggar thy neighbour' trade policies are seen as realistic alternatives.

Yet such policies are by their nature self-defeating, or at best of a stop-gap nature. They cannot in the long run succeed in achieving even the avowed objective of maintaining a high level of living for the people of the Western world, because these policies choose to ignore the fundamental causes of the current economic crisis. As long as these basic causes of international economic imbalances are not recognised the crisis will continue to feed upon itself. Although we may succeed in devising policies that may give us a temporary respite, the havoc brought by the crisis will first endanger and eventually destroy the economic order which was erected in the late 1940s (the 'Bretton Woods/UN system'), and the economic prosperity enjoyed by the West in the last thirty years or so will indeed become a thing of the past.

That the economic order devised at Bretton Woods is out of date and largely unserviceable today, is no longer a matter of debate. What is at issue is the sort of change and reform that is essential for economic prosperity to become a realisable objective for the people of all parts of the world. Perhaps the most significant deficiency of the modern international economic order is its manifest inability to spread wide the fruits of growth and prosperity. Table 1.1[1] describes the structure of the world economy in 1971.

Table 1.1   *World Economic Structure, 1971*

	Population (millions)	Per capita GNP[b] ($)	Growth rate of per capita GNP[c] (%)	Liter- acy[k] (%)	Per capita energy consump- tion[d] (kg)	Total Reserves[f] ($ million)	Popula- tion as a % of world popula- tion[a]
Poorest 40 countries	1,005·9	96	1·3	20·5	65	129[e]	26
Other LDCs	1,408·5	501	2·5	52·7	894	783[g]	37
OPEC countries[j]	257·6	1,143	5·4	31·6	1,415	1,232[h]	7
Developed countries	1,082·0	2,297	4·6	90·7	4,028	5,301[i]	28

[a] Figures do not equal 100% because of rounding.
[b] Average, 1971.
[c] Average, 1965–71.
[d] Average, 1971.
[e] Information available for only 26 countries in this category.
[f] Average, mid-1973
[g] Information available for only 41 countries in this category.
[h] Information not available for Abu Dhabi and Qatar.
[i] Information for Eastern European countries and the USSR not available.
[j] Abu Dhabi, Algeria, Ecudor, Indonesia, Iran, Iraq, Kuwait, Libya, Nigeria, Qatar, Saudi Arabia, Venezuela. (Gabon is an associated member of OPEC.)
[k] 1971.

Sources:
1 *Atlas, 1974* (Washington, IBRD Group, 1974).
2 *Statistical Yearbook, 1972* (New York, UN, 1973).
3 J. W. Howe (ed.), *The United States and the Developing Countries* (New York, Praeger, 1974).

From this table we see that the global pattern of production and consumption is marked by a high degree of inequality. The lowest-income countries, containing 26 per cent of the world's total population, have a per capita gross national produce (GNP) which is *only 4 per cent* of the per captia GNP of the developed countries, containing an approximately equal proportion of the world's population. Never before in human history has economic inequality reached such proportions.[2] Moreover, we also see that for the period covered by Table 1.1 the growth rate of the developed countries is three and a half times greater than the growth rate of the poorest countries, and almost twice as high as the growth rate of all the other less developed countries (LDCs) taken together. There is thus clear evidence that even the relative distance – let alone the actual distance – between the rich and poor countries widened during the later part of the First UN Development Decade (1960–70) – a period in which the world community had implicitly undertaken the responsibility of bridging the economic gap between the nations.

The difference in the material condition of people living in various parts of the world is reflected most graphically in two socio-economic indicators: the rate of national literacy, and the per capita energy consumption rate. Together these two indices provide a telling measure of the sophistication of the production structure of a nation, and they are much more significant than indicators based on the sectoral origin of gross domestic product (GDP).[3] Literacy in the developing countries is considerably lower than in the rich nations, as is per capita energy consumption. This structural characteristic of the economy reflects the inability of the poorer countries to exploit their economic potential. Whereas the rich countries are capable of using their economic resources in a way which maximises productivity in the long run, the developing countries are forced to tolerate the existence of disguised unemployment of labour and underutilisation of capital. They are faced with the challenge of devising or adapting a technology which can lead them to the realisation of their economic potential. Their basic motivation as participants in the international economy is reflected in their desire to obtain support for development policies which aim at bridging the technological gap – as measured by differences in literacy and energy consumption rates – between the 'have' and the 'have not' nations of the world.

To be sure, the developing world is not without cleavages. As Table 1.1 illustrates, there are significant differences in the economic structure of the various segments of the 'Third' World. At one extreme there are the forty or so hard-core poorest of the developing countries with income per capita around the $100 benchmark and imperceptible growth rates. At the other extreme are the OPEC countries with income eleven times and growth rates four times as high as the former, even before the oil price rises of 1973.[4] Yet despite this structural difference, and despite the consequent differences in the requirements and needs of the various countries, the Third World has maintained a united posture in international economic forums.

This unity reflects the essentially unchanged nature of the relationship between the rich and poor countries despite the events of the past few years. The dramatic increases in oil prices since October 1973 and the similar rise in the price of some other primary commodities have led a number of analysts to believe that the resource-rich developing countries have succeeded in achieving a breakthrough which has fundamentally altered their position within the world economy. This belief was reflected in the resolution calling for the implementation of a New International Economic Order adopted by a Special Session of the UN General Assembly in April 1974. But, though the oil crisis as well as shortages did emphasise the importance of the poor countries within the international economy, there was at that time no clear evidence of any desire to countenance a restructuring which would *permanently and irrevocably* alter the position of the developing world within international commodity, factor and money markets. The poor countries were convinced, however, that the rise in the price of oil and other commodities represented an opportunity for just such a restructuring. The handling of the energy shortages, the evolution of the food crisis, and the international trade negotiations of the General Agreement on Tariffs and Trade (GATT) have subsequently depicted a protracted conflict between the rich and the developing countries – the former attempting to retain their position of supremacy in the international economy, the latter making a bid for a decisive share in the management of world trade and finance. Moreover, the unity of the Third World (as also that of developed countries) is itself threatened by these events, for despite the public statements and resolutions in the United Nations the fact is that the position of the resource-rich developing countries within the world economy is today vastly different from that of the rest of the Third World. Hence there exists a potential for conflict within the hitherto ostensibly united Third World. The oil crisis in particular provides an apt illustration of the difference in approach and in objectives pursued by the 'have' and 'have not' countries in the last quarter of the twentieth century.

18

Introduction: The Current Economic Crisis

1.1 The Oil Crisis: Genesis and Evolution

The energy crisis did not erupt suddenly in October 1973. The world had slowly been moving towards a situation where a shortage of energy (and some other) resources would become a dominant constraint on the growth of the international economy. The basic feature of the real energy crisis is that, if present consumption trends persist, world energy demand will have doubled by the mid 1980s and the dependence of the major consumers of energy (the industrial countries) on the energy producers (the OPEC countries) will have increased substantially. The OPEC countries[5] are in a strong position today because oil is the cheapest energy resource available and because the development of substitutes (even of offshore oil) is a costly business. The rise in the price of oil since late 1973 has seemed so stupendous largely because oil prices had until then been particularly depressed since the Second World War. The oil companies which were both producing and exporting crude petroleum were large multinational enterprises. They were able to keep payments to the supply countries low and also to reduce their cost of production because of the existence of substantial economies of scale. Moreover, competition between the old and new international companies for the Western European market provided further incentives for keeping prices low. By the late 1960s, due to these low prices, oil had replaced a number of traditional solid energy fuels (particularly coal) as the major energy source in most Western countries. The United States had also emerged as a very large importer of oil, having reversed its earlier policy of restricting oil imports, and Japan's demand for oil had also risen substantially.[6] Thus the oil market rapidly became a suppliers' market and

'well before 1973 it had become clear that the countries of Western Europe, the United States and Japan would not be able to go on drawing from the Middle East as much oil as they needed. For it was evident that the oil producers were able and apparently preferred to restrict the rate at which oil production could grow. It was plain that the price of Middle East oil could rise at least to the level of alternatives produced elsewhere.'[7]

The decision of the oil-producing countries to raise the price of oil brings sharply into focus the fact that industrial growth and expansion in the West is not seen as beneficial by these developing countries. Will these countries 'continue to produce oil simply because the industrial countries need it'?[8] Clearly, some incentives are needed in order to obtain their co-operation in ensuring a continued expansion of world production.

The industrial countries are conscious of the need for the provision of incentives, but unfortunately the incentives that are offered are not in any sense sufficient from the point of view of the developing world taken as a whole. The rich countries are concerned, at least in the short run, primarily about the implications of the oil price rise on their own balance of payments. The increased cost of oil imports has already converted the surplus on the current account of their balance of payments into a substantial deficit. The developed countries are interested in reducing the size of this deficit, and in compensating for it by creating a surplus on their balance-of-payments capital account by inducing the OPEC countries to invest (recycle) their oil receipts into the Western world.

The United States and France have evolved different policies to deal with the oil crisis with these objectives in view. The United States believes that the new-found unity of the OPEC countries can be eroded and consequently that the price of oil can be brought down to 'realistic' levels and the supply of oil expanded. The United States insists on unity among the developed countries as a precondition for putting pressure on the OPEC countries. The United States's proposals have been aptly described as

'a programme of action designed to get power back to where it was thought properly to belong, that is with the Atlantic powers and Japan. The United States proposal for a continuing dialogue between rich oil consuming nations and the oil producers – seemed, at worst, to be an afterthought and at best an indication of a willingness to talk about the implementation of an already determined strategy.'[9]

Against this, France, and a number of other European countries including the United Kingdom, argue that little can be gained by appealing to the better nature of the OPEC countries or by threatening them with schemes for the rapid development of alternative energy sources in the West. Instead, France seeks to formulate 'special' bilateral arrangements with individual OPEC countries in order to ensure a regular supply of oil in the medium run. Neither of these two approaches can claim to have been particularly successful. OPEC maintains its unity, and it insists on its right to take control of the oil companies. Moreover, the price of crude oil has continued to rise.

The OPEC nations themselves have on the other hand indicated that they view the oil crisis as part of a general crisis of the international economy. It was at the initiative of the Algerian[10] President that the Special Session of the UN General Assembly was convened, and the OPEC nations supported the resolutions calling for the setting up of the New International Economic Order, though the extent to which the oil-rich countries are in fact prepared to translate the resolutions of the Special Sessions into concrete policies remains very much an open question. It is certainly appropriate that the oil crisis is seen not merely as something affecting the relationship between the 'old rich' and the 'new rich', but rather as something which has to be tackled within a truly international perspective in a manner which allows us to transcend the limits on world development imposed by the international trade and finance system that has existed since Bretton Woods.

A fundamental characteristic of this system is that it concentrates economic power in the hands of a few nations which, because of their economic strength, are capable of adjusting to the impact of disequilibria and imbalances in world markets with a minimum of friction and cost. The process of adjustment is much more painful to the weaker countries. The oil crisis illustrates graphically the difference in the effect on the economies of the rich and poor countries of the jump in energy prices. As far as the non-oil-exporting developing countries are concerned, particularly the least developed countries, these price increases will considerably aggravate the problems of unemployment and mass poverty. The increase in the price of oil has meant that the non-OPEC developing countries will have to spend over 20 per cent of their total export earnings on oil imports in the next five years. Moreover, the rise in oil prices has been accompanied by increases in the price of wheat[11] and fertilisers in particular, as well as of a number of other primary commodities. The combined effect of these price increases has been to raise the import bill for the non-OPEC developing countries by $15,000 million. 'The combined price increases are equivalent in amount to nearly five times the total of net US development assistance in 1972 and well above the $9 billion for all development assistance from industrial countries that year.'[12] To this must be added the higher prices of manufactures due to inflation in the developed countries, itself fed by the rise in the prices of oil and food.

The developing (non-OPEC) countries will be more severely affected by the rises in petroleum prices than the rich industrial nations. Table 1.2 illustrates that the current account deficit of the developed countries is higher than that of the non-OPEC developing countries – but because of the considerably lower export earnings of the non-OPEC LDCs, the relative impact of increased petroleum

21

Table 1.2   *Balance of Payments on Current Account and Annual Exports Compared ($'000 millions).*

| | Balance of payments on current account | | | Annual average exports[a] |
	1972	1973	1974	1965–72
OPEC countries	1·6	6·1	66	10·4
Industrial countries	15·6	7·9	−38	245·7
Primary-producing countries	−7·5	−9·0	−31	42·3
More developed	1·4	1·7	−5	
Less developed	−8·9	−10·8	−26	
World	3·5	8·3	−3	298·2

[a] Export earnings of Middle East countries, 1967–72.

Source: J. W. Howe (ed.), *The United States and the Developing Countries* (New York, Praeger, 1974), p. 35.

prices is more serious for them than for the developed countries. The impact is less severe for the industrialising intermediate developing countries (e.g. Brazil, South Korea and Turkey) and acute for the really poor countries (e.g. Chad, Tanzania and Bangladesh).

Moreover, it has been estimated that the OPEC countries are unlikely to be able to spend more than half of their export earnings on imports of goods and services for the development of their economies. The rest of their surplus (about another $30,000 million for the year 1974 and higher amounts subsequently) will be reinvested in Western financial markets. The OPEC countries will thus in effect transfer their surplus earnings from the poor countries to the capital markets of the rich industrial nations, this action being in sharp contrast to their avowed intentions expressed in UN forums. The recycling schemes being designed in the West may thus accentuate the antidevelopment effects of the energy crisis by increasing incentives for the investment of oil income in the industrial countries. Such a scheme is bound to transfer resources from the non-OPEC developing countries at a time when they are specially hard hit, and will inevitably force them to cut back development imports and réduce the overall development effort.

In order to reduce the injustice done to the poor countries, short-run or half-hearted measures are clearly insufficient. The suggestion that the OPEC countries should themselves provide the poor nations with the means to tide over the crisis makes sense only if the energy crisis is placed in the perspective of the general rise in the prices of all goods, both primary and industrial. The world until recently has been in the grip of an inflation which threatened to put an abrupt end to economic expansion. As far as the poor countries are concerned, world inflation has been a mixed blessing. The prices of some of their most important export commodities have risen, but so have the prices of manufactures, food, fertiliser and oil. As far as the vast majority of the people in the developing countries are concerned, there can be little doubt that the overall effect has been negative. It is for this reason that they now insist more than ever on a fundamental restructuring of international economic relations.

1.2 COMMODITY TRADE AND THE FOOD CRISIS

Table 1.3 summarises changes in the prices of commodities since 1950. The poor countries account for well over half the volume of world primary commodity trade, so that fluctuations in commodity prices are of great importance to them. Table 1.3 shows that, over the period 1950–73, the average terms of trade between primary

Table 1.3   *Commodity Terms of Trade,[a] 1950–73*

	1950–3 (1950 = 100)	1970–3 (1970 = 100)
Primary commodities	−2·4	46·3
Non-food agricultural raw material	−17·6	45.5
Mineral raw material	29·5	53·6
(Fuels)	(33·4)[b]	(68·2)[b]
Non-ferrous base metals	42·9	−0·1

[a] Percentage change of basic commodity price in relation to unit value of export of manufactures.
[b] Before October 1973.
Source: David Coetzee, 'Raw Materials Roundabout', *African Development* (July 1974), pp. 13, 14.

commodities and manufactured commodities remained almost unchanged. Despite the very considerable upsurge in commodity prices since 1970, the developing countries were by 1973 as important suppliers of primary commodities in no better position *vis-à-vis* the industrial countries than they were in the early 1950s. Throughout that decade and the 1960s, commodity prices declined. The primary commodity price index fell by 27 per cent during the 1950s and by 9 per cent during the 1960s. Moreover, the rise in the early 1970s was feared to be merely transient in character. It was caused primarily by the expanding demand for raw materials which responded to world inflationary pressures. As the expansionary process wore itself out commodity prices were bound to fall, and the poor countries felt that in order to consolidate the gains of the early 1970s it was essential to reorganise international commodity trade in a way that would stabilise commodity prices over the long run.

The rise in commodity prices was of course not of equal benefit to all developing countries. Nor was it beneficial only to developing countries. The United States was the principal beneficiary of the rise in the price of wheat, rice, cotton and soya beans. Among the developing countries, the relatively better off ones gained more than the least developed. For example, the OPEC countries gained from the increase in the price of oil; Malaysia benefited from the increase in the price of rubber, palm oil and tin; and Chile and Zambia gained from the price increase of copper. However, the net gain to any individual non-OPEC developing country of the rise in commodity prices was likely to be small, as the increase in the price of its exports was usually more or less offset by the rise in the prices of its imports.

The OPEC countries are of course the major exception, and they owe their success to the fact that since 1970 they have formed a highly effective producers' cartel which has maintained its unity while consumers of oil have become increasingly divided on their attitude towards the oil producers. Other attempts at setting up producer associations by the developing countries have not by any means been as successful as OPEC. The Copper Producers' Association (CIPEC) floundered after Allende's fall in Chile, and the bauxite association has also faced serious problems.

The poor countries have generally become aware of the problems of maintaining effective producers' associations. At the Special Session of the UN General Assembly in April 1974, the programme formulated by the developing countries did hint at the creation of producers' associations, but greater emphasis was placed on winning support for schemes which sought to link prices of raw materials to prices of industrial goods and of food ('indexation'). The developing countries were unanimous in their view that such a scheme alone could guarantee and safeguard the gains they had made since 1970. The industrial countries, on the other hand, showed little sympathy towards schemes which linked commodity and manufactures prices, and also were reluctant to commit themselves to policies which would affect their domestic agricultural sector.

This reluctance was also evident at the World Food Conference held in Rome in November 1974.[13] The Conference was convened to discuss the growing problem of food scarcity. The dimensions of the problem can be appreciated only when it is realised that death by starvation claimed the lives of no less than 100,000 people in Africa in 1973 and another 100,000 people in Bangladesh that year. Since 1951, food production in the developing countries has only barely kept pace with the growth in their population. The United Nations has estimated that, if present trends persist, by 1985 the total production of food by the developing countries will be 76 million tons less than the demand for food, if existing standards of living are to be maintained in these countries. Unless developed countries provide the 76 million tons of grain and enable developing countries to buy or obtain them, approximately 300 million people are threatened with starvation.

It is entirely within the technical capability of the international economy to bridge this 'hunger gap', but it requires a massive political and economic effort on the part of the world community. The developing countries need to reorientate their policies and accord primary importance to agriculture and rural development, and developed countries must demonstrate a willingness to transfer food resources, through trade or food aid, in quantities sufficient to meet the needs of the starving millions in Asia and Africa. At the Rome Conference two alternate proposals emerged. The plan put forward by the Secretariat envisaged greater financial assistance by the developed countries to promote self-sufficiency in food production in the Third World. The other plan, outlined by the US Secretary of State, Henry Kissinger, saw the hunger gap as being filled mainly by increased US agricultural production, which was to be sold to the needy countries. The money to finance such sales was to be provided by the OPEC countries 'as they had ample surplus funds', but was to be administered by committees in which the industrial nations exercised considerable influence. Obviously, these two plans could be complementary. There were also divergent views on such matters as food aid, food reserves, emergency aid, etc.

These divergencies were not bridged at Rome. The Conference decided to set up and maintain reserve stocks in a number of commodities and made a number of useful decisions, but action on the scale required to prevent the impending starvation catastrophe was not decisively taken. It is what Third World countries view as the inability of Western statesmen and also of OPEC countries to make more than token gestures, and their determination to safeguard their own national interest, while refusing to countenance real sacrifices even when faced with human suffering as colossal as that threatened by the food crisis, which increases the determination of these Third World countries to insist on no less than a 'New International Economic Order'.

1.3 A SUMMING UP

We have seen that the economic division of the world into the 'have' and the 'have not' nations shows no signs of being eroded. Indeed, the crisis originates from the existence of this division, but the efforts to grapple with the crisis have to date not shown real awareness of this fact. The Western countries seem bent on maintaining the essential structure of an international division of labour which favours them in a number of different ways, despite the obvious resistance on the part of the Third World to agree to schemes which do not alter the balance of international economic power to their advantage. The overriding concern of the Third World, of both its few new rich countries and its many poor countries, is the reorganisation of the international economy in a way which allows for the harnessing of international trade and finance in the interests of their own development. Such a reorganisation, the Third World recognises, is not possible merely on the basis of its new-found strength. The success achieved by the OPEC countries is something of a Pyrrhic victory. It does not represent a permanent reordering of international economic relationships. Most of the oil money benefits only a minority of developing countries, already relatively rich, and is being recycled into the metropolitan countries. The strong present bargaining position of the OPEC countries is being eroded by the rapid development of alternative energy sources. By the end of the century, perhaps a great deal earlier, the oil cartel may have been rendered innocuous, and it is an open question whether by that time the OPEC countries will have succeeded in using their revenue in a way which transforms the structure of their economies. In any case, this leaves the core of Third World poverty untouched.

The rest of the Third World has on the face of it little chance of following in the footsteps of the oil producers. With minor exceptions such as phosphates, producers of raw materials other than oil have found it impossible to organise cartels which impose their price on international markets. Moreover, the prices of most primary commodities have stabilised, and there are indications that they may well fall substantially. It is therefore reasonable to believe that the exercise of monopolistic power by Third World countries is not likely to be effective or widespread, and that unless negotiated and agreed changes in the international trade and financial system are instituted the overall bargaining power of the Third World countries is likely to remain weak in the years ahead. This is not in the best interests of mankind, nor in the real interest of the rich countries themselves.

But why are the Third World countries so much concerned with the international trading system? Is it not possible for them to formulate and implement development policies that are 'inward-looking' – i.e. that concentrate on bringing about domestic structural changes – without the stimulus of international trade or finance? In order to answer this question it is essential to describe the structure of the international economy and to understand the nature of the development process. Chapters 2 and 3 of this book deal with these questions. Chapter 4 discusses the importance of the international trade sector as an agent of development in the poorer countries. Chapters 5 and 6 review the trade policies of the rich and poor countries. Part Three then deals with the role of aid in the development process, and Part Four is concerned with international factor movements. We thus complete our review of the nature and form of the relationship of the rich and poor countries and of the sort of changes that are required if this relationship is to make a more effective contribution to the development of the poor countries.

NOTES

1 The terminology used in the book is derived from Table 1.1. By 'poor countries' is meant the 'poorest 40 countries in the world'. The terms 'developing countries' and 'Third World', used interchangeably, apply to the 'poorest countries' plus the 'other LDCs' plus the 'OPEC countries'; the latter are also referred to as the 'new rich'. The term 'developed countries' includes the Western countries and also the USSR and Eastern Europe. The book is primarily concerned with the relationship between the 'poor countries' and the 'rich Western countries'.

2 This point is developed in greater detail in Chapter 2.

3 Developed countries may or may not concentrate on the production of heavy manufactured goods, but they invariably have high literacy and energy consumption rates.

4 Some OPEC countries (e.g. Nigeria and Indonesia) have considerably lower per capita income and growth rates, however.

5 Abu Dhabi, Algeria, Equador, Gabon, Indonesia, Iran, Iraq, Kuwait, Libya, Nigeria, Qatar, Saudi Arabia and Venezuela.

6 For a review of the energy policies of the industrial countries see Peter Odell, *Oil and World Power* (Harmondsworth, Penguin, 1974).

7 MacFadzean, 'Economic Implications of the Energy Crisis' in Corbet and Jackson (eds), *In Search of a New World Economic Order* (London, Macmillan, 1974), pp. 120, 123.

8 ibid., p. 126.

9 Odell, op. cit., p. 178.

10 Algeria is a member of OPEC.

11 The developing countries are net importers of wheat.

12 J. W. Howe (ed.), *The United States and the Developing Countries* (New York, Praeger, 1974), p. 34.
13 For a discussion of the World Food Conference proposals and problems related to international food shortage see J. A. Ansari and C. Robins, *The Profits of Doom: An Investigation of the World Food Crisis* (London, War on Want, 1976).

CHAPTER 2

The International Economy

2.1 A WORLD VIEW OF THE DEVELOPMENT PROCESS

The problems of economic development[1] cannot be adequately analysed in the context of a closed economy model. This becomes clear
if an examination is made of the structure of an economy which is
in a process of development in the world of today. Typically, such
an economy is an importer of both capital and technology (as well
as consumption goods) from 'the rest of the world'. This imported
capital and technology play a crucially important part in its development. Domestic substitution for foreign capital and foreign technical
know-how is a very costly affair, often indeed impossible. This is
true whether we think of replication or genuine substitution allowing for the different needs of a poorer country. For most African,
Asian and Latin American countries (especially the smaller and
poorer ones) the external (export) sector is the leading sector – the
sector which sets the pace of development and shapes for the rest
of the economy both the pattern and pace of growth. Typically, size
by size, the poorer a country, the more dependent it is on foreign
markets and foreign sources of supply. If the external sector stag-
nates, so that the inflow of resources from abroad is constrained, the
pace of growth and rate of structural change are likely to be highly
sensitive to such a decline in the availability of foreign resources.
But there have been situations where the resulting shock and en-
forced readjustment have been beneficial; the forces involved are
political and social, not only economic. Economic planners are thus
compelled to give due weight to the problem of foreign resource inflows, in the form of export earnings, aid and foreign investment,
along with the problems of domestic resources mobilisation.

The terms on which the developing countries can obtain foreign
exchange, capital and technology reflect the relationship between the
rich and poor countries in the world economy. There are exceptions,
where the poorer countries command a strategic material or strategic
bases, or where they effectively co-operate with each other; the oil-
producing countries are a recent example. But, generally, in the face

of the existing distribution of economic power it is the rich countries which determine the terms, because in the short run the developing countries need the products and services of the developed countries much more than the latter need the output of the former. This imbalance of need is evident from the striking fact that the poor countries trade mainly with the rich countries, whereas the rich countries mainly trade among themselves. In 1972, the rich countries, with less than one-third of the world population, carried out 52·6 per cent of world trade between themselves; the poorer countries, with their much larger populations, carried out only 3·8 per cent so. Furthermore, the growth rate of exports of the developing countries has been strikingly lower than the corresponding rate for rich countries over the years since the war. As a result, the share of the developing countries in total world exports fell from 31·2 per cent in 1950 to 17·4 per cent in 1972, whereas the share of the Western developed countries rose from 60 per cent to 72·3 per cent over the same period.[2] The decline of the share of developing countries in total world trade may be a major factor in the rise of unemployment and unequal income distribution observed in these countries.

In the international commodity and factor markets the poor countries are mainly price takers, and also 'takers' until very recently in trade negotiations and trade policy formulation. This dependence of the developing countries on the industrial countries has far-reaching consequences for the development prospects of the former. It also poses a challenge to the rich nations in that, although such dependence may be a short-run advantage to them, even their own long-term economic interests point in the direction of reducing the gap. They are thus faced with a choice which is both economic and moral. The large and increasing gap between the rich and poor nations can be reduced only if sustained and co-ordinated efforts on the part of both are forthcoming. The existence of such great disparities and one-sided dependence is surely unjustifiable on moral grounds. The 'welfare state' has now become an established goal for most national economic planners or policy makers in Western countries, and strong case can be made for an extension of this concept to the international economy. The mitigation of economic inequalities between the citizens of different countries should, surely, rank high on any action agenda by the international community. On economic grounds, too, there exist strong arguments for undertaking a comprehensive international programme for a broad preferential treatment of the LDCs. In the long run the world economy cannot expand rapidly if over two-thirds of the world's population live in abject poverty and misery (and four-fifths of the world's children –

the citizens and producers of tomorrow!). The long-term prosperity of the rich 'north' depends to a great extent on its own ability and willingness to share its advantages with the deprived 'south'. If this does not happen the economic, political and social tensions that are building up in the poorer parts of the world threaten the stability, indeed the very existence, of the world order which has made the progress and prosperity of the richer countries possible. It is imperative, therefore, that we think and plan for development in an international perspective, and that we realise the interdependence of the world's constituent units.

2.2 STRUCTURAL CHANGE IN THE WORLD ECONOMY

The lopsided interdependence of nations is of comparatively recent origin. The fact that it has gained such importance is due to a number of technological as well as social factors. As long as the economic structure and economic performance of different countries (or groups of countries) were not too dissimilar, a situation could be visualised where economic independence was a meaningful concept. It was only when the gap between the rich and poor countries widened significantly and progressively that the external sector gained the importance pointed out in section 2.1, deriving from the fact that the rich countries are in a position to export goods and factors (especially technology) which are vitally necessary for the economic development of the poor countries and which are not substitutable by their domestic production. It is the existence of a wide gap between the two types of countries which determines their relations and which makes the system so interdependent that it is unrealistic, even impossible, to consider the development of the poorer and more dependent units separately from the effects of their coexistence with the richer and more powerful countries.

It is worth looking a little more closely at the more important structural changes that have taken place in the international economy. This can serve a dual purpose. On the one hand, it can provide us with a better perspective for analysing the impact of various policy measures on the development of the world economy; on the other, it can help us to understand the *nature* of the dependence of the different economic units on each other. We will then be in a position to identify the important areas of action and cooperation between the rich and poor countries and to focus attention on those policies which can bring about a significant reduction of international economic inequalities. It will then become clear that it is not merely the *quantum* of resource flows from the developed to

31

the underdeveloped countries that is important. The *type* of resources that are transferred, as well as the *terms* on which they are transferred, are of equal importance.

The resources and needs of the poor countries are determined essentially by the structural imbalances of the world economy. Up to about 1850, the world economy could be described as largely stationary or stagnant, by almost any standards. Real elements of growth could be discerned only in Britain, and a few rudiments elsewhere. It has been estimated that total output grew at about 0·1 per cent per annum, and per capita output at about 0·09 per cent per annum, in the period AD 1 to AD 1850.[3] However, the level and process of growth were by no means stable. There were wide fluctuations over different periods, but a consistent trend could just be discerned.

In the last 125 years the situation has changed radically for those countries which today are classified as rich. Their population has increased about three times, whereas their total output has increased almost twenty-five times; their rate of growth of output has risen to about 5 per cent per annum;[4] and their average level of per capita income has increased from about £150 per annum to over £1,000 per annum (in 1954 prices). It is important to note that the growth of population absorbs only a minor share of the increase in the production of the rich countries.

The structure of the economies of the rich countries has also changed significantly over the last 125 years. Before, nearly all countries produced more than half of their total output in the form of agricultural goods; now the share of agriculture in the total product of the rich countries is less than 10 per cent. But this has been consistent with big, indeed unprecedented, absolute increases in agricultural output. Whereas agricultural output has grown four or five times over this period in these countries, industrial output has grown to over forty times its original level. Within industrial output, the rate of growth of capital goods (as distinct from consumer goods) industries is even more spectacular; consumer goods production has grown twenty times over the last century, but capital goods production has grown phenomenally to more than 100 times its original level.

This big change in economic structure reflects a tremendous increase in the technological sophistication of the production mechanism in the rich countries. This becomes clear if their trade patterns are examined. When a rich country of today started its process of development it was an exporter of an agriculture-based product which had been processed, if at all, by simple and crude techniques;

32

e.g. Britain exported textiles, Sweden exported timber and Canada exported wheat. As the process of development continued, export lines, like product lines, were shifted; e.g. Britain changed from exporting wool and cloth to exporting transport equipment, mechanical goods, electrical supplies, etc. In other words, the change of the technology of production manifested itself in the foreign trade structure of the countries concerned.

The then late-developer countries, e.g. Germany, Japan and Russia, found it possible to adopt and adapt the technology that had been developed by the countries which preceded them. Indeed, the fact that the latecomers could leap over the intermediate stages and adopt the most efficient (existing) technology made their rate of growth higher than the rate of growth of the older-rich countries. No wonder economists firmly believed that the accumulation of scientific and technological knowledge would make development progressively easier and ultimately bring a golden age of worldwide development.

The transfer of technology from the old to the new growing countries in the nineteenth century – both groups now included in the rich countries – took place through the agency of a local entrepreneurial class which borrowed both capital and technology from the established industrial and financial centres but which by and large confined its production activities to one national state (and perhaps its colonies). Today's giant production unit, the multinational corporation, has attained its predominant position comparatively recently. Each national entrepreneurial class found it fairly easy to learn the production techniques from elsewhere and to adapt them to its own environment. This was so for three reasons: (a) entrepreneurial ability existed in similar degrees in the then new-rich countries; (b) the technology was not too different from the familiar traditional one; and (c) the environment to which the technologies had to be adapted were also only moderately different. These new entrepreneurial classes were usually nationalist in their interests and outlook.[5]

In sharp contrast to the experience of the rich countries, the countries now euphemistically classified as 'developing' – OPEC apart – have not grown at a significant rate during the same period of 125 years, except perhaps in the last quarter-century. Aggregate output has no doubt risen, but this has been largely matched by the increased rate of growth in the population, so that output, and income, per capita have remained little changed. Whereas the rich countries had a standard-of-living explosion, the poor countries had a population explosion. There have of course been exceptional years and countries where growth has been high, but even where *per capita* growth has been substantial it has often been of an unbalanced nature and has not really reduced the incidence and extent of poverty – for reasons which are by no means accidental. Even if the post-war period should represent a turning point – and it is too early yet to say – the growth in standards of living has remained modest, and the number of the poor and unemployed has increased rather than diminished, as was the case in the long-run development of the richer countries.

The recent rise in the income of the OPEC countries is clearly an event which cannot be compared with that which resulted from the early industrialisation of Germany or Japan. This increase in income has not been occasioned by the emergence of a private or state entrepreneurial class which has opened up its country and enhanced productivity levels. On quite the contrary, the ruling elite of the OPEC countries want to use the opportunity offered by rising oil prices to raise aggregate productivity. The increase in income *precedes*, in other words, the increase in factor productivity, and whether or not self-sustaining development occurs in even these economies of the Third World is still an open question, to be determined by the terms on which the West will permit them to transfer technology and by the degree in which the higher productivity is fed back into the various sectors of the economy and spreads among the general population.

The extent to which the gap between the rich and poor countries has widened can be realised from the following figures. In 1850, today's rich countries accounted for 26 per cent of the total population of the world and for about 35 per cent of its total income. In the 1960s the rich countries accounted for 28 per cent of the population (not much changed from 1850) but 78 per cent of the total income. The difference between the per capita incomes of the poor and rich countries increased from 70 per cent in 1850 to 900 per cent in 1960.

Moreover, the *pattern* of inequality is more important than its *quantum*. US per capita production in agriculture (taken per capita of the whole population) is twice as high as that of India, but US per capita output in industry is twenty-five to thirty times as high, and US per capita output of services is thirteen times as high. This brings to light two important facts. First of all, the absolute level of *present* inequality between the rich and poor countries is certainly not of unmanageable proportions, at least if we can afford to take a philosophical long-run view. If the poor countries were to grow at an average yearly rate of 5 per cent per capita for the next half-century, they could statistically attain the *present* output and income level of the rich countries.[6] Of course, to grow by 5 per cent per capita yearly for fifty years would be by no means an easy task if only because of population expansion, especially in the large poor countries such as India, Bangladesh and Pakistan. However, it is in no sense an inconceivable task, given the resources of the international economy and provided the full power of science and technology and other efforts are concentrated on this as a world priority objective.

The second important fact is that the poverty of the Third World countries reflects essentially the technological[7] gap between them and the rich countries. Even the oil-rich countries are no exceptions in this regard. This results in the developing countries, inability to produce by themselves goods which require modern technical know-how as an important input and, even less, to develop an autonomous alternative technology to substitute. The trade patterns of the developing countries show that they usually export crude or processed, agriculture- or mineral-based products. These countries have not succeeded in adapting or replicating for their own conditions the technological developments that have occurred in the rich countries. Although this monopoly of new knowledge cannot be strictly measured, since the *output* cannot be directly measured, the *input* – research and development expenditures – can be measured, and by that measure the rich countries account for 98–9 per cent of the world figure.

The international economy has evolved at a rapid rate over the course of the last century. This accelerated expansion has been limited to certain regions of the world, and this limitation has given rise to an imbalance in the standard of living of the different regions. The rest of this book aims at discussing some ways in which we should move if the worst effects of this imbalance are to be corrected.

2.3   THE POOR COUNTRIES' HANDICAP : TECHNOLOGY – THE CORE OF THE PROBLEM

It is the central thesis of this book that the imbalance between the rich and poor countries cannot be corrected by means of an automatic, self-operating mechanism. Specific policy measures will have to be adopted by both the rich and developing countries if the latter are to experience those structural changes which are necessary for sustained economic growth. The cliché that 'each country has the primary responsibility for its own development' is a half-truth. The statement that we are 'all members one of another' comes nearer the truth, as the world economy forms an interdependent system.

RICH AND POOR COUNTRIES

The poor countries will have to enter into an economic relationship with the rich countries; indeed, they are already deeply intertwined with them now, since both possess essential resources which the other group needs. It has been maintained by a number of economists since the late 1940s that there is a tendency for the rich countries to gain from *any* economic dealings (whether in the form of trade, transfer of technology, or investment) which they have with the poor countries.[8] Already in 1949 and 1950 the view was being put forward that the gains from international trade and investment accrued mainly to the rich countries.[9] The reason for this was seen in the fact that the rich countries produced and exported industrial commodities, whereas the poor countries specialised in primary goods. The terms of trade tended to move against the primary goods producers, and technological progress also tended to work to their disadvantage. Hence industrialisation was seen as the great panacea. The dynamic effects of industrialisation, it was maintained, would overcome any 'enclave' associated with foreign investment. Today it has to be admitted that industrialisation, even import-substituting industrialisation specifically geared to the home market, has not generated self-perpetuating growth in the poor countries. It does not lead by itself to a full transplantation and subsequent indigenous development of an effective technology, as happened for example when Japan first adopted and adapted the technology of Western Europe. Industrialisation, *per se*, does not reduce the dependence of the poor countries on the rich – in some ways it adds to it – and hence does not bridge the fundamental gap between the two.

As industrialisation proceeds in a typical 'poor country', import substitution becomes more and more difficult, for the import-substituting industries are themselves import-dependent. Hence the essential difference between the rich and poor countries is not that they produce different types of commodities, as both Prebisch and Singer initially assumed. The fact that they do, in general, produce a different 'mix' of goods is merely a symptom, or indicator, of a more fundamental difference in the structure of these two types of economies. Indeed, it has been shown that the deterioration of the terms of trade of primary products in relation to manufactured commodities really concealed, during the 1950s and 1960s, a deterioration of the terms of trade of the poor countries in all their dealings with the rich countries. Clearly, the latter relationship between types of *countries* is more significant than the former relationship between types of *products*.

Any increase in the price of the exports of the developing countries which does not translate itself into an increase in the average labour productivity of the developing country (i.e. an increase in the technological sophistication of its production structure) will inevitably be eroded by the greater adaptability of the rich countries, which by developing substitutes for the scarce or expensive Third World export reassert their position of strength in the world economy.

The fundamental advantage of the rich countries is thus, not that they produce certain types of commodities, but rather that they are the home of modern technology and the seats of the multinational corporations. It is because of this that the rich industrial countries will tend to be the chief gainers from any type of commercial relationship with the Third World – be it in the form of trade or investment. Over the long run the LDC, irrespective of the commodity it produces, will not share the gains fairly, except in the case of those groups or sectors which become integrated into the economy of the rich country. These will become oases of growth surrounded by a desert of stagnation, thus reinforcing other elements of dualism already present in the poorer countries. In this way pockets of growth may develop, but the way leads to polarisation within the poor country, clashing with the objectives of national planning and national integration. This polarisation expresses itself in widening internal income disparities, larger numbers exposed to extreme poverty, and, above all, rising unemployment.

The real source of the maldistribution of the gains from trade and investment lies in the nature of modern technology and the process of its development. Modern technology, as already mentioned, is concentrated in the rich countries and is oriented towards *their* conditions, problems and factor endowments. This goes much deeper than just the development of substitutes for primary commodities. By rendering obsolete the older, simpler, more labour-intensive, existing technology, this process creates a condition of continued and sharpening technological dependence and continued and sharpening lack of productive employment within the LDCs. Hence it is this technological dependence that has to be corrected if the poor countries are to emerge from the depths of poverty. Salvation lies not in mere industrialisation as such, but rather in the development of indigenous scientific and technological capacities within the developing countries and in a reorientation of the present system of research and development which by and large ignores their needs. In this sense, the poor and new rich countries share a common problem. It is a realisation of the community of interests which has induced them to present a common programme of international economic reform.

The traditional view, of course, is that the factor endowment of a country determines the production mix and at the same time the technology. For a poor country, this means that the abundant labour and scarce capital should lead to: (a) concentration and specialisation on labour-intensive products, and (b) choice of a labour-intensive technology within the available spectrum of technologies for each product. This situation is assumed to have the happy result for poor countries of producing a tendency towards full employment, saving of scarce capital, fruitful international trade and gradual factor price equalisation.

It is, of course, recognised that the present trade restrictions concerning labour-intensive manufactured products, the agricultural protectionism by rich countries, and the heavy effective tariff barriers against the processing of crude commodities in the developing countries prevent this advantageous process from operating in so far as it depends on the international division of labour. However, there is something much more fundamentally wrong with the idea that trade and investment benefit poor countries (as well as rich countries) by bringing into play their different factor endowments. The logic of the preceding argument is that, in fact, it should be looked at the other way round: it is the *technology* which is given which determines the production mix and factor endowment, at least in the sense of factor *use*. And since the given technology is the 'modern' technology of the developed countries (capital-intensive, skill-intensive, labour-saving, raw material-saving and raw material-substituting), neither the technology used nor the production mix corresponds to the factor endowment of the developing countries. Unemployment of labour and extreme shortage of capital outside the small modern sector result as the natural outcome of this situation. In a sense, unemployment and deprivation of the rest of the economy (outside the modern sector) act as equilibrating factors which reconcile the given technology (that of the richer countries) with the factor proportions of the poorer countries.

Another way of explaining the same situation is that it seems misleading to put so much emphasis on factor *endowment*; rather, more attention should be paid to factor *use*. As the unemployment situation and absence of new labour-intensive technologies in developing countries indicate, recent investments have not been guided in their factor use by the existing factor endowment. So, analytically, it would be more realistic to substitute for the old sequence: factor endowment→product mix→technology→factor use, the following sequence: new technology→factor use→dualism and unemployment →factor endowment. This sequence, centred upon technology, explains more of the maldistribution of benefits from trade and investment than does the previous emphasis on deteriorating terms of trade and foreign trade restrictions.

The point previously made, that more emphasis should be placed upon the characteristics of *countries* rather than upon the characteristics of specific *commodities*, can now be further elaborated. The superior technology and monopoly of technological improvement possessed by the investing countries are but one aspect of their superiority in having access to the relevant information necessary for policy making and bargaining. Here we clearly have a cumulative process at work, for information, like technology, feeds upon itself. If at the beginning there is not enough information to tell where to look for the information needed what new information should be assembled, initial inferiority is bound to be sharpened and perpetuated. This unequal bargaining situation will affect *all* relations between the investing and borrowing countries, whether labelled aid, trade, investment, transfer of technology, technical assistance or any other.

The realisation that the concentration of technical progress of a specific kind within richer countries is *the* basic determinant of the uneven distribution of gains from trade and investment, leads to the further realisation that simple manufactured products of the type capable of production in developing countries share many of the characteristics which were attributed to primary commodities ('unwrought commodities') as against manufactured goods ('wrought commodities'). The real line of division in the present day seems to lie, not between primary commodities and manufactured goods, but between primary commodities *plus* simple manufactured goods on the one hand, and the sophisticated new products – especially (but not exclusively) intermediate goods, including new equipment, as well as know-how and management – on the other hand. Import substitution shifts the geographical location of manufacturing plants, but continued technological dependence will ensure that the real terms of trade continue to go against the poor countries – except for short-run periods where effective producer cartels raise the prices of scarce commodities – and in favour of the rich countries from which the required intermediate inputs flow. Where the relationship is that between a multinational corporation and its subsidiary in a developing country, the case is particularly obvious. If the developing country believes that it is developing because of a geographical shift in the location of plants to within its own boundaries, this merely shows that the planners and politicians, no less than the economists, have become the slaves of geography. It has often been pointed out that when all the dynamic effects are taken into account

39

the net marginal social productivity of much import-substituting production may well be zero or negative, especially where the import substitute is produced by a foreign investor. This is but another way of expressing the idea that import-substituting industrialisation becomes a part of the deteriorating terms-of-trade syndrome, rather than an escape route from it.

The Third World countries thus cannot overcome the problem of underdevelopment as long as efforts are not made to bridge the technological gap which separates them from the richer countries, whatever the short-run windfall gains that may occur. The poor countries must somehow obtain and apply a technology which takes into account their factor endowment and fits their needs and requirements. The sort of technology transfer that usually takes place through the agency of multinational corporations is less than adequate in this respect. It is based upon the needs and experience of the multinational, which is primarily concerned with its own comparative advantages which include the application of a sophisticated technology developed by itself. It will tend to create an industrial structure which is based on neither the real resource potential of the poor country nor the real needs of its low-income majority and hence is incapable of generating self-sustained growth.

To reorient the system of trade, aid, and other forms of resource flows and transfer that characterise the relationship of the rich and poor countries so as to fit the factor endowments and the needs of the poor countries, is the key to the whole issue. If a method can be devised and built into the various transfer mechanisms, which ensures that the poor countries successfully adapt the technological development abroad to their own requirements and also create their own indigeneous technology based on their own resource potential, every form of association and contact between the rich and poor countries will be of much enhanced use to the latter. If the technological gap is not overcome the developing countries will remain dependent on the rich economies, and no form of assistance, trade concessions, aid, grants, technical assistance or fortuitous price rises will prove to be of lasting value. International co-operation policies must be devised which serve to remove this fundamental obstacle in the path of development.

Now the evolution of such policies cannot take place in a political vacuum. All international trade and monetary reforms have occurred as a consequence of protracted bargaining in which political factors have played an important role. The view that such reforms are mere institutional rationalisations of change occasioned by changes in the international environment and by automatic self-equilibriating forces, is based on a belief in economic determinism which is entirely unjustified. In particular, the distribution of gains between different groups must be determined by a set of political and social criteria which finds expression in specific policies. If the rich countries seek today to retain the existing international economic structure, it is primarily because they lack the political will to make the sacrifices necessary to create the new international division of labour demanded by the developing countries. The continued confrontation between the developed and the developing countries reflects both the latter's realisation that they cannot themselves bridge the technological gap and the former's unwillingness to countenance a restructuring of the international economic system which would destroy their built-in advantage in the management of the world economy.

NOTES

1 By 'economic development' is meant not simply an increase in the GNP of a country, but rather a decrease in poverty at an individual level. Probably the best indicators of poverty are low food consumption and high unemployment. If these problems are effectively dealt with along with growth of GNP and with a reasonably equitable income distribution, then and only then can genuine economic development be talked of.

2 *International Trade, 1972* (Geneva, GATT, 1973), p. 3.

3 Surendra Patel, 'World Economy in Transition 1850–2060' in R. Feinstein (ed.), *Capitalism, Socialism and Economic Growth* (London, CUP, 1967).

4 The impact of the oil crisis will shift some of this growth to the new-rich oil exporters.

5 No exception, but on the contrary an extreme example of this, was the entrepreneurial (managerial) class of Soviet Russia, which was inspired by Stalin's (no less than Preobrazhensky's) philosophy of 'building socialism in one country'.

6 This would not, of course, necessarily reduce the gap between the rich and poor countries, for the rich would be growing too. However, any country which attains the income level of a rich country of 1975 (in real terms) would no doubt have escaped the vicious circle of stagnation or downward cumulative causation.

7 'Technology is the employed or operative knowledge of the means of production of a particular group of goods or services'. Yudelman, Butler and Banerji, *Technological Change in Agriculture and Employment in Developing Countries* (Paris, OECD Development Centre, 1971).

8 The term 'economic dealings' does not cover grants and untied aid which may not be of economic benefit to the rich countries in a short-run sense.

9 H. W. Singer, 'The Distribution of Gains between Investing and Borrowing Countries', paper presented at the 1949 meeting of the American

RICH AND POOR COUNTRIES

Economic Association, *American Economic Review* (May 1950). Also R. Prebisch, *Economic Development of Latin America and the Principal Problems* (New York, UN Economic Commission for Latin America, 1950).

42

CHAPTER 3

The Poor Countries

Chapter 2 has attempted to focus attention on the nature of the imbalances that characterise the international economy in the 1970s. It has been maintained that the technological gap which exists between the rich and poor countries is the main cause of this imbalance. The fact that the rich countries are the natural home of multinational investment and of scientific and technological research and development, conforming to their factor endowment, goes a long way to explaining why – relatively speaking – it is easier for these countries to make rapid economic progress and to maintain high levels of output, employment, investment and consumption. The poor countries, on the other hand, cannot initiate or sustain high levels or rapid growth, precisely because they do not possess those institutions which can create and foster a technology that is based on their own resource endowments and which can cope with their high rates of population increase. In all the late starters of the rich world, the initial days of rapid development were characterised by the mushrooming of numerous business groups, research institutions, etc. which learnt the techniques then in vogue from the older countries and then adapted these techniques for their own use. This allowed countries like Japan and Germany to take innumerable short cuts and to profit from the experiences of the Anglo-Saxon countries. Hence the pace of development of the late starters has been much more rapid than that of the older industrialised countries.

Why is the performance of the poor countries of today so different from that of some of the then poor countries of, say, 100 years ago? The answer to this question lies in the much greater *relative* strength of the countries that are rich now, and the much greater *relative* weakness of the poor countries of today. The gap between the rich and poor countries has widened to such an extent that it is no longer possible for the poor countries to make good their deficiency in the way in which a number of then poor countries did in the last century.

Development occurs where the right kind of structural change

43

takes place within the economy. The poor countries of yesterday managed to restructure the social, economic and technological relationships that were impeding development. On the other hand, the modern LDCs find the introduction of this kind of change in their social and economic framework an extremely difficult task. In the final analysis it is this inability to accommodate the required structural change that is holding the poor countries back.

In this chapter a little time will be spent discussing the structure of the economy of a 'typical' poor country. This will enable us to understand (a) the ways in which the rich countries can help the poor countries, and (b) the extent to which the poor countries can, and must, help themselves. The fact that a country is poor reflects the existence of a set of structural relationships between sectors and between factors of production, which impede development. It is often forgotten that development means growth *plus change*. To initiate a process of sustained development it is necessary therefore (a) to alter the existing pattern of economic relationships in such a way that the released dynamism of the economic structure induces growth in production, (b) to make this growth in production self-sustaining, and (c) to spread it through the different sectors and groups of the population, especially those below the poverty line.

Development of a country thus requires the formulation and implementation of a specific strategy which identifies both the bottlenecks and the methods by which they are to be overcome. Such a strategy will, of course, vary from country to country, and over time. This follows from the fact that the factors which impede development are not related in the same way in all Third World countries. This goes a long way towards explaining the inability of economists to formulate a general theory of development.

The development strategy that is adopted must take into account the interrelationship of the different economic sectors within the country. Planners should concentrate on fostering development in the sectors with the maximum linkage with the rest of the economy. In other words, priority must be given to the needs of those sectors which, if developed, promise to propel the rest of the economy into a process of rapid growth or which, if left underdeveloped, would crucially constrain the development of the economy. The foreign trade sector, for example, deserves attention in a country where industrial development depends crucially on the availability of certain inputs which cannot be domestically produced. And all the time, any strategy of planning must be concentrated on the overriding objective of reducing poverty and utilising more fully and effectively the human and other resources available. This means that development policy must be concerned with problems of employment and income distribution.

The extent to which the rich countries can help (or hinder) the poor countries in their development depends critically on the role and importance of the foreign sector in the latter. The importance of the foreign sector is best estimated by the substitutability of domestic resources for foreign resources. Countries which do not have a high ratio of foreign trade and investment to GNP may yet be dependent on the supply of crucial imports which cannot be substituted by domestic resources and which have considerable forward and backward linkage effects. Trade may also be important because it leads to an expansion of employment or a desired change in the pattern of income distribution, even if this does not mean a rapid increase in GNP per capita. On the other hand, certain sectors of the economy may be entirely uninfluenced by foreign resource flows. Thus the balance between the use of domestic and foreign resources will depend on the extent to which the growing sectors of the economy need these resources. The structural relationships, including specifically income distribution, within the economy will determine the proportion in which domestic and foreign resources are required. Preliminary to an analysis of trade and aid, therefore, is a discussion of the structure of the economies of the underdeveloped countries and a look at the major structural changes that are inevitable if a process of self-perpetuating development is to be initiated.

3.1 THE ECONOMIC STRUCTURE OF THE POOR COUNTRIES : UNITY IN DIVERSITY

The poorer countries of the world include the whole of Asia with the exception of Japan, the whole of Africa with the exception of South Africa, and the whole of the western hemisphere except for the United States and Canada (i.e. Latin America and the Carribean area). Thus defined, the developing countries include about two-thirds of the world's population, approximately 2,500 million people. Much of what will be said also applies to the poorer countries on the southern fringe of Europe (e.g. Portugal, Spain, Romania, Bulgaria, Greece, Yugoslavia, and southern Italy).

The mention of southern Italy is a reminder of the oversimplification involved in speaking of the poorer 'countries'. Many or all of the richer countries (e.g. the United Kingdom and United States) include regions or groups which have low incomes and share many of the characteristics of the poorer or less developed countries. On

45

the other hand, many of the poorer countries have areas or enclaves of glittering modernity, and their higher income groups may live at levels of affluence greatly exceeding the average affluence of the so-called richer countries. Regional differences (e.g. those between southern and north-eastern Brazil) may span a range similar to that between rich and poor countries. This oversimplification need not worry us too much, however, as long as we take due account of the diversity of situations within the poorer countries and remember that 'development' must mean bringing forward their poorer groups and regions.

More serious is another oversimplification. The 'developing countries' include over 120 independent countries, and an additional thirty to forty dependent territories (some of which may yet become independent countries), which differ from each other in practically every imaginable respect except that, on average, they are to a greater or lesser extent dependent on the rich countries as a source of technology and knowledge. Some of the poorer countries are very large and populous (e.g. India and China), while others are tiny ministates. Some have good and stable governments; others are extremely badly governed. Some have oil or other valuable resources; others have little or nothing (presently known). Some represent natural arteries of world trade (e.g. Singapore and Hong Kong); others are remote and landlocked (e.g. Nepal, Bolivia, Chad and Afghanistan). Some are extremely primitive and have very little beyond traditional subsistence agriculture; others have sophisticated industrial, urban and social patterns (e.g. India, Brazil and Egypt). Some have shown rapid economic growth in the recent past; others have been stagnant. Some have experienced sharp social and political changes during the same recent past; others have remained bound by ancient traditions. Some are ultra-capitalist, some are communist and centrally planned, while most are mixed economies in varying degrees.

The fact is that the world is not sharply divided into two classes of countries, one rich and one poor. There is more of a continuum, and in many ways it might be more useful to distinguish three or four classes of countries representing different 'stages' of development. Three such classes would be: the really mature developed countries (e.g. the United States, Canada, the United Kingdom, France and Germany), the poorer among the more developed countries, many of which are rapidly catching up (e.g. Italy, Spain, Greece and Japan, and presumably also the USSR, Czechoslovakia, Poland and Yugo-slavia) and the more developed among the poorer countries, many of which have an intermediate status and many of which also are

46

rapidly catching up (e.g. Brazil, Mexico, Singapore, Israel and Turkey). The OPEC countries are in a class all of their own, rich in wealth but often possessing primitive and weak socio-economic infrastructures incapable of absorbing the enormous income they earn. Finally, there are the really poor countries (e.g. India, Pakistan, Indonesia, Bangladesh, Haiti, Ethiopia and Chad), which illustrate a great variety of circumstances.

The developing countries are not all poor countries, though the overwhelming majority of them certainly are. We must carefully avoid, therefore, using the increase in per capita income as an *identification* of development. This would be an extremely narrow view. Development consists of much more than an increase in per capita income; it is desired for many and complex reasons of which the increase in per capita income is merely one. An increase in per capita income, reflecting an increase in production, in many ways is merely the end product of factors or forces which cause economic development, rather than its cause or essence. Even the ultimate objective of development is a great deal more than a mere increase in per capita income; questions relating to the use and distribution of this income are as important dimensions of development policies as its increase. The good society is not identical with the affluent society, nor a better society with a more affluent one. Indeed, an important question raised by a study of development concerns ultimate aims and objectives. An increase in production at the expense of the total destruction of the ecological balance nationally or internationally is clearly undesirable. Similarly, the destruction of the national cultures and ethnic traditions of the peoples of the Third World is not necessarily a universally acceptable cost of development. The formulator and executor of development policies must recognise that development implies political and social change. The justification of specific policies may be sought, not in the application of narrow cost – benefit economic criteria, but rather on the basis of a socio-political consensus which defines the objectives of national development policy. These objectives would usually be related to the desire for material well-being, social and economic security, freedom from grave want, preservation of national institutions, etc.

The fact that the per capita GNP and aggregate GNP are inadequate as measures of the progress of the LDCs can be further substantiated in the case of India, as the result of an interesting study made by two Indian economists.[1] These two authors analysed India's progress during the decade 1954–64 on the basis of twenty-one factors which can be taken as indicators of increase in the development potential. These include: number of factory establishments; power capacity; transport capacity (various indicators); net area irrigated; postal and other communications; output and imports of intermediate and capital goods; number of bank branches; enrolments in primary schools, secondary schools, universities and polytechnics; number of wage and salary earners in factories; patents registered; and fertilisers consumed. On the basis of these indicators, the authors concluded that the rate of progress of India during that decade was 7·3 per cent per annum – over double the rate of growth in national income at constant prices, which was only 3·5 per cent per annum. The authors concluded that 'this appears to suggest that, provided the momentum of the development process is maintained, the growth rate in national income could accelerate after the adaptation lags are completed'. A similar discrepancy would seem to apply to the LDCs in general, though the relationship between real growth and GNP growth might be reversed in some cases. Yet on the other hand there is evidence, for India as well as many other countries, that the situation, as measured by the number and proportion of people living below a very low poverty line, has actually worsened rather than improved.[2] The evidence is thus confusing and difficult to interpret.

Although the physical environment and the resource endowments of the developing countries differ widely, it is nevertheless possible to identify a more or less common set of economic processes and relationships which prevent a full utilisation of their resources. Economists often indicate these processes by stressing that development is hindered by the operation and domination of a series of interlocking vicious circles. Different characteristics of the economy are related to each other in such a way that a general breakthrough is difficult, if not impossible. We can identify, in an aggregative and general sense, a number of characteristics that determine the structural relationships peculiar to poor countries.

One important characteristic which has held back the expansion of per capita production has been their rate of population growth. It would, of course, be hazardous and perhaps unrealistic to argue that a specific country had reached, or exceeded, its optimum population level. The latter is a limit which recedes continuously with increases in the efficiency of factor utilisation and with technological progress. However, in the poor countries today, unlike in the developing countries of the last century, population growth pre-empts much of the growth in productive capacities.

The rate of population increase in the poorest countries stands out as statistically the main factor explaining why even the relative gap, not to mention the absolute gap, in per capita incomes separating

48

them from the rich countries has continued to increase, even though the poorest countries have recently kept up with the rich in terms of the rate of growth in aggregate production. Moreover, the rate of population increase for the 1970s projected by the United Nations is even higher than that for the previous decade, i.e. 2·65 per cent per annum as against 2·5 per cent. The high rate of population increase has, of course, other and more profound significances for development, in addition to the purely statistical effect of reducing the rate of per capita growth to only half or less that of aggregate growth.

The higher birthrate of the poor countries means that the proportion of children and young people at any point of time is very much higher there than in the richer countries. Typically, in the poor countries nearly half the population is under fifteen and almost two-thirds is under twenty-five. This means that the poor countries have to devote much more of their resources to the task of raising a new generation of producers, besides providing services of a given standard to an enlarged and rapidly urbanising population.

The low per capita incomes of the poor countries prevent the generation of a sizable investable surplus. New sectors of modern economic growth thus remain very small, especially in terms of employment, and are often foreign-controlled. The national economy at large remains deprived of new capital infusion. In the poor countries agricultural production accounts for about 40–50 per cent of GNP, while in the rich countries the ratio is 5–10 per cent. Moreover, about three-quarters of the total population of a poor country is engaged in the agricultural sector. It has been contested ever since Ragnar Nurkse proposed turning the rural 'surplus labour' into capital, and since Arthur Lewis in his famous Manchester School paper talked of 'unlimited labour supply' in developing countries, whether the people in the agricultural sector could be said to be unemployed or underemployed. The problem of lack of productive employment in the poor countries is, however, by no means confined to agriculture. It also exists in the urban and non-agricultural sectors to a significant degree. Indeed, the underutilisation of all factors of production (capital, labour, etc.) is a central feature of the economy of a poor country. The underutilisation of labour is both the cause and effect of a distortion of the consumption and investment patterns and of high and rising inequalities of income distribution. The poor country cannot afford to allocate resources to any but the most essential uses, and yet such a concentration may clash with the demand structure reflecting a highly unequal income distribution. The result is that investment in the socio-economic infrastructure is well below its optimum level. The low level of expenditure on education, health, transportation facilities, credit and marketing arrangements, etc. leads to the prevalence of high mortality rates, the inadequate provision of health, education and nutrition needs, inadequate access to public services and support, and a widening of the gap between the different income classes within the poor country. Countries often, and usually wrongly, believe that such conditions must be tolerated and unequal income distribution fostered in order to create an investable surplus, and that this leads to growth of the economy which will later benefit the masses.

These structural bottlenecks of a 'typical' poor economy reflect its basic inability to evolve and use a technology which caters to its own resource endowments and resource potential and deals with rapid population growth. The great scientific and technological upsurge that the world has been experiencing since the turn of the century has almost completely bypassed the poor countries. These countries are, with few exceptions, dependent on the richer countries to meet their technological needs.

The well-off Third World countries (not only the oil-producing ones but also some other which may benefit from rises in the prices of their primary commodity exports) are not confronted with low investment rates. They have financial resources in plenty, but the underdeveloped socio-economic infrastructure of these countries impedes growth and structural change. Thus despite abundant foreign exchange and investment funds, investment opportunities are severely limited and technological backwardness thwarts their development effort. The desire to participate in the management of the international economy and to influence the diffusion of technology internationally is thus shared by all nations of the Third World.

Almost all world expenditures on science and technology take place inside the richer countries, and research and development are therefore quite naturally directed towards solving *their* problems by methods suited to *their* circumstances and resource endowments. The problems of the poorer countries, however, are not the same; for instance, they need research to design simple products, to develop production for smaller markets, to improve the quality of and to develop new uses for tropical products, and above all to develop production processes which utilise their abundant labour. Instead, emphasis is placed on sophisticated weaponry, space research, atomic research, sophisticated products, production for large high-income markets, and specifically a constant search for processes which save labour by substituting capital or high-order skills.

50

THE POOR COUNTRIES

The accumulation of knowledge in directions broadly irrelevant and sometimes harmful to the poorer countries hurts these latter in so far as the new knowledge inevitably tends to destroy or submerge the old knowledge, which often was more relevant and useful to them. Thus, where the long line of economists looking hopefully to science and technology for easing the task of development went wrong, was in placing great emphasis on the *volume* of knowledge without paying equal regard to the *composition* of that volume. What has in fact happened is that, while more and more knowledge has accumulated, it has on the average become less and less suitable for the development of the poorer countries. Some economists and other scientists have the rather naive idea that the accumulation of scientific and technological knowledge provides a growing stock or inventory of possibilities, and so constantly widens the spectrum of technological possibilities open to LDCs. What this view neglects is that in practice only the 'latest', most 'advanced' or most 'modern' of the known technologies is actually available; the others have been displaced or destroyed. Thus the spectrum of technologies available to developing countries is not widened; on the contrary, the range of *suitable* technologies – suitable that is for the LDCs – is constantly diminished. Partly this is no doubt the fault of the LDCs themselves, since they often accept the identification of 'suitable' with 'modern' or 'advanced'. As 'modern' and 'advanced' nearly always mean more capital-intensive and less labour-intensive, i.e. less employment-intensive, the use of such technologies exacerbates the rising unemployment and underemployment which have now often assumed frightening proportions in the poorer countries, particularly among the younger job seekers pouring from the rapidly expanding ranks of primary and secondary school leavers.

Paradoxically, simply to increase scientific and technological expenditures within the underdeveloped countries within the present system may be no remedy at all. Their present expenditures are much too small and scattered to be effective and they also suffer from the shortage of trained research people (particularly those just below the top level). To be more effective, these expenditures would have to be multiplied to a degree clearly beyond the resources of many of these countries without extensive financial or technical assistance. More important and feasible is a reversal of policies which presently often discourage and harrass such elements of national and labour-intensive technologies as are found particularly in the informal sectors of these countries. In the case of private foreign investment, all the forces are working in the direction of the investors, especially the multinational corporations, using their own home-made tech-

51

nology; the widespread use of labour is often further discouraged by the relatively high wages – high relative to rural incomes – paid to regularly employed workers, wages strongly pressed for and often readily conceded. Aid and technical assistance work in the same direction; aid is available for imported capital goods, but much less so for local employment-creating expenditures, while technical assistance also lacks in adaptation to different local conditions especially considering the short duration of the assignments of most experts from the more developed countries. Training fellowships for nationals of the poorer countries all too often are synonymous with training in methods which are more suitable for rich countries and possibly harmful for the trainees' countries.

The social and economic structure of a Third World country is characterised by what, for want of a better word, is called 'dualism'. Most LDCs have a large, stagnant, agricultural sector which is linked to the small, modern, large-scale, industrial sector mainly through the supply of resources, both labour and capital, from the former to the latter. The growth of the industrial sector neither initiates a corresponding growth process in the rural sector nor generates sufficient employment to prevent a growing population in the stagnant sectors. The industrial sector of the poor countries is really a periphery of the metropolitan industrial economies, critically dependent on them for the technology it uses. Hence its pattern of production fails to make an impact on the economy as a whole. The central task of development planners is to integrate the industrial and agricultural sectors in such a manner that growth and structural change in one sector initiate and support corresponding developments in the other, while the human and natural resource potentials of the country are more fully utilised. The flood of migration from the depressed rural sector, combined with the small employment potential of the modern industrial sector, results in the growth of a large, overflow, shanty-town district in urban areas.

This section has looked at a few of the salient characteristics of a 'typical' less developed economy. Such an economy, we have seen, is characterised by low income levels, high rates of population growth and technological dependence. These characteristics lead to low saving rates, small foreign exchange earnings and lack of integration between the rural and the urban sectors of the economy. The process of economic development must break up the vicious circles of poverty and stagnation that prevent economic growth and structural change. The few rich Third World countries do not experience this vicious circle, but even here dualism is no less pronounced and real development is limited by the absence of an adequate technology. Section 3.2 is addressed to an analysis of the major aspects of this development process.

3.2 THE DEVELOPMENT PROCESS

The theoretical literature on economic development has been growing at a very rapid rate since the end of the Second World War. There exists no central body of doctrine that is generally accepted as *the* theory of economic development, as different authors have emphasised different aspects of the development process. A strikingly important aspect of the development process is its complexity; economic, political, social, demographic and cultural factors all interact to produce growth and change. A comprehensive analysis of the relationship and the behaviour of all these factors is not possible given the existing state of knowledge in the social sciences. Social, and particularly economic, theory deliberately seek to abstract from the complexity of the process, in order to focus attention on those relationships considered to be crucial. All unifactor theories of development attempt to identify the dominant vicious circle, in the sense that they hypothesise about the particular set of relationships between a few variables which are considered the prime cause of underdevelopment.

It is impossible, and unnecessary, in a book of this nature to undertake a comprehensive survey of the major theories and schools concerning development. Excellent surveys are available.[3] We are here interested mainly in understanding the role of the external sector as a stimulant for development – more specifically, the role of foreign trade, foreign capital, foreign technology and foreign skills in the process of development. We wish to know not only how the level of production is affected by different levels of foreign resources, but also what would be the effects of substituting foreign for domestic resources, and vice versa.

One analytical tool developed by economists that could help in this is the production function. This is a technical relationship expressing the quantity of output in a production process as a function of the quantity of inputs consumed. *For a given technology* a production function indicates how the level of output varies with different levels of inputs. It enables the marginal productivities of the different inputs of production to be calculated, and also their degree of substitutability. For our purposes, therefore, we could use a production function to assess the contribution of foreign resources to production and the consequences (in terms of output) of substituting domestic for foreign resources.

53

RICH AND POOR COUNTRIES

The constant elasticity of substitution (CES) production function[4] in particular enables estimates to be made of the extent to which different factors of production can be substituted for each other. If domestic saving or production can easily be substituted for foreign exchange earnings or imports respectively, the external sector is not critically important for development policy and a vigorous fiscal policy or other promotional policies may suffice. On the other hand, if such substitution is difficult, the domestic economic policies of the government will not be adequate to meet a foreign resource shortage. The value of the substitution parameter in a CES production function is an important measure of the structural characteristics of an economy. Theoretically there is no reason why we cannot first define a CES production function which specifies as its inputs domestic resources and foreign exchange, and then estimate the elasticity of substitution between those factors. The importance of the external sector, and hence the importance of trade and aid in the development process, can be indicated (albeit roughly) by the value of the substitution parameter in a CES production function of this sort.

The formulation of the CES production function has enabled economists to focus attention on the problem of factor substitutability. Most of the relatively newer theories of economic development, especially the 'two-gap' models[5] first put forward in the early 1960s, have recognised the importance of factor substitutability. All the main approaches to the problem of economic development have made assumptions about factor substitutability. The 'classical' theory assumes that the only limit on development is the savings of the society; given this saving, which is thought of in the form of a surplus over 'subsistence' consumption, factor substitutability is infinite. The 'stage' theories in the tradition of Walt Rostow assume, like the classical theory, that savings is the only constraint on development. The 'balanced growth' theories stress external economies, market conditions and demand in general. Hirschman, in his theory of 'unbalanced growth', stresses the low substitutability between capital and the 'ability to invest', i.e. entrepreneurial and managerial skill; he recommends concentration of effort on 'induced' rather than 'autonomous' investment because in the former increase in capital is matched by entrepreneurial ability. Finally, the 'capital' theories in the Harrod–Domar tradition and the 'labour surplus' theories (Lewis, Ranis and Fei, etc.) assume that factor substitutability is infinite and that savings is the only constraint on growth.[6]

The problem of factor substitutability has been dealt with extensively in the two-gap models. Growth may be constrained because the resources which are available cannot be substituted for resources which are not available; i.e. a minimum amount of each factor of production is necessary if the structural bottlenecks which limit development are to be overcome. The 'three-gap' models identify a 'savings constraint', a 'balance-of-payments constraint' and a 'skill constraint' which may limit development. These constraints represent gaps between the demand and supply of capital, foreign exchange and skills respectively. It is assumed (and considerable empirical support has been provided to back this assumption) that capital, labour and foreign exchange cannot be substituted for each other freely, i.e. that the elasticity of substitution between these factors is low. Investment and growth in most developing countries may be regarded as being highly influenced by the foreign exchange available to import capital goods. Chenery has shown that the development of a large number of poor countries is limited mainly by their lack of foreign exchange and that these countries cannot substitute domestic resources for foreign exchange in order to achieve their planned growth targets. Similarly, Weiskopf and Marris and a large number of other researchers have shown that poor countries have extensive foreign exchange requirements. Half the countries in Marris's sample had their growth limited by the scarcity of foreign exchange; the other half had the required foreign exchange and skilled manpower but were short of domestic savings. This shows that the external sector can play a crucially important role in determining the pace and direction of a poor country's development.[7]

The growth rate that can be attained by a poor country under given supply and demand conditions of the factors of production is determined at the lowest level where the *tightest* constraint becomes operative. If the economy functions at this level the other factors of production are, of course, not fully utilised, because they cannot be substituted for the factor which is limiting growth. The gap may therefore be defined as the difference between (a) the quantities of the factors of production that are required if the country is to grow at a maximum possible rate (where the least limiting constraint is operative), and (b) the existing supplies of the factors. For example, if the attainable growth rate on account of domestic savings availability is higher than that on account of the availability of foreign exchange, the foreign exchange constraint may be said to be dominant and an import gap exists.

The view of the development process thus unfolded is a complex one. It emphasises the importance of the availability of the requisite factors of production in the *right proportions* to the developing societies. The two-gap models have shown that the strategy of development must concentrate on the alleviation of the dominant constraint. An increase in foreign exchange earnings will not be useful when the savings gap is dominant, and an increase in domestic savings will be of little value when the skilled labour shortage is the main constraint, except to the extent that substitution exists or can be promoted.

3.3 DEVELOPMENT STRATEGY: NATIONAL AND INTERNATIONAL

Most developing countries have tried to eliminate the structural bottlenecks that limit growth and change through the extensive use of national economic plans. In most developing economies in Asia, Africa and Latin America economic planning has taken place within the context of a 'mixed economy'.[8] This has meant that the planners have usually thought in terms of financial balances. The core of a 'typical' development plan of a 'typical' poor country in the 1950s was the sections which described how savings (private and public) were to be mobilised and to be allocated between alternative (private and public) investment uses. Implicit in the plans was a preoccupation with growth models of the Harrod–Domar type, which see a saving deficiency as the main hurdle for a developing economy. Admittedly, some plans adopted a more disaggregated approach and identified a number of different sectors of the economy. Professor Mahalanobis's plan for the Indian economy deserves special mention in this connection.[9] However, neither the aggregate nor the disaggregated approach dealt explicitly with the problem of factor (or resource) substitutability.

In the 1960s some poor countries adopted the two-gap models as the framework within which their plans were constructed. Pakistan's Third Five-Year Plan (1965–70) and Perspective Model (1965–85) were based on the two-gap theories. The planners sought to use the foreign resources available along with other factors in such a way that dependence on foreign assistance would be eliminated by 1985. This, the planners foresaw, would involve both an increase in the capacity of the economy to earn foreign exchange and a substitution of domestic produce for imports. In other words, a change in the coefficients of the inputs of the aggregate and sectoral production functions was envisaged, by substituting (a) foreign assistance for domestic savings and export earnings in the initial stages, and (b) domestic savings and export earnings for foreign assistance in the later years.

There are very real constraints on the usefulness of foreign assistance. In the 1940s and 1950s, when underdevelopment was thought of merely as a state of capital scarcity, it was assumed that all money obtained as foreign assistance by a poor country would be spent entirely on investment and capital imports. There was nothing in conventional theory on which such an assumption could be based, for clearly some of the foreign assistance would be allocated to consumption purposes.[10] Recently it has been claimed that foreign aid and investment contribute very little in the way of additional saving. A number of time series and cross-section studies have found that a negative association exists between foreign inflows (including foreign assistance and investments) and domestic saving rates. The greater the foreign inflows, the lower are the domestic savings. This may be so because increased foreign aid may permit governments to lower public savings (realised through taxation) or because foreign capital may reduce investment opportunities for domestic savers and thus induce them to increase their consumption levels.[11] The estimates have limited validity, however, because of the rather imprecise concepts and methodologies on which they are based. To find a negative correlation between two variables is not synonymous with discovering a causal pattern. That domestic savings are negatively associated with foreign inflows need not mean that foreign aid availability causes a reduction in domestic savings. Both saving rates and foreign inflows may be associated with another factor which causes the former to fall when the latter rises. According to Papanek, the relationship between domestic savings and foreign inflows is a complex one. Low savings and high foreign inflows are both caused by exogeneous factors, and the negative statistical association between the two variables says nothing about the contribution that foreign aid and assistance can make in the development process. The utility of foreign assistance differs from country to country. Countries well endowed with natural resources, e.g. the oil-rich, Middle Eastern states, have no serious savings or balance-of-payments problems. Trade receipts are, however, a vitally important source of development finance for these countries, and foreign aid can make very little contribution towards their development. On the other hand, countries that have limited natural resources and low levels of export earnings depend critically on foreign assistance. Semi-industrialised countries, experiencing difficulties in selling their manufactured exports, find foreign aid and capital inflows very useful in the alleviation of savings and balance-of-payments problems. The importance of foreign inflows varies according to the need of the developing countries.

An important fact pinpointed by Papanek and other researchers is that, whatever the relationship between saving and foreign aid, the association between savings and growth on the one hand, and between savings and export earnings on the other, is significantly positive. A country with low export earnings has less chance of developing. The external sector is thus of crucial importance; it can stimulate growth and facilitate structural change by providing resources that cannot be obtained domestically.

However, the economic planners of a poor country are usually confronted with a large number of factors beyond their control when they attempt to accelerate the inflow of foreign resources. This reflects the generally weak position of the poor countries in the international goods and factor markets. Because the production methods and powers of technological innovation of the richer countries are much more efficient than those of the poor countries, the former can substitute for the produce of the latter much more easily or can totally dispense with the need for it. In the short run, however, this may be difficult, and the OPEC countries have in the recent past demonstrated their ability to influence the volume of their export earnings and to determine the terms at which their exports will be traded in international commodity markets. However, they now face the problem of safeguarding their gains by negotiating favourable terms for their developmental imports. On the other hand, as things stand, the development of the poor countries is critically constrained by the availability of certain imports. The advantage which the rich country has is articulated in the trade patterns and tariff arrangements that exist in the world today.

There is therefore a need for the formulation of an international development strategy, supported and indeed pioneered by the rich countries (both new and old), providing assistance in an increasing flow of resources through trade, aid capital and the transfer of skills and technology to the poor countries. Both multilateral organisations and individual rich countries have a vital role to play in this. Such a strategy must provide for some discrimination in favour of the poor countries in international trade and payment arrangements. The trade and aid policies of the new- and old-rich countries and of the multilateral organisations (which they largely finance and control) must be designed to supplement the ability of the poor countries to obtain those products and services from the outside world which are required to overcome the bottlenecks now limiting development. This implies that the poor countries must have at their disposal not merely a larger volume of goods but also a more appropriate one. They must be able, in the main, to import a technology that allows them to increase employment, raise productivity levels, improve income distribution patterns and develop their socio-economic infrastructure. Such international strategies were developed by the United Nations for both the First (1960s) and Second (1970s) Development Decades, though these strategies may be criticised in detail and in any case have not been effectively implemented.

NOTES

1 V. V. Divatia and V. V. Bhatt, 'On Measuring the Pace of Development', *Banca Nazionale del Lavoro Quarterly Review* (June 1969).
2 Dandekar and Rath, *Poverty in India* (New Delhi, Ford Foundation, 1971).
3 For detailed bibliographies see Gerald M. Meier, *Leading Issues in Economic Development* (London, OUP, 1970), pp. 119–20. Also see Lloyd Reynolds, 'The Content of Development Economics', *American Economic Review*, Papers and Proceedings (May 1969).
4 The CES production function was first presented by Arrow, Chenery, Minhas and Solow in 'Capital Labour Substitution and Economic Efficiency', *Review of Economics and Statistics* (August 1961).
5 The two 'gaps' are the foreign exchange gap and the domestic savings gap.
6 A detailed discussion of these theories is not undertaken because this is a book on trade and aid, not on development in general. Readers are referred to: Singer and Schiavo-Campo, *Perspectives of Economic Development* (Boston, Houghton Mifflin, 1970), and I. Adelman, *Theories of Economic Growth and Development* (Baltimore, John Hopkins, 1961).
7 These studies are discussed in Papanek, 'The Effect of Aid and Other Resource Transfers on Savings and Growth in Less Developed Countries', *Economic Journal* (September 1972), pp. 934–50.
8 The exceptions, of course, are North Vietnam, North Korea, Mongolia, Albania, Bulgaria and Cuba, which are judged to be within the category of poor or developing countries.
9 The Indian Second and Third Plans were based on the Mahalanobis model.
10 This is by no means totally undesirable. If foreign assistance leads to an increase in the consumption level of the children, the rural workers or the urban poor, it may in effect contribute more towards development than the proportion of foreign assistance which finances a highly capital-intensive project which, while inflating the GNP, does not contribute towards an increase in employment or an improvement in the pattern of income distribution.
11 For a discussion of these studies see Papanek, op. cit., pp. 939–50.

PART TWO

TRADE

CHAPTER 4

Trade and Development

4.1 INTRODUCTION

Chapter 3 has shown that the importance of the foreign trade and investment sector in the economy of a developing country is determined by the cost at which domestic resources can be substituted for foreign inputs during the process of development. But development is not synonymous with an increase in GNP per capita. The cost involved in substituting domestic resources for foreign exchange may entail changes in the level of employment, the pattern of income distribution or the structure of public revenue and expenditure, which may be detrimental to the long-run development prospects of the poor country. The concern with overall growth rates tends to obscure the fundamental objective of reducing poverty. Consequently, attempts to isolate the determinants of GNP growth are by their very nature incapable of going to the real causal links in the development chain. Little is to be gained therefore by concentrating attention on the relationship between growth of GNP per capita and changes in the size of the foreign sector of the poor country. Foreign trade orientation is not merely reflected in an association between levels of GNP per capita and ratios of trade to income. In any case, attempts to relate foreign trade fluctuations to aggregate variables such as investment, government expenditure and prices have failed to identify any simple consistent form of association.[1] The only quantitative relationship that seems firmly established associates the ratio of exports to investment (both public and private) with the size of the country. The smaller the country, the greater is the importance of exports relative to investment. Otherwise, it has also been estimated that the impact of changes in export earnings on income generation will be rather limited in the short run in most poor countries.[2] This finding, however, has been questioned on the basis of more recent analysis, and clearly much depends on the nature of the exported commodity, its mode of production and the policies of the exporting country.

Yet trade has traditionally been regarded as the main engine of growth. The theory of comparative advantage itself provides a rationale for holding the view that trade would equalise world prices of commodities and eliminate international differences in the incomes of factors of production. Developing trade between rich and poor countries may thus be expected to induce international specialisation in accordance with the comparative advantage and factor endowments of the trading partners, and to raise labour incomes and reduce the cost of capital in the poorer countries. It should be noted that this factor price equalisation is achieved as a consequence of international specialisation based on corresponding international differences in the true social costs of production. If trade patterns do not reflect such specialisation, there is no reason to believe that trade will lead to development.

International trade in the modern world does not reflect the assumptions that underlie the simple (Ricardian) theory of comparative advantage. The theory assumes: (a) that technological knowledge is a free good, or at least is equally available in both countries; (b) that the trading countries are not too different in their relative availabilities of capital and labour; (c) that trade is free, i.e. unencumbered by the existence of tariffs, quotas, etc.; and (d) that the prices of factors and products represent their true scarcities, values, etc. However, technological knowledge is not a free good. It is concentrated in rich countries, and much of it is exclusive to the international firms. Trade patterns are determined by domestic policies which require barriers to be placed by governments to regulate the quantity and the direction of imports and exports. The international differences in resource endowments are enormous, and all the existing evidence suggests that the gap is widening. Moreover, the differences are complex and by no means reducible to simple capital/labour ratios. International trade patterns between rich and poor countries reflect the bargaining power and institutions of the trading partners. Because the world markets in which trade takes place are characterised by the existence of oligopolistic competition, there is no indication that the economic bargaining position of the poor countries is being strongly improved (though this may be the case for some strategic materials and also politically). Factor and commodity prices are distorted in all countries by multiple government and institutional intervention.

If trade is not a simple engine of growth and even less one of development, it is because the pattern of world trade thwarts international specialisation in accordance with the principle of comparative advantage. Hence trade does not equalise commodity prices or factor income. Myrdal, Prebisch and Singer[3] separately have argued that there are systematic forces at work in world markets which tend to reduce the gains of the poor countries in international trade; consequently, trade may actually widen the gap between the rich and poor countries. Furthermore, the adverse movement in the terms of trade of the poor countries transfers the benefits of techno-logical innovations from the poor to the rich and, what is more important, acts as an impediment to the development of the poor countries. Trade cannot be an agent of development if it does not facilitate structural change within the economy, for development is growth *plus* change. In the case of the oil-producing countries, for example, trade had phenomenal growth long before OPEC. The bargaining power of these countries has now dramatically improved, but in the past the impact of trade on their economic structure – on poverty, on employment and income distribution patterns – was less than optimal. The argument that foreign trade and foreign investment may tend to sustain dualistic tendencies within the developing economy reflects the view that the benefits of inter-national specialisation in the existing framework of world markets are not shared either efficiently or equitably between different regions and different social groups within the developing country. This brings us to a consideration of the relationship between trade, employment and income distribution.

4.2 TRADE, EMPLOYMENT AND INCOME DISTRIBUTION

If development is conceived of as a human (rather than a technical or mechanical) process, it becomes immediately obvious that we cannot speak of development without reference to employment and income distribution. If the GNP of a poor country is growing at a rapid rate but more and more people are finding themselves to be socially and economically useless, and if the wealth and income of the country are being increasingly concentrated in the hands of a microscopic elite of businessmen, landlords and government officials, it is surely wrong to think that such a country is develop-ing. Policies aimed at growth maximisation to the exclusion of employment and income distribution considerations have often proved to be disastrous. Pakistan in the past is a case in point. The economic planners of that country, backed by the experts of the Harvard Development Advisory Group, devised and implemented an economic strategy which sought to increase growth by increas-ing the share of the rich in the national income. For some time the economy boomed, and Pakistan was cited as a major success story

65

by the professional developmentalists. Then the economy collapsed. Imbalances in the interregional and interpersonal distributions of income, coupled with an unexpected shortfall in foreign aid on which the economy had been increasingly dependent, put an end to the growth process. Mounting labour and peasant unrest together with the reduction in foreign exchange and capital imports strangled the economy, and the interregional and other differences led to political disintegration.

The most important lesson that must be learnt from such cases is that a great deal of harm can be done by those theorists and practitioners who (explicitly or implicitly) assume a necessary contradiction between growth and equity. There exists no convincing empirical evidence in support of this presumed contradiction, but much to the contrary. Indeed, real development can only occur if there is a sustained increase in the skill and productivity of the mass of the workers and producers of the country concerned. This implies that output growth must go together with improved incomes in the poorer groups, as a result of the more productive employment of labour in the developing sectors. A growth process that substitutes scarce capital for abundant labour cannot be regarded as development-inducing, for it is not inducing the required structural changes within the economy. The increase in production is not being balanced by a corresponding increase in the ability of the producers to harness the production process and to operate at a level where optimum use is made of the existing factors of production.

Development thus necessitates an increase in productive employment. This implies an increase in the share of the poorer sections of society in the national product. In particular, development policy must be concerned with preventing the impoverishment of the rural sector – especially of small farmers – as a consequence of growth, for an industrialisation programme that feeds upon the agricultural hinterland and effectively reduces the marginal productivity of agricultural labour is by its very nature a self-defeating programme. The agricultural sector generates an overwhelmingly large proportion of the surplus that is necessary for investment in most poor countries. A reduction in agricultural productivity is a sure sign of an impending decline in domestic resource mobilisation. Development policy must therefore encompass an agricultural strategy which promotes the productivity of the rural producers.

Employment expansion and equitable income distribution are most important elements of development policy. Now that the obsession with overall GNP growth rates as conventionally measured is becoming widely questioned, we are gradually becoming aware of the fact that the success of development policies and strategies is best depicted by changes in the quality of human life in the poor countries. The objectives of increasing employment and of re-distributing income in favour of the poorer sections of the population are much more adequate as indicators of development than is the overall GNP per capita, for they reflect improvements in living and working conditions.

The impact of trade on development, as indeed the impact of any other factor, can only be properly assessed if we look at the relation between trade and changes in employment and in the pattern of income distribution. A country which uses its export proceeds to import sophisticated capital goods for capital-intensive projects benefiting a small elite, cannot expect to derive real benefit from an expansion in trade. The same is true of a country which has no proper policy of maximising the linkage or indirect employment and income effects of export production, or of concentrating export production among smaller farmers and indigenous firms so as to place the export and related activities within the context of a proper development policy. The oil economies now have immense export revenues each year, but unless the use which is made of these funds ensures an increase in both the living standard of all – including the poorest sections of the population of these countries – and the productivity of their labour force, they will simply squander their money. Despite the favourable trade position of these countries, it cannot be assumed that this will necessarily or automatically lead to a transformation of their economies. Such a transformation can occur only if the export earnings are used to increase employment and productivity and to improve income distribution patterns within their economies.

Existing patterns of trade do not automatically contribute to-wards desired changes in income and wealth distribution in the poor countries. The emphasis upon the small 'modern' urban sector and the neglect of agriculture, rural development and small-scale industry have invariably resulted in increased levels of income concentration in the poor countries. This change in the pattern of income distribution has in no small measure been assisted by the trade policies of both the poor and the rich countries. The develop-ing countries have often sought to emphasise the necessity for becoming 'self-sufficient', in terms of presently imported goods, and 'industrially modernised'. In the past it was thought this could be achieved if emphasis were placed on import substitution,[4] i.e. on producing goods that were previously being imported for home consumption. Such import substitution was conceived of as a fairly simple process, involving a transfer, usually with the help of aid and foreign investment, of capital and technology. Ambitious programmes of industrialisation were drawn up, and attempts were made to divert resources towards the financing of these programmes. Poor countries ran up enormous foreign debts, and the dependency of these countries on the industrial countries increased rather than diminished. This dependency was mainly technological, for the developing countries essentially failed to devise an indigenous technology based upon domestic resource endowments and capable of increasing the skill and efficiency of the labour force. (Nor did the technologically powerful countries do so on their behalf.) Moreover, the domestic financing of the import-substitution industrialisation programmes invariably involved the impoverishment of both the rural sector and the unskilled urban workers. The gap between the rich and the poor within the developing countries continued to widen, with the result that the goods produced by the newly established import-substituting industries faced a limited market. This tended to reduce the incentive for further saving and investment, and it became difficult either to operate these industries at full capacity or to invest in more sophisticated import-substituting industries.

Trade patterns that can lead to employment expansion and desired changes in the pattern of income distribution in the poor countries are easily conceivable. A country specialising in the export of processed mineral and agricultral goods, or of labour-intensive manufactures, should be able to link trade expansion with employment levels and income distribution patterns. A nation importing relatively simple technology and inputs geared to the small producer in country and town (e.g. small tractors, fertilisers, light software and licensed know-how) should also be able to relate growth through trade to desired structural changes in employment and income distribution. The strategy of development suggested above (provided the trade policies of the rich countries make it possible – a big proviso!) is essentially different from the import substitution strategy in that it emphasises the relevance of increasing the productivity of the whole mass of the working population of the poor country and of reorienting its production structure so that it finds it possible to specialise in accordance with its long-run dynamic comparative advantage. The trade strategy, in both export and import structure, of a country must reflect its overall development policy. Most developing countries have a comparative advantage in

the production of labour-intensive manufactured goods and processed agricultural commodities. Economic policy must aim at
developing a production structure in which specialisation in the
production of those goods, and the use of the resulting foreign
exchange proceeds, increase the skill and efficiency of the labour
force, so that expansion in the economic production of more sophisticated manufactures and in agricultural mechanisation becomes
possible in the future – the comparative advantage of the country
changing as its production structure becomes more complex.

Even the OPEC countries have to ponder carefully on the best use
that can be made of the enormous oil revenues for the transformation of their economies. A gradual diversification of their production structure requires that they undertake investment programmes
which spread the benefits of development to all sectors, and though
capital-intensive techniques may not be out of place in their case,
these must only be introduced at a pace which reduces (and does
not perpetuate) the existing dualism of the economic structure of
these countries. The desire of the OPEC countries to nationalise or
jointly manage the oil companies is no doubt partly related to their
desire to increase the backward and forward local linkages of the
oil industry.

But is it possible to advocate that most developing countries
should specialise in the production of processed goods and labour-
intensive manufactures? Exports of these goods have been growing
at a fast rate, but they still constitute a very small proportion of the
total exports of the poor countries. Moreover, the growth of such
exports is handicapped chiefly by the present 'escalating' structure
of industrial countries' tariffs and by the widespread use of formal
and informal 'voluntary' quantitative restrictions against low-wage-
manufactured imports. Trade can only be a means of development
if the international environment is favourable to the poor countries.
It is obvious that only if world markets do respond to the developing
countries' efforts to specialise in the production of processed commodities and simple manufactures, will international trade be able
to play a major role in the development process. The international
environment, reflecting as it does the economic relations of the rich
and poor countries, is an important determinant of development and
of world trade patterns. Let us now look at the actual patterns of the
international trade of the developing countries.

4.3 DEVELOPING COUNTRIES: TRADE PATTERNS

Table 4.1 summarises the structure of world trade. It shows that

Table 4.1 *World Exports by Origin and Destination, 1961–72*

Exports to	Developed Market Economies		LDCs		Centrally Planned Economies	
Exports from	% of exports	Growth rate (%)	% of exports	Growth rate (%)	% of exports	Growth rate (%)
Developed market economies						
1961–6 av.	73·8	10·8	22·0	6·3	3·8	13·0
1967–72 av.	76·7	15·3	19·1	12·7	3·8	12·9
LDCs						
1961–6 av.	71·9	7·5	21·3	5·7	5·7	11·1
1967–72 av.	73·6	11·2	19·8	10·3	5·4	11·7
(Middle East)						
(1961–6 av.)	(73·4)	(10·9)	(21·1)	(7·4)	(2·2)	(12·4)
(1967–72 av.)	(75·5)	(11·9)	(19·0)	(12·5)	(2·3)	(18·2)
Centrally planned economies						
1961–6 av.	20·9	13·7	14·4	11·8	64·6	5·4
1967–72 av.	24·1	13·2	15·0	9·9	60·7	11·1
World						
1961–6 av.	67·1	10·2	21·0	6·6	11·4	7·7
1967–72 av.	70·5	14·5	18·8	11·6	10·2	11·6

Source: *Annual Report, 1973* (IBRD/IDA), pp. 84–5.

over the period 1961–72 the share of the LDCs in world exports declined, whereas the share of the developed market economies increased. The growth rate of the exports of the developed countries was 9·8 per cent in the period 1961–6 and 14·6 per cent in the period 1967–72. Against this, the exports of the LDCs grew by 9·2 per cent in the first period and 11 per cent in the second period. Exports from the Middle East, consisting of the major oil-producing countries, grew by 10 per cent and 12 per cent respectively – growth rates higher than those of any other group of developing countries. The oil-exporting countries of the Third World thus retained their share of world exports till 1972, before improving their position considerably with the 1973–4 price rises.

Another important characteristic of Third World trade as revealed by Table 4.1 is 'West-centricness'. The share of the total exports of LDCs going to Western market economies increased from 71·9 per cent in the period 1961–6 to 73·6 per cent in the period 1967–72.[5] On the other hand, interregional trade within the developing world declined; it accounted for 21·3 per cent of the total exports of LDCs in the first period, but only 19·8 per cent in the second period. LDCs' trade with the developed socialist countries tended to remain more or less constant.

This information has to be viewed, moreover, in the context of the facts that the increase in commodity prices after 1970 only just restored the developing countries to their 1950s terms of trade and that even these primary commodity prices seemed vulnerable – except perhaps for the oil producers. Traditionally, primary commodities did not represent a vigorous export growth area for the developing countries. The growth rates of raw material and fuel exports from developing to developed (Western) countries were only 2·7 per cent and 9 per cent respectively over the period 1965–72; in interregional trade in the Third World they were 3·9 per cent and 4·8 per cent respectively. By contrast, exports of light machinery and light manufactured goods from developing to Western developed countries increased by 30 per cent and 13·6 per cent per annum respectively over the 1965–72 period (but of course from much lower initial levels); similarly, in interregional trade these exports expanded by 16.6 per cent and 11 per cent per annum respectively.

Admittedly, these aggregative trends conceal important variations. Nevertheless two facts emerge: (a) the overwhelming importance of the Western market economies for the developing countries as sources of export earnings; and (b) the importance of the manufactured goods sector as a source of export expansion – except for the OPEC countries in the short run. In their quest for a reform of the international trade system, the developing countries are therefore concerned primarily with opening up the market of the developed countries for their products, as well as with improving their terms of trade.

NOTES

1 See, for example, A. MacBean, *Export Instability and Economic Development* (London, George Allen & Unwin, 1966), pp. 58–108.
2 MacBean, op. cit., p. 94.
3 See G. Myrdal, *An International Economy* (New York, Harper, 1956); R. Prebisch, *Towards a New Trade Policy for Development* (UNCTAD Document E/Conf/46/3, 1964); and A. W. Singer, 'The Gains from Trade', *American Economic Review, Papers and Proceedings* (1950). The theme of 'unequal exchange' has more recently been further developed,

e.g. by Arrighi Emmanuel, *Unequal Exchange* (Monthly Review Press, 1972).

4 The import substitution strategy is explained in detail in Chapter 5.

5 Middle Eastern trade displayed a similar pattern. It increased with the Western economies and fell with the other developing countries in the two periods.

CHAPTER 5

Trade Policies of the Rich Countries

Chapters 1 to 3 have outlined the general environment within which the trade between rich and poor countries is conducted. In Chapter 5 the specific trade policies pursued by the rich countries will be examined, in order to identify the sort of changes that could increase the impact of trade on development.

Leaving aside the oil producers, the international economy in the 1970s is characterised by a sharp division between the rich and poor economies. The gap between the two blocs, moreover, has been increasing at an accelerated rate. If international trade is to be restructured so as to enable the poor countries to orient their production structure towards specialisation in light manufactures and processed commodities, and to use their primary exports as a proper basis for development, the rich countries must be prepared actively to encourage such a reorientation. The need for rich country support in the task of building an international economic system which facilitates development is widely recognised. The UN International Development Strategy for the 1970s emphasises the importance of implementing the General System of Preferences (GSP) negotiated through the UN Conference on Trade and Development (UNCTAD) and of eliminating tariff and non-tariff restrictions on exports from the developing countries. It also calls for an increased flow of relevant technological knowledge to poor countries. But is the international economic system in fact evolving in accordance with these objectives? We may examine some major changes in the pattern of international economic relations in order to estimate the trade prospects for the poor countries in the foreseeable future.

5.1 TRADE IN PRIMARY COMMODITIES

The predominant role of primary commodities in the trade of the LDCs cannot be ignored. If the broad category of primary products includes raw materials, fuels and unprocessed edibles, exports of primary products constitute over 80 per cent of the export earnings of the LDCs in the recent past. Even if oil is excluded from primary products, exports of the latter still account for about 60 per cent of the total.

The share of primary products in the world trade – barring oil – however, has been declining since 1950–1 – the short-lived Korean War boom. Long-run prospects for expanding (or even maintaining) the level of external demand for both food and industrial raw materials are rather limited, despite the boom of the early 1970s. According to Engel's well-known 'Law', as income rises expenditure on food tends to constitute a smaller proportion of consumer spending. Hence the overall income elasticity of food exports is low (though there are exceptions), and this is often also the case with exported industrial raw materials. As modern industrial production expands there is a relative economy in the use of raw materials. Moreover, industrial raw materials produced in the poor countries are confronted in world markets today with competition from synthetic substitutes. The relatively high price and output instability of the raw materials of the LDCs may also tend to work against an expansion in export demand in the long run, despite the spectacular gains made in the early 1970s.

Yet the sluggishness in the world demand for the primary goods (excluding oil) exported by the LDCs cannot be attributed entirely to the change that has occurred in the structure of production in the developed countries. Nor can it be explained merely by reference to the very real increase in productivity of the agricultural sector of the rich nations. An important element in the reduction of the import demand for primary goods exports from the poorer countries is the protectionist policies that are being pursued by the industrial countries with respect to their agricultural sector.

By almost any standards, the protection rates of the rich countries against the exports of the LDCs are excessive. Levels of agricultural protection are substantial. The Common Agricultural Policy (CAP) of the European Economic Community (EEC), to which the United Kingdom subscribes, maintains high domestic prices for agricultural commodities by a system of 'variable levies' which ensure that prices do not fall below those specified by the CAP.[1] The European countries have used quotas and other quantitative restrictions for limiting agricultural trade even among themselves. Under the aegis of the EEC these have been removed, but intra-EEC specialisation in the agricultural field has invariably taken place at the expense of third countries. The United States also has a

74

highly protectionist policy concerning agricultural trade; there, support to domestic farm policies is given by a whole range of import quotas. The traditional UK method was less directly protectionist, relying on income deficiency payments to farmers instead of import levies or controls.

The national agricultural policies of the rich countries constitute the most important impediment in the way of liberalising trade in agricultural commodities. Such policies have entailed substantial cost to the rich countries themselves. The rich EEC countries, the United States and Japan have devised farm policies in order to increase the income of their rural population and to reduce dependence on food imports. This is usually done by raising the price of agricultural goods and limiting the import of agricultural commodities into the economy. This is by no means the most efficient method of giving assistance to the farming sector, if such support is considered necessary. Support could and should be given in the form of direct income subsidies and the extension of auxiliary agricultural services. This would at least allow for a reduction in the domestic prices of agricultural goods in the rich countries and enable the LDCs to compete through their agricultural exports. In particular, policies that discriminate heavily against LDC-produced agricultural commodities should be abandoned. The EEC system of export subsidies financed by variable import levies should be revised. Significant progress towards the reduction of agricultural protection by the EEC has been made through the Lomé Convention signed in 1975.

At present, agricultural trade patterns are disadvantageous from the point of view of the poor countries. The (effective) protection of agricultural production is increasing over time in most countries.[2] The rich countries dominate international agricultural trade, both as sources of exports and as destinations of imports. During the 1960s the share of the poor countries in agricultural trade declined and their reliance on food imports increased.[3] Thus high food prices do not, on balance, benefit the LDCs. If present protectionist policies are not relaxed the situation is likely to be even more grim in the future. The trade policy of the rich countries is a major contributor to the increasing lack of productive employment in the rural hinterland of the Third World. Improved agricultural technology has made it possible for agricultural production to increase considerably, but if the fruits of this increased productivity are denied to the small farmers and agricultural workers of the poor countries the 'Green Revolution' will not facilitate these countries' development. Despite the availability of the new techniques, we will not be able to come to grips with an international food crisis which threatens death by starvation to countless millions. It is not enough to produce enough food in the rich countries, if the needy in the LDCs cannot buy it for lack of incomes and foreign exchange earnings. The poor countries are seriously threatened by the agricultural trade policies of the rich and have sought to circumvent these threats by specialising in the production of light, labour-intensive manufactures, including the processing of their agricultural products.

The existence of tariffs, administrative barriers, quota restrictions, etc. on the imports of agricultural commodities, required as a consequence of subsidies and high prices granted to local farmers, is often economically irrational and very harmful to the poorer countries, especially to the poorer sections within this group. Their removal, however, is rendered difficult by the simple fact that they have existed for so long. It is commonly recognised, for example, that little or no political or economic disadvantage would accrue to the developed countries if trade restrictions on coffee, cocoa and spices were to be considerably lowered. This is so because these products do not compete with commodities produced in the industrial countries; nor have synthetic substitutes for coffee, cocoa or spices as yet been found.[4]

For the majority of primary product exports from the LDCs, however, competition from synthetic substitutes is a very important problem. Synthetic substitutes for both textiles and rubber have now established world markets for themselves. Moreover, once a market has been created for a synthetic commodity, occasioned perhaps by a rise in price and a relative scarcity of the competing primary good, a subsequent fall in the price of the primary good has little effect. The advantage that the synthetic industry enjoys in terms of economies of scale and low variable costs is usually overwhelming.

Some synthetic fabrics, synthetic rubber and synthetic leather are all part of 'petrochemical' production, and their production processes have the technical and financial characteristics of the petrochemical industry. The characteristics of the petrochemical 'parent' industry are as follows:

1   It is a highly sophisticated technology.
2   It exhibits marked economies of scale.
3   It has a long gestation period.
4   It requires heavy financial investment.
5   It is highly capital-intensive (in the factor proportions sense of a high capital/labour ratio).

76

6 It is dominated by large international concerns and the financial barriers to entry are formidable.

It is not suprising therefore that the product of such an industry has important technological competitive advantages over the 'natural' product of perhaps the most backward sector of the poorer countries. Some of these advantages are: (a) synthetic products can be standardised to a degree that is not possible with corresponding primary goods; (b) it is usually much more possible to cater for quality changes in demand in the production of the synthetic products; (c) synthetic goods are usually more durable than primary products; and (d) because primary goods are produced by a large number of small units in many different countries, whereas their synthetic substitutes are produced by a few large and highly sophisticated industrial enterprises, co-ordination of decisions and forecasting of market trends is considerably easier in the case of the synthetic products. Thus, whatever the scarcity-induced advantages that occur to primary products from time to time, in the long run the synthetic products have the most important advantages – unless of course the production of the synthetic product is based on a scarce or very costly raw material (e.g. oil) which cannot easily be substituted.

It is quite clear that in the long run the comparative advantage that the rich countries have in the production of synthetic substitutes for primary commodities, and also for food, will force the poorer countries to hunt for new channels of export expansion. The poorer countries cannot in the foreseeable future hope for major domestic development of any of the big synthetic substitute industries because, as pointed out earlier, the financial and technological barriers to entry into such industries are formidable. A number of LDCs can, however, especially within the context of a comprehensive regional integration programme, aim at the establishment of an economically viable synthetic fibre or synthetic rubber industrial complex. Even so, it would be quite some time before such an industry became truly competitive in world markets.

But this is perhaps too bleak a picture of the prospects of agricultural export products, as in a short-run sense, primary commodities undoubtly stand a much better chance than synthetics. When a synthetic substitute is introduced for the first time the public is (in general) quite slow in its response. It takes some considerable time before synthetic goods create their own markets. The growth in the demand for such commodities is gradual, and the primary good which is under threat from a synthetic substitute can expect to hold its own for quite some time; e.g. despite the availability of different types of synthetic fibre since about the turn of the century, natural fibres still have the greater share of the market, though the proportion is continuously declining.[5] Moreover, the successful large-scale introduction and public acceptance of most synthetic substitutes often depends upon a critical impulse provided by the existence of abnormal circumstances; e.g. the case of both rubber and fabric synthetics, the two world wars, the Great Depression of the 1930s and the Korean War provided the critical impulses necessary for their worldwide popularisation.

Hence most of the poorer countries have a chance of planning for the change in their production structure that takes into account the growth of synthetic products. Export diversification is an unavoidable necessity for those of the LDCs that have to depend critically on their external trade sector to initiate and/or sustain the development process. This is as true for the oil economies as for other LDCs.

Two important conclusions emerge from the foregoing analysis. First, if export diversification is to become possible for a large majority of the poor countries, it is clear that international co-operation and co-ordination are inevitably required. Moreover, it is futile to talk of international action to thwart the development of synthetic substitutes; such action will be strongly resisted not merely by multinational corporations but also by the governments concerned. (Additional technical research on natural products and tropical materials and production problems may, however, be more easily conceded.) It is much more realistic and sensible to urge the developed countries to assist the LDCs in their programmes of export diversification by easing the social cost of resource reallocation in both the rich and poor countries. Above all, it is time to begin to distribute research and development expenditures and technological progress more evenly over the rich and poor countries. Such international action will in the long run prove much more fruitful than action aimed merely at slowing or preventing the development of synthetic substitutes.

Second, it is also important to tackle the problem of price and revenue instability which confronts the primary exporters. The introduction of synthetic substitutes for primary goods will in fact tend to increase the price stability for primary products. There exists at this moment little doubt that export instability is a far greater problem for the poor than for the rich countries, though it is not possible to make blanket statements about the relative importance of this problem for all LDCs taken together. Clearly, not all developing countries suffer from significant and frequent fluctuations in their export earnings, but a large proportion of them do find their development effort restricted by wide fluctuations exports.[6] It has been estimated that during the immediate postwar period (1946–58) export instability for the LDCs was greater than for the developed countries by about 30 per cent.[7]

What are the determinants of the relatively higher level of export instability for the LDCs? A number of factors might be enumerated. One is that these countries usually export a few commodities to a small group of importers, whereas a diversified export portfolio would allow fluctuations in the export earnings of some commodities to be offset by counteracting fluctuations in other commodities. Moreover, most LDCs are exporters of primary goods, and primary goods markets are characterised by inelastic demand and supply and by frequent shifts in the supply curve, which are factors adding to the export revenue instability of primary goods.

Export instability is inextricably related to both the structure of production within the poorer economies and the trade practices of the rich countries. Ultimately, the problem can be adequately tackled only through planned export diversification by the LDCs, but it is again impossible for most LDCs to implement such a programme without international support. Such support may come in the form of commodity agreements, compensations, financing schemes or supplementary financing schemes.

It is significant that despite the boom in oil and other commodity prices the LDCs have continued to show concern about stabilising their export earnings from primary exports. The UN Sixth and Seventh Special Sessions advocated renewed efforts at establishing commodity agreements between the producer and consumer nations of specified primary commodities, in order to minimise fluctuations in the export receipts of the developing countries. Recently, the Lomé Convention of the EEC and forty-six developing countries have adopted a plan to stabilise the export earnings from primary products. Similarly, UNCTAD has proposed an Integrated Commodity Plan which aims to stabilise the export earnings of primary producers.[8]

5.2 TRADE IN MANUFACTURES

Developing countries have sought to expand manufactured exports, as this promises to offset the uncertainties and fluctuations in their primary export receipts. As early as 1964 a major theme at the first

UNCTAD conference was the need for both the rich and poor countries to take measures that would enable the latter to expand their exports of manufactured goods to the former. Chapter III of *Towards a New Trade Policy for Development*, the report prepared by UNCTAD's first Secretary-General, Raul Prebisch, for the 1964 conference, discussed the problem of accelerating industrialisation in poorer developing countries, laying particular stress on (a) the difficulties created by policies of import substitution based on excessive protectionism, and (b) the consequent uncompetitiveness of so many products on world markets. The report also drew attention to the substantial tariff and non-tariff barriers in the industrialised countries against the import of manufactured goods produced in the poor countries.

The duties and other restrictions on the import of manufactured goods from poor countries are still relatively high. Table 5.1 shows both the average nominal and average effective rates of protection on manufactures as being higher on imports from the poor countries than on imports from other rich countries. Moreover, the Kennedy Round of the GATT negotiations for tariff reductions seems to have actually increased the relative level of discrimination.

Table 5.1 *Average[a] Nominal and Effective[b] Tariffs on Rich Countries' Imports of Manufactures (%)*

	Average Nominal Tariffs on Imports from:		Average Effective Tariffs on Imports from:	
	All countries	Poor countries	All countries	Poor countries
Pre-Kennedy Round, 1967	10·9	17·1	19·2	33·4
Post-Kennedy Round, 1972	6·5	11·8	11·1	22·6

[a] The weights used in calculating these averages are non-preferential imports.
[b] The effective rate of protection is a measure which indicates protection given by tariffs etc. to a production process. The nominal rate of protection measures the increased cost that the tariff structure imposes on the consumer in the protected market.

Source: B. Balassa, *The Structure of Protection in Industrial Countries* (IBRD Report No. EC-152), quoted by the Economic Planning staff, Overseas Development Administration in 'International Trade: A Background Paper' (Cambridge Development Conference, mimeo, 1972).

In 1967 the effective rate of protection on all manufactured imports into rich countries was 19·2 per cent, but on manufactured imports from poor countries was 33·4 per cent. In 1972 the comparable rates were 11·1 per cent and 22·6 per cent respectively. Thus, while in 1967 the effective rate of protection on manufactured imports from LDCs was about 84 per cent higher than that on all manufactured imports, in 1972 the former was 109 per cent higher than the latter. In part this increase reflects the fact that the poor countries in general produce and export goods that have higher import duties.

Textiles, clothing and light manufactures constitute about half of the total manufactured exports of the poor countries. Rich countries, on the other hand, export mainly heavy-engineering products. The textile and clothing industries, and industries included in the 'light manufacturing' category, are generally speaking labour-intensive. Besides clothing, the poor countries export footwear, sports goods, travel goods, toys, etc., and such exports from the LDCs have grown at a much faster rate than textile exports. The differential growth rate is explained above all by the commercial policies of the rich countries. Whereas textile imports into the rich countries are restricted by high tariffs and also are subject to (discriminatory) quotas and quantitative limits, the labour-intensive 'other manufactures' may encounter high effective tariff barriers but are only rarely subject to quantitative restrictions. Engineering product exports from the poor countries have also been growing very rapidly. These products are often manufactured and exported by the multinational corporations operating in the LDCs,[9] and consist mainly of 'components [and] re-exports of products brought in for contract processing'.[10] Lower protection rates on these products are thus of mutual benefit to both the rich and poor countries.

The trade policies of the rich countries can best be analysed through looking at the way they behave in world markets, for it is in these markets that the rich and poor bargain with each other and it is this bargaining process which determines the relative shares of the total gains from trade. We have already seen that, generally speaking, the rich countries are in a strong position and that in the past they have sought to exploit the opportunities that this strength has given them. An examination of the conduct and practice of international trade in different world markets reveals the striking facts that the development needs of the poor countries are very rarely taken into consideration and that trade in manufactures and in primary goods is not in general organised on lines that facilitate the development of the LDCs.

The measures that might be taken by the rich, and that in some cases are now beginning to be implemented, are of two main types. First, there are those measures which are intended to remove or mitigate the effects of the various tariff and non-tariff barriers that inhibit the free flow of processed and manufactured products in international trade; UNCTAD's GSP scheme, for generalised non-reciprocal preferences, is the outstanding example. Second, there are those measures designed to offset the adverse consequences of an increasing flow of imports on domestic industries in the importing countries; the textile industry is the most obvious example. Several countries have introduced such 'adjustment assistance' programmes of one kind or another.

Before we go on to consider any detailed policy questions, however, it is important to try and sort out the real nature of the problem with which they are intended to deal. The most superficial study of the arguments and policy proposals concerned with the expansion of the poorer countries' trade in manufactures suggests that there is a good deal of confusion as to whether the purpose of such arguments and proposals should be merely to permit the realisation of existing comparative advantage in favour of the poor countries. In other words, would the desired growth of trade take place if barriers were removed, or is it necessary to go beyond merely removing barriers to introduce positive measures to help developing countries improve their competitive position?

The answer depends on the country and the product. Some of the poorer countries are competitive in some products; these countries usually either are strongly resource-based (e.g. metals, timber and timber products, and processed foods) or have deliberately set out to build up the export potential of parts of their industry.[11] Other countries would find it difficult to compete on the open market in almost any product, either because their own industries are very high-cost – often as a consequence of excessive protection – or because, as in the case of many smaller African countries, the economic base is so small that industries of the necessary size and sophistication do not exist. Finally, there are a few countries that are competitive in a wide range of manufactured products, possessing a broad industrial base and the management skills needed to make effective use of the potential cost advantage imparted by their low wage rates – an advantage which in most poor countries is largely dissipated by low productivity, management deficiencies and government policies that discourage its exploitation. Hong Kong, South Korea and perhaps Mexico are current examples of economies in this last position, and fifteen or twenty years ago Japan might also have been so regarded. The difficulties that are still being

82

experienced in integrating the Japanese economy with the other free-market economies of the industrial world are perhaps a pointer to problems that lie ahead as other developing countries achieve Japanese levels of industrial efficiency.

Only in cotton-type textiles does it appear that almost all the poorer countries with significant domestic textile industries are competitive with almost all industrial countries. However, it does not follow that the removal of barriers is the only action necessary, at least not if considerations of the relative needs of individual developing countries are allowed to influence policy. Of the poorer countries that have a significant share of international trade in cotton-type textiles, India is probably the least competitive. But India and its problems loom so large in the Third World, and foreign currency earnings are so essential to the country's economic survival, that it may be desirable for importing countries to take special measures to protect India's share of the market – or at least to prevent the lowest-cost exporters from snapping up all the business going. This sort of reasoning, which is applicable to many different exporters in different product groups, underlies the provision in the EEC's general preference scheme that restricts any one exporting country to 50 per cent of the total tariff-free imports of any given product.

Lastly, it should be observed that a similar degree of confusion exists over the attitudes adopted towards affected domestic industries in the importing rich countries. Put in its sharpest form, the question is: should adjustment assistance measures be designed to slow down the rate of change – and even perhaps, through re-equipment subsidies and training programmes, to encourage these industries to develop a 'positive' competitive response – or should they be directed towards accelerating structural change in the rich countries and enabling labour to move out of the declining industries? Most of the measures so far considered or adopted have reflected an uneasy compromise between these two opposing objectives, with, on the whole, a balance in favour of slowing down rather than speeding up change. It will be argued that the emphasis should be the other way round, because more rapid structural change is in the best long-term interests of rich as well as of poor countries.

5.21 *Measures to Remove Barriers to Trade*

In practice, the application of the most favoured nation principle in GATT has meant that all developing countries and not just those that are signatories to the Agreement, have benefited from the various tariff reductions that have been achieved in successive rounds of GATT negotiations. However, by the early 1960s it had become apparent that this equitable treatment was not enough to satisfy the demands of the developing countries – demands that were increasingly coming to be recognised by the rich countries as having a basis in the facts of the situation and the scale of the problem. During the general debates and discussions that preceded the formal opening of the Kennedy Round of negotiations in GATT and the first UNCTAD conference (both of which took place in 1964), it emerged that the poor countries were dissatisfied because they felt that products of particular interest to them were not given sufficient prominence in GATT deliberations and, more fundamentally, that they needed special preferential advantages in the markets of industrial countries to enable them to compete.

These feelings led to the formulation of UNCTAD's preference scheme (i.e. the GSP). They also helped to focus the attention of ministers in GATT on the need to complete the new Trade and Development chapter that had been under discussion since 1958. In this chapter (which was approved in November 1964) the Contracting Parties gave recognition to the special problems and needs of developing countries, and the developed Contracting Parties explicitly stated that they 'do not expect reciprocity for commitments made by them in trade negotiations to reduce or remove tariffs and other barriers to the trade of less-developed Contracting Parties' (Article XXXVI, paragraph 8). This statement paved the way for the UNCTAD scheme by making it possible for countries to contemplate granting non-reciprocal preferences without contravening GATT rules.

Six years were to elapse, however, before the resolution passed at the first UNCTAD conference calling for the establishment of a generalised non-reciprocal preference scheme in favour of poor countries resulted in formal proposals. The main difficulties encountered in devising a workable scheme were product coverage, the depth and extent of the tariff cuts that importing countries were prepared to make, the special problems arising from the fact that some of the countries classed as 'developing' are more competitive than others, and the need to take account of different existing preference systems.

In effect, what has happened in the development of the UNCTAD scheme is that the 'donor' countries – the term is significant – have agreed to differ in the scope of their offers. The language used to describe the scheme – 'donors', 'recipients', 'offers' – is indicative of some muddled thinking about its purpose. Many leading exponents of international trade theory (e.g. H. G. Johnson) would argue with undeniable logic that a scheme which enables consumers in industrial countries to increase their real incomes by buying imported goods more cheaply than goods from their own domestic producers, and which thus also helps to reduce inflation, benefits importing as well as exporting countries. But in practice it is clear that the rich countries see the scheme as a concessionary one in which they are being asked to give away something (i.e. tariff protections) without any return, and this attitude of mind explains why so much stress seems to have been laid on equitable burden-sharing in the discussions that have taken place – mainly in the Development Assistance Committee (DAC) of the Organisation for Economic Co-operation and Development (OECD). The major reason why the rich countries have taken this view is their apprehension about the adverse effects of increased imports on competing domestic industries – their fears that unemployment might rise and both money and real incomes fall despite the increased purchasing power of given domestic incomes. The question as to how far these apprehensions are justified, on the basis of experience to date and such estimates as can be made of what might happen in the future, will be examined in subsection 5.23.

5.22 Non-tariff Barriers

The most familiar examples of non-tariff barriers to the exports of manufactures from poor countries are in the field of textiles and related products (e.g. clothing and leather goods). It is in this area that the competitive advantage of developing countries has become most evident. Moreover, these industries are important because they are more employment-inducive than the capital-intensive heavy industries that large poor countries (e.g. India and Brazil) have made great sacrifices to establish. However, in this area many industrial countries have, as part of their own industrial history, created domestic industries that are important enough to make claims for protection which governments find it difficult to resist.

More generally, it can be said that non-tariff barriers are probably more significant in relation to trade between the poor and rich countries than in relation to trade among the latter, if only because the poor countries are less well informed about the nature of the barriers they face and much less well placed to find out how these can be overcome in practice.

A GATT document lists over 800 barriers, ranging from quotas – now few in number but quantitatively still important in terms of the volume of trade affected by them – to rules determining government procurement procedures, health and safety standards, and many minor administrative and customs regulations that restrict the free flow of goods across national frontiers. Additionally, there is growing concern about the extent to which multinational corporations can control the trade of their subsidiaries in different countries, as regards both the products marketed and countries of marketing. In certain circumstances, for example, a chemical or fibre company might seek to prevent its subsidiary in a developing country from exporting or to restrict its exports to a limited range of markets where they would not come into competition with the exports of a subsidiary in another country. The government of the developing country involved might well be prepared to co-operate in this policy if it needed the subsidiary badly enough, with the capital and know-how it represented.

As yet, nothing much has been done to tackle these problems, though Article XXXVII of GATT (also part of the Trade and Development chapter) does commit Contracting Parties to refrain from introducing or increasing the incidence of non-tariff barriers, as well as tariffs. A further measure which it is hoped will do something to reduce ignorance and improve the developing countries' knowledge of market conditions and regulations is the establishment of the joint GATT/UNCTAD International Trade Centre. Bargaining capacity with multinational corporations is to be improved by a new UN Committee and Information Bureau on transnational corporations and by training courses in developing countries. The Tokyo Round of GATT negotiations which began in 1975 and at which the developing countries are playing an active part will, it is hoped, lead to significant changes in the non-tariff barriers that restrict trade in manufactured goods between developed and developing countries.

5.23 Adjustment Assistance

In the field of manufacturing trade, high tariff walls and quantitative restrictions imposed by the developed countries make it increasingly difficult for the poor countries to specialise in the exports of those labour-intensive manufactures in which they have a comparative advantage. These protectionist policies are in sharp contrast with the general willingness of the rich countries to permit each other to reap the benefits of international specialisation based on their respective comparative advantages by reducing protection on engineering products and other 'technology-intensive' goods. The differences in policy, as in the case of agriculture, can be explained by the fact that the social goals of the rich countries commit them to maintaining the income of workers in the classical labour-intensive industries. Often these industries are low-wage and located in old now 'depressed', industrial areas, and strong 'income distribution' arguments are used in favour of subsidising the income of people in them (both workers and employers). This is usually done by reducing competitive pressure and inflating the prices of labour-intensive manufactures in the domestic markets of the rich countries. Such practices usually harm both the rich and poor countries. They impede the evolution of a pattern of international specialisation that is based upon the changing comparative advantages of the trading partners. The real forces in the international economy are constantly altering the international division of labour. The integration of the present economy reflects the 'increasing diffusion of technology, transportation and communication developments [and] the new forms of transnational enterprise [all of which] are technical elements of [the] new international industrial revolution'.[12]

In order to reap the advantages of this new industrial breakthrough we have to facilitate the transfer of the simpler industrial processes to the developing countries, a move which will require the extension of adjustment assistance to the people employed in these industries in the rich countries. This will make it possible for the rich countries to reconcile their social goals with liberal trade policies. Efforts must be made to increase the occupational mobility of the industrial labour force in the rich countries.

The US Trade Expansion Act 1962 incorporated the first serious direct attempt by an advanced industrial country to introduce a major programme of adjustment assistance for industries affected by a growth of imports. The Trade Expansion Act 1951 had enjoined the Tariff Commission to consider, *inter alia*, the impact of imports on domestic production, employment, prices, wages and salaries when deciding whether or not to recommend tariff increases under the escape clause mechanism. But the 1962 Act made provision for direct financial assistance to firms and workers affected, and indeed made it clear that this type of action was to be regarded as preferable to a tariff increase. The 1962 Act was drafted not long after the founding of the EEC, when the prime objective of US commercial activity was to lower the Community's common external tariff through negotiations in GATT – the negotiations that subsequently became known as the Kennedy Round. Its adjustment assistance clauses were not, therefore, drafted with the poorer countries primarily in mind.

Another statute that may be said to have incorporated a range of adjustment assistance measures, though they were not explicitly identified as such, is the UK Cotton Industry Act 1959. The 1959 Act did in fact incorporate three adjustment assistance measures:

(a) cash payments to firms scrapping plant, with a bonus to those leaving the industry altogether; (b) grants to firms undertaking approved schemes of re-equipment; and (c) compensation to workers who were losing their jobs as a result of this subsidised contraction and modernisation.

These two measures, together with the Bill put before the US Congress by Congressman Wilbur Mills in 1970, provide a starting point for discussing the concept of adjustment assistance and the formidable practical difficulties that arise in drawing up programmes for its application in specific circumstances. The problems of promoting industrial change in rich economies – which is really what adjustment assistance is all about – are, *par excellence*, problems of political economy, and the student who wants to reach a full understanding of the issues involved needs to investigate the political and institutional aspects of the subject as well as its economics. It is not possible, however, to go fully into these aspects within this text.

The first question to be asked about adjustment assistance programmes is whether they are intended to promote or to slow down the pace of change, either within the industrial structure as a whole or within a single industry. To give an example: at one extreme a programme intended to maximise the rate of change might consist simply of special unemployment pay, of retraining schemes for displaced labour, and possibly also of provision for financial compensation to owners of assets made useless on condition that the money was not reinvested in the same industry; while at the other extreme a programme intended to moderate the rate of change might involve a mixture of special grants and/or investment incentives and tax provisions, together with tariff and/or quota protection.

The UK Cotton Industry Act 1959 is particularly interesting in that it reflects much confusion about objectives. It both established a system of cash grants to firms scrapping plant (with premiums to those getting out of the industry altogether) *and* made provision for financial subsidies to companies re-equipping in order to be able to compete more effectively.

The second problem area concerns the question of eligibility. Underlying the idea of adjustment assistance programmes is the assumption that certain special circumstances will arise in which it will be desirable to provide additional help to the people immediately affected, over and above any generally available unemployment pay, redundancy pay, training programmes, regional investment incentives, etc. But defining these circumstances so as to limit the availability of special measures without making them totally inaccessible is a difficult matter.

The US Trade Expansion Act 1962 adopted a narrow definition of eligibility, making it necessary for imports to be the major cause of disruption, and this is the main reason why so little use was made initially of the Act's adjustment assistance provisions. In 1969, however, the definition was relaxed, the Act now requiring evidence that imports were a substantial rather than 'the major' cause of injury; since then there have been many more applications for assistance, of which about a quarter have been granted. The Mills Bill 1970 proposed further relaxation of this criterion, to the point that all that would be required is evidence that imports have 'contributed substantially' to disruption. Apart from the crucially important practical questions of defining 'major' and 'substantial' – and indeed the scope of the industry or industrial sector which is claiming disruption of its normal business – there are clearly attempts to widen adjustment assistance at work here.

Another need is to identify accurately the recipients of adjustment assistance. Usually affected workers are helped, but little thought seems to have been given to the desirability or otherwise of helping the owners of the companies going out of business, though small family-owned firms often may face problems of readjustment as great as their employees'. The UK Cotton Industry Act 1959 was in fact oriented towards companies more than towards workers. The government of the day believed – and to a large extent was justified in believing – that, provided the general level of economic activity was kept high, workers would be absorbed elsewhere without too much difficulty. However, most subsequent general discussions of the problems of structural change and adjustment assistance have concentrated on labour and largely ignored the difficulties to which immobility of capital and management resources can give rise.

The principle of adjustment assistance, i.e. that the rich countries should bear the cost of adapting to changes in the structure of world industrial production and trade, commands general assent, but more consideration and more experimental programmes are required if it is to be applied successfully. Adjustment assistance programmes generally make it easier for the governments of rich countries to take the initiative in liberalising trade and enabling the poor countries to expand their processed and manufactured exports.

5.3 PROSPECTS FOR THE 1970s

The removal of restrictions on manufactured exports from LDCs has not taken place at a satisfactory pace. The developing countries in 1974 called for 'the improvement, implementation and enlargement of the generalised preference scheme for exports of agricultural primary commodities, manufactures and semi-manufactures from developing to developed countries'[13] at the Sixth Special Session of the UN General Assembly. Discrepancies in the different preference schemes of the rich countries remain considerable, and their implementation leaves a lot to be desired. The developed countries regard preferences as voluntary and are likely to make this abundantly clear during the Tokyo Round of GATT negotiations. They do not consider the 'erosion' of preferential margins emerging from general tariff cuts as justifying the award of compensation.

5.31 Trade Prospects of the Poor Countries and the Tokyo Round of GATT Negotiations

The GATT Contracting Parties have launched a new round of multilateral trade negotiations, known as the Tokyo Round.[14] One of the main aims of these negotiations is, in the words of the Director of the Trade Division of GATT, to 'promote the growth of production capacity of less developed areas by integrating it more closely with that of the more advanced regions, while allowing the . . . [latter] to control the accelerating transformation of their own economies . . . without impairing the economically vital features of their interdependence'.[15]

In order to achieve these objectives the rich trading nations will have to co-operate on a wide range of policies, which would involve the granting of concessions in areas in which a great deal of political tension has been generated. The negotiations are likely to focus sharply on escape clauses and safeguard provisions and, moreover, will be very wide-ranging. It has been agreed that they should cover tariffs and non-tariff barriers on both industrial and agricultural products, and special attention is to be given to the export problems of the poor countries. The negotiations are likely to be influenced by the broad agreement reached in September 1972 on the reform of the international monetary system and the subsequent endorsement of the floating exchange rate system. In particular, a greater willingness to alter exchange rates will allow imbalances in international payments to be corrected with greater ease. The balance-of-payments consequences of trade liberalisation are likely to be less important if an adequate adjustment is operating. This is likely to be of considerable value to the poor countries, for in the new circumstances reciprocity in tariff reduction will not be sought by the rich countries in order to deal with the deflationary effect of decreases in import duties. Similarly, the importance of the OPEC countries in particular and of the LDCs generally has been enhanced in the Tokyo Round by the rise in the price of petroleum and other primary commodities since October 1973. Events since that date have increased the determination of the developing countries to see that nothing short of a fundamental restructuring of international economic relations is achieved as a result of trade and monetary negotiations.[16]

All the developed countries are in broad agreement that import duties and tariffs are inefficient policy measures. The rapidly increasing comparative advantage of the poor countries in the traditional labour-intensive industries is already too large to be frustrated by tariff barriers. The tariff is also incapable of protecting domestic industry against foreign firms, especially in the fields of science-based capital goods production, for multinational corporations tend to invest behind high tariff walls. It is therefore being advocated by very powerful trade interests that the GATT negotiations should aim at eliminating all industrial tariffs according to a predetermined time schedule. The proposal has the support of the US Administration. Such a scheme would, it is argued, avoid the discrimination involved in the formation or enlargement of regional groupings among the rich countries (e.g. the EEC). Other suggestions have also been made advocating another conventional round of GATT tariff reductions, harmonisation of national tariff schedules, and the adoption of a sectoral approach which aims at achieving maximum reductions for each economic sector. The Tokyo Round of negotiations is, however, taking place against a background where the threat of regionalisation is never absent from the minds of the participants. However, the eventual elimination of all tariffs may not be unwelcome to even the Europeans.

As far as the poor countries are concerned, the gradual phasing out of tariffs would amount to a reduction in the effectiveness of the general system of preferences that has been initiated through UNCTAD. It is of course difficult – some would argue impossible – to determine with any degree of confidence the actual value of the advantage that a particular set of preferences gives to a poor country. Yet provision should certainly be made to obtain adequate compensation for the elimination of the preferences. The poor countries should try to safeguard their markets in the rich countries by negotiating for additional commitments. The poor countries must also actively seek to seize the opportunities that arise when trade expansion among the rich leads to a shift of resources from the declining industries (which usually compete with the export industries of the LDCs).

However, the poor countries may well find that tariff elimination

91

will not have a very great effect on their exports. The exports of the poor countries, both manufacturers and primary agricultural commodities, are subject to extensive non-tariff restrictions and barriers. In 1972, non-tariff barriers accounted for almost 50 per cent of total effective protection for US imports of primary goods, and of intermediate and consumer goods; on the other hand, US capital goods had *negative* effective protection from non-tariff barriers.[17] Primary goods and intermediate and consumer goods are extensively exported by the poor countries.

GATT rules to control quantitative restrictions have been rendered largely inoperative by the Protocol of Provisional Application under which most countries apply the GATT Treaty. The Kennedy Round left the non-tariff barriers virtually untouched. This does not mean that non-tariff barriers to trade cannot be negotiated; however, it is not possible to identify a comprehensive negotiation technique to cover all non-tariff barriers. It is essential that attempts must be made to evolve international rules of fair competition to which governments are committed, if GATT is to have any effect whatsoever in the realm of agricultural protectionism.

Agricultural protection is usually of the non-tariff kind; moreover, reducing agricultural trade barriers will invariably involve tampering with domestic farm policies. This, for instance, must involve the limiting of export subsidies and the setting of maximum levels for farm support. Such action may be of great benefit to the least developed countries which specialise in agricultural exports and will also go a long way towards compensating poor countries for the reduction in the effectiveness of the GSP resulting from the removal of tariff barriers. The relaxation of quantitative restrictions on manufactured and agricultural exports from the poor countries can be jeopardised if exceptions and safeguard measures are used to protect industries (e.g. textiles, plastics, etc.) in the rich countries with which the poor can compete effectively.

The Tokyo Round of GATT negotiations provides an excellent opportunity for the rich and poor countries to reorientate international economic relations in such a way that trade becomes a major development-inducing factor. Trade can lead to development only if it contributes towards a restructuring of the domestic economy in a way which allows a maximum use of human, as well as natural, resources. Trade must lead not merely to growth, but also to more employment, a better pattern of income distribution and higher levels of health, nutrition, education, etc.

It is encouraging to note that the changed international environment since the more than fourfold increase in the price of oil has induced the developed countries to adopt a more positive attitude towards the Third World. There is still considerable resistance to programmes which are seen as capable of bringing about a fundamental interrelationship, but clearly co-operation on specific issues between the developed Western and Third World countries is increasing; e.g. witness the change in the attitude of the EEC since the United Kingdom became a member of it.

5.32 *The Impact of UK Entry into the EEC*

The United Kingdom's entry into the EEC in 1973 was at that time viewed with some alarm by the governments of most Commonwealth countries. Traditionally, the United Kingdom had discriminated in favour of the commodities it imported from Commonwealth countries under a system of imperial (later retitled Commonwealth) preferences; e.g. the price of Indian textiles in the United Kingdom was not inflated by import levies, whereas French textiles were subject to custom duties, etc. before UK membership. The United Kingdom not merely had to end the preferences that were previously accorded to Commonwealth products, at least gradually and subject to compensating action, but also had to discriminate against these goods and imports; thus, the United Kingdom has had to impose the common EEC tariff on Indian textile imports as well as subject India to the quota restrictions stipulated by the Community. As Professor Meade pointed out: 'The problem is not simply one of facing the abolition of imperial preferences as it is so often falsely presented; it is one of facing not only the abolition of imperial preferences but also the institution of an important system of discrimination against Commonwealth products.'[18]

For the poor Commonwealth countries the institution of such a system of discrimination could have created enormous problems. The EEC had over the years developed a trade policy that was then generally regarded to be highly unfavourable for the poor countries. The major exceptions were of course the African countries that had been 'associated' with the EEC, i.e. the countries that were French colonies and had been associated with the EEC for nearly a decade. The Commonwealth countries in Africa, the Caribbean and the Pacific – but not those in Asia – became 'associable' as a consequence of the agreement that marked UK entry into the EEC. Later, special arrangements were arrived at between the EEC countries and some Mediterranean developing countries also, including both Arab countries and Israel. The countries that were not made 'associable' were the Asian Commonwealth countries, including populous and poor countries like India, Bangladesh and Sri Lanka.

These envisaged serious trade problems, as their exports to the United Kingdom (which represented a very important source of demand for most of their products) dwindled and as the associated countries gradually took advantage of their position. The associated contries are, in general, allowed free entry into the EEC, and are in effect allowed to protect their own import industries by imposing duties on imports from the rich EEC countries. But even they are prevented from freely exporting agricultural products which compete with those of the EEC countries themselves.

Why were some Commonwealth countries denied EEC association while others were accepted? The reasons become obvious when the Community's CAP and attitude towards labour-intensive manufactured imports are considered. The CAP discriminated heavily against the import of temperate zone foodstuffs (e.g. cereals, fruits, vegetables) by maintaining high domestic 'support' prices for agricultural products; this tended to reduce their consumption as well as to raise import duties and increase quota restrictions. Moreover, the generally high 'support' prices were likely to increase the agricultural production substantially in Europe and thus to reduce the import demand for these commodities. It was perhaps true to argue that the adverse effects of the United Kingdom's adherence to the EEC agricultural policy would be mainly felt by the rich Commonwealth countries, though effects both inside and outside the Commonwealth (e.g. among the cane sugar producers) were also feared to be substantial. After all, the United Kingdom was a larger importer of foodstuffs (as a percentage of total domestic consumption) than any other EEC country. More recently, however, the rise in world food prices has overtaken the EEC prices – a development not foreseen in the discussions on the occasion of UK entry.

EEC trade policy also discriminated against the import of light manufactured goods. Countries like India, Pakistan and Hong Kong envisaged finding themselves deprived of a large UK market, as Continental light manufactures were substituted in UK imports. It was precisely in order to protect their light manufactures industries that the Six insisted upon excluding the large Asian Commonwealth countries, as well as Canada and Australia, from association with the EEC.

It is difficult to assess the overall impact of UK entry into the EEC on the poor countries. The poor Commonwealth countries of Asia are likely to be the worst off. Since these countries are among the poorest in the world and contain a population considerably larger than that of the associated LDCs, the net effect of the United Kingdom's entry into the EEC was a source of great concern to developmentalists. Compensatory action was pressed for and obtained, including the extension of EEC food aid as well as trade concessions in special agreements.

The enlargement of the EEC has had a marked positive impact on its attitude towards the developing countries. In January 1973 the EEC offered associated status to twenty Commonwealth countries and the latter evidenced great enthusiasm for association. Moreover, the rise in the price of oil since October 1973 has also considerably influenced the posture of the EEC *vis-à-vis* the Third World countries. France in particular has been advocating increased co-operation between the developing countries and the EEC. This has resulted in the improvement of trade relations as well as of the development assistance performance – as estimated by the OECD – of the EEC countries.[19] In early 1975 the EEC and forty-six developing countries from Africa, the Pacific and the Caribbean signed the Lomé Convention, which considerably extended the concessions that had been granted .by the EEC under the First and Second Yaounde Conventions. Developing countries that have signed the Lomé Convention have a population of over 268 million and include the whole of independent black Africa. The Lomé Convention provides for continuous consultation between the EEC and developing countries and for the elimination of all tariff and non-tariff barriers on most exports from developing countries that are a party to the Convention. These concessions, however, could not be granted to products covered by the CAP of the EEC. The Convention reorganises the principle of non-reciprocity of trade concessions granted to the developing countries and has established an Export Stabilisation Scheme.[20] The Convention aims to strengthen the socio-economic structure of the developing countries, to promote rural development, to support schemes for regional and inter-regional co-operation and to provide aid to small-sized industrial firms.

The change in the attitude of the EEC has not gone unnoticed by the developing countries. At the Jamaica Summit Conference of Commonwealth leaders in 1975, the developing countries – even those like India, Bangladesh and Sri Lanka, which are not direct beneficiaries of the Lomé Convention – gave support to the United Kingdom's continued membership of the EEC. This does not, of course, amount to an unqualified endorsement of EEC policies, but it does indicate that there is some appreciation of EEC policies in the developing world.

Co-operation rather than confrontation must be the watchword for the 1970s. The world is in the grip of an economic crisis which is perhaps more serious than the recession and slump of the 1930s. Astute and farsighted international economic management is indispensible for recovery. Co-operation between the developed and developing countries is a prerequisite for devising adequate policies to deal effectively with the world's economic problems. Such co-operation is possible only if the present encouraging trend evidenced by Western nations, towards modifying their trade policies so as to improve the development prospects of the Third World, is strengthened and supported by the international economic community.

NOTES

1 Suppose the domestic price of commodity X is fixed at £100 per ton and the import price is £50 per ton; then the levy will be £50 per ton. If the import price falls to £10 per ton, the levy will rise to £90 per ton in order to maintain the CAP-determined domestic price. More recently, however, CAP prices have at times been below world market prices, so that the need for variable levies has disappeared.

2 See D. Gale Johnson, *World Agriculture in Disarray* (London, Fontana, 1972).

3 W. Schmidt, 'An Enlarged European Community and Agricultural Trade Policy Choices for Third Countries', paper presented to the Agricultural Economic Society (Oxford, 1972); and J. Ansari and C. Robins, *The Profits of Doom* (London, War on Want), 1976.

4 However, synthetic substitutes may not be long in coming, unless the industrial countries exclude such matters from their research and development programmes.

5 Natural fibres held 80 per cent of the market in 1955, 77 per cent in 1961 and 67 per cent in 1966.

6 We have assumed that export instability is a 'bad thing' but it can conceivably be argued that this is not so. The large majority of economists would certainly agree with our view, as would UN opinion. However, see also A. MacBean, *Export Instability and Economic Development* (London, George Allen & Unwin, 1966).

7 See MacBean, op. cit.; also Erb and Schiavo-Campo, 'Export Instability: Level of Development and Economic Size of LDCs', *Bulletin of Oxford Institute of Economics and Statistics* (November 1969).

8 Both these schemes are discussed in detail in Chapter 6.

9 In some Latin American countries more than four-fifths of such exports are supplied by multinational corporations.

10 Jan Tumlir, 'Trade Negotiations in the Field of Manufactures' (Cambridge Conference on Development, mimeo, 1972); also in P. Streeten, *Trade Policies for Development* (London, CUP, 1973).

11 This is well discussed in a study by Little, Scitovsky and Scott, *Industry and Trade in Some Developing Countries*, prepared in the OECD Development Centre (London, OUP, 1970).

12 G. M. Meier, 'Outward Looking Strategies: Policies of Developed Countries' (Cambridge Conference on Development, 1972), mimeo, p. 10; also in P. Streeten, op. cit.
13 *Monthly Chronicle* (New York, UN, May 1974), p. 72.
14 These negotiations were to have begun in the autumn of 1973, but actually were delayed until 1975 due to a hold-up in the vital US Congressional authorisation.
15 Tumlir, op. cit., pp. 5–11.
16 For a summary of the position of the developing countries in the international efforts to deal with the current economic crisis, see Chapter 1.
17 Figures cited in Overseas Development Administration, 'International Trade: A Background Paper' (Cambridge Development Conference, mimeo, 1972).
18 James E. Meade, *UK Commonwealth and Common Market*, Hobart Paper 17 (London, Institute of Economic Affairs, 1970), p. 45.
19 See DAC, *Development Co-operation, 1974* (Paris, OECD, 1974).
20 For a discussion of this scheme, see Chapter 6.

CHAPTER 6

Trade Policies of the Poor Countries

6.1 INTRODUCTION

The developing countries have pursued trade and commercial policies which have generally been regarded as highly protectionist by the development economists of the rich countries. The OECD[1] and the International Bank for Reconstruction and Development (IBRD or World Bank)[2] have sponsored a number of studies into the trade structure of the developing countries, and the researchers concerned have reached strikingly similar conclusions. For a very wide range of LDCs they estimated that the degree of protection to domestic industries was quite high and that the intersectoral price distortion which had been introduced by trade and commercial policy had considerably worsened the terms of trade of the agricultural sector. This is not surprising. Throughout the nineteenth century the then developing European and American countries adopted policies that protected domestic industries, policies for which List and a number of other economists belonging to the German Historical School provided academic justification. Moreover, the post-1945 world inherited a tradition of neo-mercantilism from the days of the Great Depression. Only slowly and haltingly have the protectionist walls been lowered among the developed countries, though even here it is dangerous to indulge in generalisation, for to date the tariff reductions within Europe remain the only *success* story whereas the United States and especially Japan have in recent years shown little enthusiasm for trade liberalisation. The rich countries have particularly strong protectionist policies against the kinds of agricultural and manufactured exports which the developing countries are most successful at producing.

The LDCs have reacted to developed country protection by attempting to produce an increasing proportion of their import requirements domestically, except of course for the OPEC countries

98

which have put little or no restrictions on imports. The policy of rapid import substitution has also been viewed as a key factor determining the rate of industrial growth, a theory to which Chenery gave empirical support in his famous 1960 article.[3] But import substitution can only occur if a high protectionist wall is erected to allow local industry to develop. It was hoped that industries established in these circumstances would eventually become competitive and that planners would then be able to justify the initial protectionist policy on the basis of the 'infant industry' argument. In section 6.2 will be presented the empirical evidence that has been produced with regard to the protectionist policies of the LDCs. The important question from the point of view of economic development is not the absolute level of protection of a particular industry, but rather the effect of protection on the competitiveness of that industry.

6.2 EMPIRICAL EVIDENCE OF LEVELS OF PROTECTION IN DEVELOPING COUNTRIES

To measure the average levels of protection implied by a particular tariff structure is by no means an easy task, even in the analysis of single commodities. Nominal rates of protection (as measured by the levels of import duties) are an imperfect guide to their economic consequences, because the demand and supply characteristics of the products involved must also be taken into account. For this reason economists use the concept of effective protection as a simple and more direct measure of the influence of tariff structures on the protection afforded to domestic industries. The *effective rate of protection* (ERP) is measured as the additional value added generated in the protected industries as a consequence of the implementation of a protective tariff structure. A more detailed account of the measure may be found in the Appendix to this chapter.

Recently, the two expert groups just mentioned (the OECD and World Bank) calculated ERPs for a number of developing countries. These estimates are not directly comparable due to substantial differences in concepts, classification schemes and time periods, so the results of the two studies will be discussed separately.

According to the OECD study the average ERP varies very considerably from 27 per cent for Mexico to 313 per cent for India. The level of protection in India, Pakistan, Argentina and even perhaps Brazil would be regarded as alarmingly high by almost any criteria. The OECD researches found that for four out of five countries for which data is available the ERP is higher, often considerably higher, for consumer goods than for intermediate and capital goods. These higher rates for consumer goods industries reflect the import substitution bias in the trade and development policies of many LDCs. However, the continuing survival of these industries has become chronically dependent on protection ('once an infant always an infant'). Some are highly inefficient while others are the source of very large profits, but in either case there is need for revision of trade policy.

More comprehensive evidence on the structure of protection in the LDCs has been provided by Balassa in the World Bank study;[4] his ERP calculations are given in Table 6.1. It is, as has already been pointed out, difficult to compare these figures with the OECD estimates. The concept of the 'net' ERP is different from the measure used by Little *et. al.* Net ERP is calculated by adjusting the ERPs for the extent of overvaluation of the exchange rates as compared to their value in a hypothetical free trade situation[5] and is therefore a more realistic measure of the extent of protection that is accorded to a particular set of economic activities.

A most striking feature of the structure of protection revealed by Table 6.1 is the discrimination in favour of the manufacturing sector. All the countries in the sample, except Malaya, pursued trade and commercial policies that protected the manufacturing sector, but for five of the six countries included in the sample the ERP for the primary (agricultural and mining) sectors was negative. The average net ERP for the manufacturing sectors of the countries in the sample was 55 per cent, and for the primary-producing sectors was approximately −12 per cent.[6] This discrimination in favour of the manufacturing sector was most pronounced in the case of Pakistan, Philippines and Chile and less important though still significant for Mexico and Brazil.

There are, as has been shown, important reasons for the evolution of this pattern of protection. The LDCs have been convinced that specialisation in the production of primary commodities is unlikely to enable them to acquire foreign resources on a scale commensurate with their increasing development needs. The rise in the price of primary commodities (except, of course, oil) has taken the LDCs by surprise, but as they are not certain that these trends will persist unless negotiated settlements are arrived at they continue to place emphasis on the expansion of manufactured production and exports. This is not to deny the importance of agricultural development or the likelihood that a number of LDCs will recognise this importance, but it is difficult to see how, in view of the trade policies of the rich countries,

Table 6.1 Net ERP in Selected Developing Countries[a] (%)

Industry	Brazil (1966)	Chile (1960)	Mexico (1960)	Malaya[b] (1965)	Philippines (1965)	Pakistan (1963-4)
Agriculture	21	−11	−6	−4	−13	−40
Mining	−1	−42	−13	−20	−34	n.a.
Primary production total	20	−28	−7	−10	−14	n.a.
Processed food	48	1,676	−3	−4	28	−238
Construction	47	−2	−7	−6	31	1
Intermediate goods I	66	1	26	−26	1	13
Intermediate goods II	—	—	27	4	62	92
Non-durable consumer goods	115	128	19	58	34	10
Durable consumer goods	98	30	77	−6	915	−1,433
Machinery	58	18	27	−10	77	59
Transport	—	—	26	—	53	—
Manufacturing total	68	68	16	−10	41	147

[a] The concept of net ERP is explained in the text. The ERPs have been adjusted for overvaluation as compared to the hypothetical free trade situation.
[b] Western Malaysia.

Source: B. Balassa, et al., The Structure of Protection in Developing Countries (Baltimore, IBRD, 1971), p. 56.

101

increased agricultural productivity will increase the LDCs' ability to import industrial goods. Hence an emphasis on industrialisation is likely to remain an important characteristic of the economic policy of most developing economies, even if more attention is paid in future to rural development.

The OECD study offers evidence supporting the view that the structure of protection in the LDCs discriminates in favour of the consumer goods industries, as these are the industries in which import substitution is relatively easy. In general, Table 6.1 also tends to support the hypothesis that ERP is lowest on capital goods and highest on durable and non-durable consumer goods. The value of the net ERP displays a trend towards escalation from inputs to final goods; the average net ERP is lowest for construction goods, higher for intermediate goods at lower levels of fabrication, higher still for machinery and highest of all for 'final' consumer goods. It is dangerous to read too much into these observations. The only assertion that can be made without substantial qualifications is that they do not contradict the finding that the LDCs in general tend to protect consumer goods industries more than capital goods industries.

Similar aspects of the structure of protection in the poor countries are also revealed by the evidence concerning the difference in the impact of protection on the import-competing and export industries. Table 6.2 shows that the net ERP is negative in the case of all four primary categories; on the other hand, the net ERP for manufacturers is negative only once – in the case of the export-manufacturing industries of Malaya.

Table 6.2 lends support to the view that protectionist policies have discriminated in favour of import-substituting manufactures. The level of protection accorded to these industries is generally high, while the net ERP of export industries is usually negative. The bias against exports reflects the general bias against agricultural and other primary goods, and the discrimination in favour of import-substituting industries mirrors the bias in favour of manufacturing. Even within export industries the net ERP is generally positive for manufacturing industries. A number of LDCs (e.g. Pakistan[7]) have tried to reduce the bias against manufactured exports by the use of specific policy measures. Since the rise in the prices of primary commodities these policies may have been changed, but the fact that the improved terms of trade for primary commodities occurred despite the absence of favourable policies indicates that they were occasioned by fortuitous circumstances. Whether or not the LDCs

Table 6.2   *Net ERP[a] for Export, Import-Competing and Non-Import-Competing Industries[b]* (%)

Sector	Chile	Mexico	Malaya	Philip-pines
Export Industries				
Primary	−36	−7	−11	−32
Manufacturing		12	−19	9
Total	−36	−5	−12	−28
Import-Competing Industries				
Primary	−11	—	1	−2
Manufacturing	14	39	7	39
Total	0	39	3	8
Non-Import-Competing Industries				
Primary	−23	−7	0	1
Manufacturing	153	5	17	86
Total	124	−1	0	9
All Import-Substituting Industries				
Primary	−12	−7	0	0
Manufacturing	68	16	7	57
Total	30	6	1	9

[a] For explanation see Note 6, this chapter.

[b] Export industries are those where more than 10 per cent of production is exported, import-competing industries are those where imports provide more than 10 per cent of domestic supply, and non-import-competing industries are those where international trade does not exceed 10 per cent either way.

Source: B. Balassa *et al., The Structure of Protection in Developing Countries* (Baltimore, IBRD, 1971), p. 61.

will in the future be capable of consolidating these gains will depend on their ability to reshape their own trade policies as well as to influence the trade policies of the Western countries.

In summary, two outstanding features of the structure of protection in the LDCs may be noted: (a) the level of protection is high and (though there is little quantitative evidence for this) has in all probability been increasing over time; and (b) the structure of protection discriminates in favour of import-substituting manufacturing industries. The rationale of such a trade policy lies in a desire to achieve industrialisation. Since the infant manufacturing sector is small and weak, economic policy has been used to manipulate the structure of prices prevailing within the economy so as to facilitate the development of industry. However, the cost that is incurred by the economy as a whole for accelerated industrial expansion is substantial, at least in the short run. But whether or not the recent developments in international commodity trade are sufficient to induce the LDCs to reorientate their trade policies depends ultimately on the extent to which these countries feel that existing commodities can be stabilised in relation to the prices of manufactured goods. If the international system cannot guarantee such a stabilisation, the costly and generally inefficient trade policies of the LDCs will, in the main, remain unchanged.

6.3 THE EFFECTS OF PROTECTION ON THE STRUCTURE OF DOMESTIC PRODUCTION IN THE LDCS

The cost of protection to the LDCs has been high due to the artificial reduction of the relative price of agricultural commodities on the one hand and to the restriction of imports on the other. It is no easy matter to assess what the cost of protection is to a particular country. The dynamic, i.e. long-run, effects cannot be adequately assessed by means of the methodology that is currently employed to measure the cost of protection.

The static costs of protection reflect the allocative effects of protection. These result from the distortions which are introduced by protectionist policies into the domestic price structure. The country is forced to forego the advantages of specialisation in accordance with existing comparative cost advantages both on an intersectoral level (i.e. between primary production and manufacturing) and on an intrasectoral level (i.e. within the manufacturing sector itself). These price distortions entail both a consumption cost, which arises from the fact that by distorting prices protectionist policies interfere with consumer choice, and a production cost, which exists because protectionist policies induce a shift of resources from low-cost to high-cost activities.

However, if all protection were abandoned most LDCs would find that an expansion in their exports would be offset by a reduction in export prices and an inevitable exchange devaluation. Therefore, the static costs of protection should not be measured at existing exchange rates. They should be measured by the net ERP of the import-competing goods, against which should be set the higher foreign prices that the smaller volume of exports obtains under protection.

A number of countries producing consumer durables have found the c.i.f. value of material inputs to exceed the value of output, if valued at world prices. Pakistan is a good example.[8] In cases like these it is obvious that, even allowing for gains from exchange overvaluation, the static costs of protection are formidable.

Protection is usually justified on the grounds that as time goes on the static costs will be reduced and eventually the protected industries will become efficient and competitive. This is the gist of the 'infant industry' argument, according to which protection is justified if a reallocation of resources increases national economic productivity sufficiently to offset the initial static costs of protection. But there are important reasons why the protected industries never seem to outgrow the 'infancy' stage: they are sheltered from foreign competition and are induced to produce for relatively small domestic markets. The production patterns thus established entail a very important dynamic cost of protection. Moreover, it has commonly been observed that industries producing for sellers' markets and deliberately ignoring economies of scale due to low levels of demand usually lag behind in terms of productivity and efficiency.

Protectionist policies induce producers in LDCs to set up plants that are well below the optimum size to realise scale economies, and underutilisation of capacity is a common phenomenon. Gordon Winston has shown, however, that in the case of Pakistan underutilisation of capacity is not primarily the result of irrational policies. It appears because of employees' preference to work at a 'normal' time.[9]

Protectionist policies that aim at the development of import-substituting industries encourage production for the home market rather than for export and thus opt for a development strategy that sacrifices the short-run gains of international integration along lines determined by existing national comparative advantages. This is one dynamic cost of protection.

Another dynamic cost is the impact of protectionist policies on technological change within the industries of the poor countries. The structure of protection of the LDCs has discriminated strongly against technological innovation, a bias resulting from two factors. First, import substitution has meant a concentration on the development of the light consumer goods industries and a discrimination against the production of investment goods. The result has been an inappropriate pattern of industrialisation as far as the technological development of the poor countries is concerned. The protected consumer goods industries could easily import the capital and technological know-how from the West and have, therefore, paid no attention to developing indigenous technologies and production methods which are more labour-intensive and which exploit indigenous resource endowments more appropriately.

Indeed, the oligopolistic position of firms in protected LDC markets has been a second obstacle to technological development. Both domestic and foreign firms have found that import-substituting policies have invariably resulted in assured high profitability levels. The restriction on imports has led to an elimination of competition, with the consequence that firms operating in such insulated markets have increasingly adopted monopolistic practices and, in the absence of incentives, have imported technology from abroad despite its obvious unsuitability. They have tried to compensate for inefficiency by insisting that the level of protection should be raised even more, so that they can offset the high cost of maintaining and replacing their capital equipment by corresponding increases in product prices and in their profits.

The unwillingness of developing countries to protect production processes which promise to lead to the development of appropriate technologies has had serious consequences. It is maintained throughout this book that the problem of international development cannot be tackled adequately without there being reduction in – and eventually elimination of – the technological dependence of the poor countries on the rich. The technological developments that have taken place in recent times have been geared to the needs and the resources of the developed world, so that modern technological and scientific processes and products are, generally speaking, quite unsuitable for the LDCs. The LDCs must therefore themselves recognise the importance of encouraging the development of an indigenous technology that caters more specifically to their requirements. Unfortunately, the protectionist policies that the LDCs have followed – and it must be remembered that the concept of ERP shows that protection of a production process is determined not only by tariffs and trade restrictions but also by domestic fiscal policies – have neither encouraged local producers to develop an indigenous technology nor induced foreign investors to import more suitable technical and scientific materials. In fact, the net effect of the protectionist policies has been to discourage technological innovation. Most LDCs have allowed the so-called import-substituting consumer goods industries to import capital goods at subsidised prices, and no one in the LDCs – business, government or public opinion – has stopped to question the suitability of the technology being imported. The cost involved in deliberately permitting the introduction and consolidation of alien and unsuitable technologies into developing countries is colossal. It cripples the chances of a balanced development for the economy and of full employment and leads to a chronic dependency of developing on developed countries. There is no indication that the oil-rich developing countries are paying adequate attention to the question of the impact of their trade policies on the technology transfer process, either (though for some of them with very small populations a capital-intensive technology may well be 'appropriate', at least as long as the oil lasts).

The effects of the protectionist policies of the LDCs have not been what one would have wished. Protection has involved both short- and long-run costs. Protectionist policies have aimed at promoting the rapid industrialisation of the LDCs, but the type of industrialisation that they have in fact promoted has entailed a heavy cost in terms of economic efficiency. Such industrialisation has usually had a negative impact on the pattern of income distribution within the developing countries. More often than not the industries that have been encouraged are capital-intensive, employ a relatively small labour force and tend to accentuate income disparities. Moreover, the import-substituting industries that have been developed often show no sign of becoming competitive in the foreseeable future. It seems that protectionist policies have resulted in more poor countries having the worst of both worlds: on the one hand, by promoting import substitution they have discriminated against exports and thus reduced their own ability to earn foreign exchange, while on the other they have increased their technological dependence on the developed countries.

There are no simple and universally applicable ideal solutions to these problems. Obviously the policies of different countries will differ. The size of the domestic market, the geographic position of the country, its relationship with foreign countries and its resource endowment will be important factors in determining its protectionist policies. But a few general conclusions may be drawn about the nature of the protectionist policy that is most likely to be conducive to development, given the general economic characteristics of most developing countries.

To begin with, the LDCs must pursue a *consistent* protectionist policy. This is a point that has to be stressed, for in most LDCs the system of protection has evolved in a very haphazard way. Tariffs and taxes have been imposed, modified and withdrawn at different times in response to the pressure of circumstances and of individual investors, and the effect of these sporadic measures on the different industries has been very varied. The standard deviation (i.e. the average variability) of the ERP among industries is very large in most LDCs.

Protectionist policies must also aim at providing incentives for the growth of the technological resources potential of the poor country. It is important to realise that unless the technological backwardness of the developing world is eliminated the poor countries will find it impossible to tackle the problems of low productivity levels, economic inefficiency and high unemployment rates. An overriding aim of policy in developing countries should be to promote the development and use of local resources (including labour resources) and the development and import of suitable technological capacity. These considerations apply with equal force to both rich and poor developing countries.

Beyond this, it would be difficult to specify an 'ideal protectionist' policy for the whole developing world. Currently, Western development economists are advocating a radical change in the trade policies of the LDCs. It is being argued that trade liberalisation and specialisation in accordance with international comparative advantages are likely to be of great benefit to the LDCs.[10] Developing countries are being advised to reduce their protection of manufactured products, to emphasise production for export (as against import substitution) and to explore the development of world markets for non-traditional primary commodities. They are being asked to refrain from setting up producer cartels. It is difficult to be enthusiastic about these recommendations. For one thing, the rich countries seem reluctant to ensure the stabilisation of commodity prices and their linkage to the prices of manufactured products. For another, the acceptance of these policies will leave unchanged the nature of the relationship between the rich and poor countries. The type of international economic integration that is envisaged by the authors of these policies will tend to perpetuate the economic and technological dependence of the LDCs on the industrial countries and will increase the gap between the haves and have-nots on both a national and an international level. It is therefore not surprising that many LDCs have not responded very favourably to the advice and recommendations of the economists of the World Bank and the OECD, and have sought to improve their bargaining position in world markets by establishing producer associations committed to obtaining more revenue from the flow of scarce resources from the developing countries. They are also calling for basic changes in the relations of rich and poor countries – a 'New International Economic Order'.

6.4 ECONOMIC INTEGRATION AMONG THE POOR COUNTRIES: SOME CASE STUDIES

The relatively high levels of protection prevailing in most LDCs reflect the fact that the poor countries remain unconvinced of the desirability of specialising in the production and export of goods in which they have comparative cost advantages. The studies quoted above have shown that the LDCs have foregone substantial economic gains by distorting their domestic price structures. The current commodity price boom also seems to lend force to this opinion. What remains to be proved is the proposition that the long-run economic interests of the poor countries can be served by development strategies which emphasise specialisation in the production of primary commodities and semi-manufactured goods. Such a policy, in their own view, would increase the economic dependence of the LDCs on the rich countries. It would promote international integration, but along lines that would perpetuate existing international economic imbalances. The bargaining power of the LDCs would be likely to be reduced as time went on, because they would be exporting commodities which often have income-inelastic demand functions and importing commodities for which demand rises sharply with income. Even the existing strong position of the oil producers would be eroded as substitutes were developed, so that even they need to diversify their economies to prepare for the depletion of their oil. For these reasons the LDCs quite naturally tend to opt for industrialisation, even though it may involve heavy initial costs in terms of economic efficiency and even though commodity export trade may be highly profitable in the short run. This policy entails the development of a production structure which, it is hoped, will eventually reduce the dependence of the poor countries on the rich and hence permanently increase the relative bargaining power of the former.

Programmes of industrial development within the LDCs are severely constrained by both supply and demand conditions. On the supply side there is a general scarcity of capital, managerial ability, technical know-how and skilled labour. On the demand side the smallness of the domestic market thwarts growth and expansion. The size of the market is primarily determined by income levels, and on this count even such large countries as India, Pakistan and

Bangladesh have significant demand constraints on industrial expansion. One possible solution to the problem of market size is offered by the establishment of common markets and economic integration. The forging of strong regional economic ties is, however, no easy task, because at present the national entities of the developing world seldom have strong economic links. They buy from the rich countries and sell to the rich countries; more than 75 per cent of the LDCs' exports are to the rich countries, and imports from the developed world into the LDCs are an even larger proportion of the LDCs' total imports. Thus, regional economic integration among developing countries implies the necessity of developing new economic relations between them, which is bound to be a long drawn-out process. Conventional custom union theory, with its emphasis on the overall benefits of economic integration, tends to ignore the problem of assessing the 'durability' of a particular regional integration scheme. Two regional unions among developing countries are looked at below, attention being focused on the question: To what extent are these unions successful in establishing new economic relationships between their members with the gradual reduction of their dependence on the metropolitan country in whose 'periphery they at present are? The two cases examined are the Latin American Free Trade Association (LAFTA) and the East African Community (EAC).

6.41 *The Latin American Free Trade Association*

LAFTA was established in 1961. Its founder members were Argentina, Bolivia, Brazil, Chile, Colombia, Ecuador, Mexico, Paraguay, Peru, Uruguay and Venezuela. The Montevideo Treaty, signed in 1960, which led to the formation of LAFTA, considered the establishment of a free trade area to be a first step in the evolution of a Latin American economic community, and provided that within twelve years the members of LAFTA would abolish virtually all restrictions on trade within the area. In order to attain this objective, periodic negotiations were to be arranged between the member countries on both a bilateral and multilateral level. Special arrangements were agreed upon to discriminate in favour of Bolivia, Ecuador, Paraguay and Uruguay – the relatively poorer members. The agreement also envisaged that the member countries would attempt to co-ordinate their industrialisation policies and would develop complementary lines of industrial production.

A number of negotiation 'rounds' have now been held under the Treaty, and a large number of minor tariff and trade concessions have been granted. There has, however, been a noticeable decline in the success of negotiations as the years have passed, many more concessions being granted in the earlier years. Semi-manufactured goods have been favourably treated, but very few concessions have been granted for new industrial products. Negotiations with regard to changes in the Common Schedule (which lists the products whose duties are to be eventually abolished) have generally been difficult, and little seems to have been achieved in this area. Hence investors in new products generally have no guarantee that they will have access to the regional market. Attempts to regulate trade in agricultural goods have also sometimes run into difficulties. All this has led to a modification of the original LAFTA treaty. In early 1969 it was decided at Caracas at the end of the liberalisation programme was to be postponed from 1973 to 1980, and that new regulations were to be drawn up for the compilation of the Common Schedule. The annual tariff reduction that the member countries are required to make has been reduced from 8 per cent of the (weighted) average import duties (to non-member countries) to only 2·9 per cent.

Despite the obvious need for co-ordination of national economic policies by the member countries, little progress has been made by LAFTA in this direction. In the absence of a common external tariff it was necessary to negotiate area-of-origin agreements in order to ensure the equitable distribution of benefits from free trade. There was also a need for the co-ordination of import policies and the harmonisation of fiscal, monetary and industrial policies. Success has, however, been achieved in the field of production agreements, where some industrial agreements with private firms have been reached. However, policy harmonisation among the members of LAFTA remains at an early stage.

Trade among LAFTA members tended to grow at an uneven rate during the 1960s. However, it has accounted for only about 11–12 per cent of the region's total exports[11] and is concentrated between a few large neighbouring countries and consists mainly of primary products. The poorer countries within LAFTA have not in general shared in the benefits from freer intraregional trade, the pattern of which has tended to widen the gap between the rich and poor countries of the region. It is the rich who have mainly benefited from the incentives that LAFTA has provided and also from the 'escape clauses' of the Montevideo Treaty.

The limitations to the success of LAFTA emanate chiefly from two main sources: (a) its organisational defects and (b) the economic conditions of its member countries. With regard to the first group of factors, it is quite obvious that the methods used and the institutions established by LAFTA are by their nature rather inadequate for the comprehensive integration of the national economies of the region. The extraordinarily cumbersome method of annual item-by-item negotiation is perhaps not suitable for the achievements of economic co-ordination between countries at that level of development, partly because it is quite incapable of taking into account new products. Agricultural imports are also treated as special exceptions. Indeed, the whole emphasis seems to be on reaching arbitrary compromises without reference to a common set of procedures. This lack of procedures for the automatic elimination of tariffs prevents policy harmonisation, restricts regional investment and increases the problem of the distribution of benefits from free trade. The LAFTA agreement does not provide for the implementation of a regional investment policy and does not lay down the procedures by which the fiscal and monetary policies of the member countries are to be brought together. It also fails to take into account differences in the levels of development of the member countries. All these factors have reduced the usefulness and effectiveness of LAFTA.

The second most important group of factors which have limited LAFTA's success is the economic structure of its member countries. Most of the members do not have complementary production and trade structures. They remain oriented towards Europe and the United States and communications and transportation among even neighbouring member countries can be difficult and expensive. Moreover, these countries have been facing problems of inflation and balance-of-payments deficits, and have been pursuing inward-looking import-substitution industrialisation policies during the 1960s. All this has hindered the development of complementarity within the region. However, the existence of LAFTA has induced members countries to increase their trade with each other, which is in itself a healthy sign. Furthermore, the fact that the Latin American countries continue to work through LAFTA despite the many problems they have faced indicates that LAFTA has established itself as a permanent feature of the Latin American economy and that if sufficient attention is paid to administrative problems etc. its contribution to the development of the region can increase.

6.42   The East African Community
The EAC Treaty was signed in June 1967, but its members (Kenya, Uganda and Tanzania) had been associated before in one of the oldest economic integration systems among the LDCs. The EAC was a common currency area during the days of UK administration. Interregional trade accounted in 1963 for 20 per cent of total area trade, of which half consisted of industrial goods. The independence

of the three countries in the region led to a disintegration of economic relationships, as economic integration had been achieved by a colonial administration and had little relevance to the development needs of the individual countries of the region. Moreover, the distribution of benefits was very unequal; Kenya, because of its more advanced socio-economic infrastructure, attracted most of the investment and hence benefited the most from regional free trade.

In 1961 a Distributable Pool Fund was created so as to ensure a more equitable distribution of common market benefits, but the redistribution was regarded as wholly unsatisfactory by Uganda and Tanzania and effected no sufficient decrease in regional inequalities. In 1964 and 1965 further attempts at preserving the EAC structure were made. In 1966, however, the common East African currency was abandoned, and both Tanzania and Uganda imposed quota restrictions on a wide range of industrial imports within the region. The 1967 Treaty was signed to prevent the total disintegration of the EAC system.

This Treaty aims at the development of a common external tariff structure, but does allow for some exceptions to this rule. It disallows all quotas on industrial goods produced within the region, but permits the retention of quantitative restrictions on a few key agricultural commodities. Import restrictions are also permitted for balance-of-payments reasons.

The Treaty also envisages harmonisation in the area of fiscal policy. It calls for establishing a common excise tax within the region and proposes to introduce a 'transfer tax'. This new instrument aims at protecting the less developed industries of the region. The transfer tax may be levied by a country with an interregional trade deficit in manufactured goods, and has mainly been employed by Tanzania and Uganda. It is hoped that the transfer tax will allow for a redistribution of the gains from the common market and will spread out the pattern of industrialisation within the region. The Treaty also aims at setting up an East African Development Bank, which will give priority to the industrialisation of the less developed parts of the region and will also contribute towards a redistribution of the gains from free trade.

The effects of the 1967 agreement have generally been positive, and some co-ordination of development plans have been achieved. The EAC does not specify the procedure by which harmonisation is to be achieved; nor does it suggest specific measures for the allocation of industries and the co-ordination of industrial projects. Furthermore, a large section of agricultral production is excluded from the common market. Nevertheless, interregional trade within the EAC remains high and a number of neighbouring countries (Burundi, Ethiopia, Somalia, Rwanda and Zambia) have applied for membership. What is most significant is that, despite the acute political tension between Tanzania and Uganda since Amin came to power, neither country has opted out of the EAC and like LAFTA it seems to have established itself and is likely to play an important role in the development of the countries of East Africa.

6.43 Prospects for Regional Collaboration

The two cases discussed above illustrate some of the major problems faced by economic integration policies between the LDCs. Despite such difficulties, attempts at economic integration by the poor countries are quite common. In 1975 at least twelve major schemes envisaging some form of economic union among the LDCs could be identified: in Latin America, the Central American Common Market (CACM), the Punta del Este Programme, the Caribbean Free Trade Association and LAFTA; in Africa, the EAC, the West African Customs Union and the Maghreb Permanent Consultative Committee; in Asia, the Arab Common Market, the Regional Co-operation for Development (RCD – Iran, Turkey and Pakistan), the Asian and Pacific Council (ASPAC), the Association of South East Asia (ASEA) and the Association of South East Asian Nations (ASEAN).

The progress that has been made towards regional integration in these schemes is rather small. Most regional groupings have low and widely fluctuating intraregional export levels, and the proportion of intraregional exports to total regional exports is also small. A few large countries tend to dominate intraregional trade; e.g. Pakistan accounts for more than 80 per cent of exports within the RCD and Malaysia for 61 per cent of exports within ASEA. However, the dominating nation usually has a low share in the region in terms of the proportion of its total exports going to the region; e.g. Pakistan exports only 1·5 per cent of its total exports to the RCD region, and Malaysia exports just over 2 per cent of its total exports to members of ASEA. On the other hand, Thailand, which is the least dominating member of ASEA (accounting for about 9 per cent of intraregional exports) exports more than 10 per cent of its total exports to the ASEA region. Such imbalances lead to dissatisfaction among member countries about the distribution of the gains of market integration. The smallest countries with the highest participation in the region, in terms of the proportion of their total exports going to regional trading partners,[12] usually complain bitterly about the methods and criteria of benefit distribution. The larger countries have a very low level of integration, as they tend to export largely to non-member countries. The United States absorbs most of the exports of LAFTA, CACM and ASPAC and, together with Japan, also of ASEA and ASEAN. Japan is also the main trading partner of the RCD region. The United Kingdom and France dominate the trade of the African regions. Trade between different regional groupings of LDCs, like that between individual LDCs, remains insignificant.

In view of the evidence presented here it becomes difficult to understand why the LDCs keep on trying to build schemes of regional co-ordination. The low trade levels reflect the similarity of the production structures of most LDCs, i.e. they tend to produce and trade in the same type of goods, so that as a group they fail to produce what they need to import. Pakistan textiles can replace UK textiles in African markets and African processed food can replace American packaged food in Pakistan, but clearly there is a limit to which this type of trade expansion can be pushed. Ultimately the LDCs will have to develop a complementarity within their production structures if they are to become the main buyers and sellers of each others' products. Economic co-operation between countries which have non-complementary production structures can only occur if the countries concerned co-ordinate and synchronise their industrial development schemes through conscious and deliberate planning.

Such difficulties should not be allowed to obscure the fact that the fundamental rationale for economic integration among the LDCs is to be found, not in static trade creation and trade diversion effects, but rather in the long-run advantages of industrial co-ordination and market expansion. Economic unions are established because, given the existing patterns of world trade and the existing policies of the rich countries, they appear to provide one of the few solutions to the problem of dependence on developed countries which is experienced by the majority of developing countries. Another way of putting this is that customs unions increase the bargaining power of the poor countries in world markets. A regionally integrated group should be more capable of successfully pursuing the strategies of import substitution and export expansion with respect to the developed countries than a single country. Moreover, the industries that are established within an economic union may prove to be relatively more efficient because they are based upon specialisation and division of labour on a regional, rather than a national, basis. The creation of a larger market also allows for the better exploitation of opportunities. Resource mobilisation is easier.

115

Technological innovations are encouraged, and due to increased competitive pressures firms are induced to rationalise production methods.

The LDCs as a group have realised the potential of economic integration, and despite the very slow progress that the various schemes have made the countries concerned display a genuine desire to continue negotiating with each other for economic co-operation. Very few integration schemes have been abandoned altogether. Regional integration provides an important channel through which such co-operation can be achieved. It may therefore be predicted that attempts at regional integration will be in the forefront of the issues with which the trade policies of the LDCs will be concerned in the future. In particular, attempts at regional integration among countries that are members of a producers' union (e.g. the Arab oil producers) may be specially important.

6.5 LIMITATIONS OF TRADE POLICIES

In many developing countries the import substitution strategy of industrialisation has run into serious difficulties. Export earnings have been fluctuating and unpredictable. Attempts at economic integration have proved slow in yielding results. Trade policy can be effective if monetary, fiscal and general planning measures are used to support them. Unfortunately, most LDCs have tended to use conflicting domestic and external economic policies and have only rarely attempted to rationalise these policies in accordance with the economic objectives laid down in their national development plans. The impact of trade policy measures has been reduced due to the lack of overall economic co-ordination.

The overall economic dependence of the poor countries on the developed world is the most significant reason for the ineffectiveness of their own trade policies. The greater this dependence, the lower the ability of the LDCs to undertake comprehensive programmes of economic reform and reorientation unilaterally.

The LDCs are aware that the developed world will have to play a prominent role in the restructuring of international economic relationships which is necessary to make trade an instrument of development. Since the early 1960s they have displayed a remarkable unity in international economic forums, a unity which seems to have been strengthened by the recent boom in the price of oil and other primary commodities. The Third World wants to preserve its recent gains and to extend them by reforming the international

116

economic system. The New International Economic Order envisaged by the Special Sessions of the UN General Assembly on Raw Materials and Development would make possible a reorientation of trade and investment policy in the interests of the developing countries. It is only if such a reorientation is achieved that the trade policies of the developing countries themselves can become instruments for promoting international development. This, however, is not to deny that for a handful of LDCs, particularly the OPEC countries, expanded export revenues have created opportunities which are denied to the vast majority of the Third World.

6.6 INTERNATIONAL EXPORT STABILISATION SCHEMES

The LDCs have sought co-operation with the developed world through international export stabilisation schemes, the most important of which are commodity agreements.

Commodity agreements are set up for a number of reasons, but traditionally they have been justified as a means of stabilising the export earnings and/or prices of a particular commodity. Compensatory financing schemes deal with the problem of stabilising the aggregate export earnings of poorer countries, and supplementary financing schemes are devised to offset the effects of unexpected deficits in a poor country's budget as a result of shortfalls in export earnings. In the following paragraphs some of the more important export stabilisation schemes will be discussed.

6.61 *Commodity Agreements*

Commodity agreements may take several forms, but basically they involve agreements between producers and consumers. The countries concerned agree to regulate the price and/or production of the commodity in question so as to prevent fluctuations in export prices beyond a predetermined range. In practice it has been found extremely difficult not only to fix this range but also to adhere to it over a number of years. Commodity agreements have had a high failure rate. Largely as a result of the divergence of interests between sellers and buyers there is disagreement about what constitutes a 'reasonable' price range. One popular economic objective is that agreements should aim to smooth short-term fluctuations in prices that do not reflect long-term changes in supply and demand. An opposing view is that agreements should aim to maintain prices at current levels either in money terms or in terms of the manufactured products for which the export earnings can be exchanged. A further

117

suggestion is that agreements should incorporate an element of aid; i.e. they should affect the market so as to allow an additional flow of resources from the rich to the poor countries.

One of the biggest drawbacks to the idea of widespread international commodity agreements is that the poor countries do not always benefit from maintaining (or raising) price levels. There are only a limited number of commodities that have a sufficiently inelastic demand for any benefit to arise from increasing the world price or maintaining the price against falling demand. Most exports of temperate foodstuffs that compete with domestic demand in the rich countries have high elasticities. Similarly, many raw materials exported by the poor countries face stiff competition (actual or potential) from synthetics. Petrol and tin have low elasticities of demand, but copper (from Zambia, Chile and other poor countries) has to compete with aluminium. However, among the category of tropical foods and beverages, several commodities would benefit from price increases. The Food and Agriculture Organisation (FAO) cites coffee, cocoa, tea, bananas and citrus as having particularly low elasticities of demand.[13]

The significance of low demand elasticities becomes apparent on consideration of those commodities in which agreements have been made. The four principal agreements operating for varying periods since 1945 have been for coffee, sugar, tin and wheat. In addition, there was a limited agreement for olive oil and an agreement for cocoa was also worked out. These are all formal agreements involving some degree of international supervision. There have also been intergovernmental informal agreements for tea, sisal, abaca and jute. Not all these agreements have worked to the benefit of the poor countries. For example, one study[14] suggests that Tanzania has suffered financially as a result of the informal agreement to raise and stabilise the price of sisal. As the world's major exporter of sisal, Tanzania has found herself undercut by non-participants in the agreement and seriously hit by the relatively elastic demand for sisal. This elasticity seems to result from the availability of synthetic substitutes for sisal.

Undoubtedly the most successful attempt of the Third World countries in managing an international commodity market has been achieved in the case of oil. The oil-producing countries came together in the early 1960s and established a producers' association, OPEC, initially in order to resist moves by international oil companies aimed at reducing their tax commitment to the host countries. It was expected that OPEC would not last very long, for it contained member states with widely different economic and

118

political interests. However, OPEC has not merely survived; it has enormously increased its influence in the oil market. The OPEC member states have succeeded in maintaining unity on the question of changes in the price of oil, despite the considerable difference in the views of those like the Shah of Iran, who press constantly for higher prices, and those like the Saudis, who prefer more moderate prices. OPEC is subject to strain and stresses, especially on issues related to the limiting of total output. There are many who prophesy that OPEC will not be able to maintain its unity for much longer, but as long as it does remain united OPEC will continue to demonstrate the ability of primary-producing countries to stabilise, by unilateral action, commodity prices at levels which are significantly higher than those that would exist in the absence of a producers' cartel. Primary-producing countries that do not produce oil have found it difficult to organise producers' associations. They have lent support to international commodity agreements between producing and consuming countries.

The actual mechanisms used to 'stabilise' world prices have varied with different commodities, the principal devices used being buffer stocks, production quotas and multilateral contracts. A look will now be taken at how these devices have been utilised in four major agreements.

The large-scale usage of buffer stocks has only proved possible in the case of the non-perishable commodity tin. The *Fourth International Tin Agreement* of 1971 allows for the setting up of a buffer stock with a value equivalent to 20,000 tons of tin (comprising both tin metal and cash). Under the supervision of the International Tin Council (ITC)[15] this stock is used for the purchase of tin when the price falls below the agreed 'floor' level and for the sale of tin when it rises above the 'ceiling'. From time to time the ITC may review and alter the range within which it aims to stabilise the price. The 'buffer stock' system has the advantage (in the eyes of many economists) that it does not distort the long-term supply and demand forces of the market. It is seen as a device for ironing out erratic short-term fluctuations in price, and there is some evidence to suggest it has been successful in this objective.

However, by itself a buffer stock does little, if anything, to increase the export earnings of the poor countries which are the major tin exporters. In the Tin Agreement it is especially stated that such an increase in export earnings is a desired objective.[16] To achieve this end it has been necessary to introduce a production quota system, under which quotas are allotted to each producing country and are subject to revision by the ITC. This introduces a divisive influence among the exporter countries, which tend to compete among themselves for higher quotas.

Such a conflict of interests played a major part in the evolution of the *International Coffee Agreement*. This agreement rests almost exclusively on the control of production through export quotas.[17] It was initiated in 1962 with almost total support from all consumer and producer nations after a steady decline in the price of coffee from a peak in 1954. Since then the price decline has been halted and increases have occurred in some years. Export earnings by the producers, all of which are poor countries, have risen. Thus despite disagreements among themselves about the allocation of export quotas, the exporting countries were content to sign a second agreement in 1968. This agreement gave marginal quota increases to many of the new producer countries (in Africa and Latin America) at the expense of the big traditional producers (Brazil and Colombia). The latter, nevertheless, still retain their dominant role in the world market, and there is no doubt that they consider their interests better preserved with an agreement than without one. One significant innovation in the 1968 agreement has been the setting up of a diversification fund to assist the structural changes necessary to prevent the recurrence of oversupply. Minor alterations have also been made to the enforcement procedures that proved a major weakness during the first agreement. In general it is the big producer countries that press for strict enforcement of quotas, while the smaller ones consider they have most to gain from exceeding them.

On the consumer side, one of the principal objectives of the Coffee Agreement is to 'assure adequate supplies of coffee to consumers . . . at reasonable prices'.[18] A stable coffee market is regarded by many consumer countries as desirable for both economic and non-economic reasons. Since the late 1950s, US governments have seen stable coffee prices as a prerequisite to political stability in Latin America. France, with the objective of retaining its political influence in Africa, actively canvassed for an increase in the price of coffee during the 1962 negotiations. There is therefore a degree of self-interest uniting all signatories to the agreement. Recently there have been signs that the major exporters are trying to follow the oil producers' example in co-operating more closely with each other. This precipitated a crisis during the negotiations for the 1972–73 price–quota relationships, and there is now a serious possibility that some of the importer countries will opt out of the agreement if the exporters continue pressing for higher prices. Since the importers' co-operation has in the past proved essential for the enforcement of the quota system, such a withdrawal might lead to the total collapse of the organised market.

International Sugar Agreements, though structured similarly to the Coffee Agreement, have proved less resilient to internal destructive forces. They have never covered more than that residual portion of the market which is not covered by preferential schemes such as the (now expired) Commonwealth Sugar Agreement. With this basic structural weakness the 1959 Sugar Agreement never recovered from the US unilateral boycott of the Cuban quota in 1960. By 1962 the agreement had ceased to function. During the mid 1960s the price fell below 2 cents per pound weight, about half the planned price of the 1959 agreement. A new agreement was signed in 1968, and since then the situation has improved dramatically. Prices have been rising steadily and have already passed through the upper price limits of the agreement despite the selling of national reserve stocks. This improvement in the position of the producers can certainly be partly attributed to the agreement, but it can also be seen as a consequence of the response of producers to the very low prices of the mid 1960s. The gestation period for sugar (cane) is such that it takes a number of years to build up production again after it is cut back during a price slump.

The third mechanism used in commodity agreements is the multilateral contract. Such contracts have operated in the past for wheat and have been allowed for under the terms of the 1971 *International Wheat Agreement*. In practice, however, the supervisory body, the International Wheat Council (IWC), has in recent years preferred to act simply as a clearing house for trade in wheat rather than encouraged price negotiations. The significance of this agreement to the poor countries is different from that of the other commodity agreements, in that for most of them wheat is not a major export crop but a source of food imports. One part of the agreement allows for the use of wheat as 'food aid'. Certainly there are advantages to the poor countries in encouraging the smooth flow of wheat when they need it; on the other hand, the incentive to expand wheat production for export by the poor countries themselves is severely reduced.

In an assessment of the role of commodity agreements, the issues of economic inefficiency and waste should certainly not be ignored, for on these grounds they are often criticised. However, our concern is primarily with the question: do the poor countries benefit from commodity agreements? Perhaps this can be best answered by pointing to the facts that the poor countries have considered it in their interests to sign a number of agreements already and that at the fourth UNCTAD conference in 1976 they advocated the spread of further arrangements. Perhaps a more relevant question is therefore: what form of commodity agreements will most benefit the poor countries? To recapitulate some of the points made earlier, the poor countries should benefit from agreements affecting their exports that include the following:

1 Measures to reduce sharp fluctuations in their export earnings.
2 Measures to increase the prices of those of their exports that have low elasticity of demand.
3 Measures to encourage diversification of production where the prospects for expanding a particular commodity export are slight.
4 Measures to increase consumption of a commodity in the rich countries.
5 Measures to encourage the smooth flow of exports.

Recently the UNCTAD Secretariat has put forward an Integrated Programme for Commodities (sometimes referred to as the Correa Plan) which is likely to be discussed in great detail at the fourth UNCTAD conference in Nairobi in 1976. The aims of this programme are to ensure export diversification, stable and remunerative prices, expanded access to markets, improvement in marketing systems and a reduction of inflationary pressure in world markets.

The Correa Plan envisages:

1 The establishment of international stocks of commodities on a scale sufficient to provide assurance of the disposal of production undertaken on the basis of a realistic assessment of demand, as well as assurance of adequate supplies at all times for importing countries. Stocks held should also be adequate to offset excessive movements, either upwards or downwards, in price through market intervention.
2 The creation of a common fund for financing international stocks on terms capable of attracting international capital to the fund while reflecting in the fund's composition the responsibility of the governments of trading countries.
3 The building up of systems of multilateral commitments on individual commodities, whereby governments on the basis of a multilateral appraisal of trade requirements enter into purchase and supply commitments as a means of improving the predictability of trade requirements and of encouraging rational levels of investment in commodity production. Commitments should be

linked to the operation of international stocking mechanisms and to compensatory schemes.

4 Compensatory arrangements for commodities for which international stocking etc. could not secure suitable price-production incentives.

5 The reduction of discrimination against processed products and encouragement of the transfer of technology, to secure rapid development of the processing of raw materials in the producing countries so as to encourage export expansion and diversification.

The Integrated Programme recognises the need for producers' association and for linking the prices of primary commodities to the prices of manufactured goods. The idea that we should move towards what the 1975 Commonwealth Conference held at Jamaica called a General Agreement on Commodities, and that we should abandon the traditional commodity-by-commodity approach, is certainly gaining ground.

The present commodity agreements, as has been shown, include several desirable features, but because of the difficulties involved in the conclusion and implementation of these agreements other mechanisms and methods have also been developed to stabilise the export earnings of the poor countries. Compensatory financing schemes may be viewed with greater hope, for they are addressed more directly to the problem of export earnings stabilisation than are commodity agreements, which are rather ineffective and inappropriate as export stabilisation devices. Export instability is detrimental to growth mainly because it reduces *total* export earnings and jeopardises development planning. The solution to this problem surely lies in the adoption of a stabilisation mechanism that is basically of a *macro-economic* type, for such a mechanism would deal directly with the problem of export revenue instability on an aggregate level. The commodity agreement approach tends to obscure the macro-economic problem of the stabilisation of exports receipts, by concentrating on the maintenance of prices for individual commodities. Compensatory financing schemes, on the other hand, concern themselves directly with the problem of export stability. Hence they enjoy relatively greater popularity among economists and development planners.

6.62 *Compensatory Financing Schemes*
The major difference between the effects of a commodity agreement on the one hand and a compensatory financing scheme (CFS) on the other may become clearer with the help of a little geometry.

In Figure 6.1 the initial equilibrium in the market for a certain commodity is established at the intersection of S and D. Total revenue at this point is measured by p_2q_3. If demand falls to D_1, total revenue will fall to p_1q_2. If a commodity agreement is in operation in order to maintain revenue at the level of p_2q_3, changes in price and output of the commodity will be manipulated; the new price will be p_3 and the new output q_1 (since $p_2q_3 = p_3q_1$). On the other hand, if a CFS exists the new equilibrium price in the market will be p_1 and the new equilibrium output will be q_2. The CFS will ensure that the difference in revenue between p_2q_3 and p_1q_2 is made up in the form of compensation; alternatively, the compensation may only be partial.

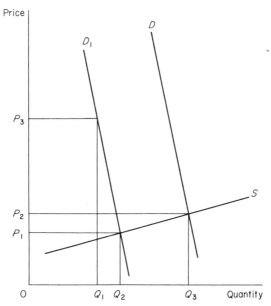

FIG. 6.1 Effect of a compensatory financing scheme on revenue.

In any case, the main point is that under the CFS (unlike the commodity agreement) the market will be allowed to find its own equilibrium and the necessary compensating adjustments will not directly interfere with the market-determined pattern of resource determination. In the real world, it is found that if a CFS is operative the exporting country is tempted to restrict output so as to extract the maximum benefit from the CFS in question. In such a situation, of course, the neutrality of the CFS on the resource allocation process is no longer maintained.

A large number of CFSs have been proposed since the early 1950s. Some can hardly be called a CFS at all. They are specific commodity compensatory schemes, which compensate exporters for deviations of the price and/or output of specified commodities from agreed 'normal' levels. The most far-reaching commodity CFS aims at evening out total export proceeds from the specified commodity.

On the other hand, general compensation schemes focus attention on the fluctuation of the total export earnings or the terms of trade of a particular country. A number of sophistications have been suggested within the compensation mechanism. UN proposals, for instance, have argued that compensation should be automatic on specified shortfalls in export proceeds. It should not be left to the discretion of the compensator to determine the action to be taken in each specific case, for invariably political and strategic considerations will influence decisions if this procedure is adopted. It has been suggested that compensation should come out of a permanent insurance fund rather than in the form of *ad hoc* payments, or alternatively that compensation should be in the form of interest-bearing loans rather than outright grants. Both of these proposals aim at increasing the automaticity of the compensating mechanism. The rich countries have, however, argued that some exporting countries may deliberately limit sales so as to maximise their gain from the CFS; hence some discretionary element in the compensation procedure is called for. If a durable and successful CFS is to be launched it is essential that some form of compromise between these two opposing standpoints should be worked out.

Two important CFS proposals will now be briefly considered. The CFS of the *International Monetary Fund* (IMF) inaugurated in 1963 stipulates that if a country's export earnings are lower than the average of the earnings of the present and last two years, the IMF will allow the country concerned to draw up to 25 per cent of its IMF quota. The scheme applies only to earnings from merchandise exports, and IMF allows a country to benefit from the scheme only if it is convinced that the decline in export earnings has not been deliberately created and is of a relatively short-run nature. Repayment is expected within three to five years. At the instigation of UNCTAD, the IMF extended the scheme to allow an additional compensatory drawing of another 25 per cent of the members quota. However, this facility can be availed of only if the IMF is satisfied that the country concerned is strictly following the recommendations of the IMF to deal with the problem of export instability. The LDCs have generally refrained from making extensive use of the IMF's CFS, though the situation has improved since 1966 when the scheme was liberalised. There are two reasons for this lack of enthusiasm. First, there is a link between ordinary drawings and compensatory drawings; although the revised IMF scheme places the compensatory financing facility outside the structure of ordinary drawings, it is nevertheless true that in practice a use of the CFS facility jeopardises the chances of getting future requests for ordinary drawings granted. Second, and more important, the LDCs strongly resent an increased IMF interference in their domestic economic management and decision-making processes. Hence the terms of the CFS sponsored by the IMF have generally been unacceptable to the poorer countries.

The *Organisation of American States* sponsored a CFS in 1962. The scheme envisaged the creation of a 'revolving fund' of $1,800 million; the rich countries within the scheme would provide $1,200 million and the LDCs $600 million. This fund would be used for compensating two-thirds of the export shortfall of the LDCs within the scheme. The export shortfall would be calculated as the difference between the current export earnings and the average export earnings of the last three years. The CFS proposed that compensation should be entirely through loans repayable over a period of five years. Refinancing would be possible only if the country concerned faced serious balance-of-payments problems. If the decline in export revenue was chronic, refinancing under the scheme would mean an increased debt burden for the LDCs. The scheme was tested extensively in no less than 136 variants by IMF economists, and it was found that the effect of the implementation of the scheme would be at best marginal as far as the exchange requirements of the LDCs were concerned. Consequently, the scheme has never been put into practice.

A number of other CFSs have been proposed.[19] In February 1975 the Lomé Convention was signed between the EEC and forty-six African, Pacific and Caribbean states. The Convention has set up machinery for permanent dialogue between the EEC and the forty-six poor countries. Trade concessions, including the removal of quantitative restrictions, have been granted with respect to a large number of products. Most important, a system stabilising the export earnings of the LDCs (known as STABEX) has been established. The products covered by STABEX include groundnuts, cocoa, coffee, cotton, coconuts, palm and palm kernel products, hides and skins, wood products, bananas, tea, raw sisal and iron ore. The producers of these commodities are guaranteed a certain level of earnings, provided the commodity concerned represents a certain minimum proportion of the total export earnings of the producer country. If a country qualifies on this criterion it may request a transfer from the EEC when exports of the product fall by 7·5 per cent compared to the moving average of export earnings from this product over the preceding four years.

Most CFSs seem to raise a controversy about the 'automaticity versus discretionary control' issue. It is difficult to devise a CFS that does not lead to a net transfer of resources over time. If such a scheme could be devised, the rich countries could have no case for insisting on discretionary control. The IMF has maintained that conditions have to be imposed due to the necessity of rationing the scarce amount of credit among different LDCs. However, as international liquidity increases, this argument will increasingly lose its relevance; if we can *plan* for an increase in world liquidity, we can also *plan* to take into account the requirements of the LDCs that arise from the instability of their export earnings.

If, on the other hand, there is a net transfer of resources from the rich to the poor countries as a result of the operation of a CFS, the rich can argue for the principle of some discretionary control. But the LDCs will be quite right in classifying assistance received under such schemes as tied aid, and, moreover, in order for such aid to be at all acceptable to the LDCs it is inevitable that grant-based supplementary financing schemes should gradually supplement CFSs.

5.63 *Supplementary Financing Schemes*

A supplementary financing scheme (SFS) aims at providing additional resources to LDCs so that they may deal with the problem of export instability. The best known of the SFS proposals is the one formulated by the *World Bank* in 1964. It was designed with the intention of allowing for adjustment to take into account the varied effect of export earnings instability on different economies. The amount of finance to be provided and the conditions under which it would be made available would be determined by the conditions existing in the recipient country. The World Bank's SFS is quite complex, and its application is more difficult than that of CFSs, which are aimed at aggregate export earnings stabilisation. The primary concern of the World Bank's SFS is to offset the disrupting effects of export earnings shortfalls on the national plans of the poorer countries. The scheme aims at supplementing the efforts of these countries in adjusting to unexpected export shortfalls.

Only that part of the shortfall which would pose a serious problem for the implementation of the LDC's development plan would be offset under this scheme, export shortfalls being estimated on the basis of the development plan's own projections of export earnings. Each country would be offered a 'policy package' in accordance with its requirements and circumstances, and the supplementary finance offered as part of the 'policy package' would of course, be additional to the aid funds already committed to the LDC.

The scheme has been criticised on a number of counts. The rich countries have been sceptical of accepting export projections of the poorer countries' plans as a basis for estimating supplementary financing requirements, while the poor countries have expressed suspicion about the 'policy package' which they regard as yet another infringement of their national economic sovereignty. Given this attitude of the recipients, the 'policing' of supplementary financing arrangements would be very difficult. Moreover, the poor countries suspect that money provided under the World Bank's SFS would in one way or another come out of aid funds and would not amount to additional resource transfer. They view the SFS of the World Bank as another form of aid administration and are therefore somewhat lukewarm and unenthusiastic about its inauguration. In view of these factors, it is unlikely that the World Bank's original scheme will be accepted in the near future. In 1975 the World Bank and the IMF increased their assistance of the Third World by the opening of the 'Third Window' and the extension of the 'oil facility' to developing countries particularly affected by the international economic crisis.

Another important SFS proposal was the *United Nations' Development Insurance Fund Scheme* formulated in 1961. A fund was to be established to offset the (downward) fluctuations of the export earnings of the LDCs, contributions to the fund by different countries being determined on the basis of each country's share of world export proceeds and world income. Fluctuations in export earnings were to be computed as the difference between the current year's export earnings and the average of the last years' export earnings. Compensation would be in the form of outright grants or contingent loans that were to be repaid if and when the trend in export revenue was reversed for the country concerned. There would thus be an increasing net transfer of resources to those LDCs which suffered from a chronic problem of export earnings shortfalls. Despite the academic interest aroused at the time of its first proposal, the scheme has never been put into action.

The inability of the international community to evolve a satisfactory mechanism for dealing with the problem of export instability mirrors the fact that there are no universally accepted criteria of what would constitute a satisfactory CFS or SFS. The developed countries generally feel that such a scheme should not involve a long-term net transfer of resources and that, if it does so, an element of discretionary control should be incorporated into the financing mechanism. On the other hand, the LDCs feel that a CFS/SFS of this nature would offer no more than marginal help in their endeavours to cope with the problems of fluctuations in export receipts. Empirical tests of the Organisation of American States' CFS and of the United Nations' SFS tend to bear out this point. If a financing scheme is to have real rather than symbolic significance, it must involve a transfer of funds much larger than the fund transfers envisaged under the current schemes. Moreover, the poor countries actually resent the fact that the rich countries want to use the compensatory or supplementary financing mechanism as a means for ensuring that the former accept some limitation of their national economic sovereignty. The fact that the poor countries are obliged to listen to the IMF and World Bank and not to the United States or EEC countries is of little relevance here, for in the 1970s the World Bank and IMF are not bodies that are regarded by the poorer countries of the world as highly representative of their interests. A compromise between the radically different positions taken by the rich and poor countries on this issue is necessary before the problem of export instability can be effectively tackled through a comprehensive international financing scheme.

The developing countries have become disillusioned with institutions like GATT and the IMF and consider that they cannot serve as the forum where a meaningful dialogue on international economic restructuring can be conducted. UNCTAD is generally regarded as the place where the rich and poor countries can meet on a more equal basis; hence the Third World has been firm in its support for UNCTAD since the birth of this organisation.

5.7 THE IMPACT OF UNCTAD

UNCTAD was established in 1964, with the main purpose of co-ordinating international effort in order to promote the development of the poor countries. The poor countries felt that the United Nations was the right place for negotiating economic arrangements with the rich countries. UNCTAD has provided a forum for the poor countries to express their views on international trading arrangements and on the economic policies of the rich countries in general. However, UNCTAD's achievements in the course of the last ten years have not been as spectacular as the optimists expected. In the field of international trade its main contribution has been the pioneering in 1971 of the General System of Preferences (GSP) already mentioned, designed to cover the manufacturing exports of the poor countries. A look at the GSP is a useful introduction to the limitations involved in UNCTAD-sponsored negotiations.

The main idea behind the GSP is that manufacturing exports from developing countries should be given preferential access to the markets of the rich countries. However, in a sense it is erroneous to talk of the GSP as an entity, because the rich countries were not able to agree on one single scheme. The United States, Australia, the Nordic countries, the EEC countries and Japan all came up with different preference schemes, which differ with regard to product coverage and the method of preferential treatment. The rich countries argued that processed agricultural goods and other semi-manufactures should be excluded from the scheme, and different rich countries gave different product classifications. Generally speaking, the schemes evolved by the Nordic countries were the most liberal, those of the EEC countries and Japan were the most restricted, while those of the United States and United Kingdom[20] were intermediate. The rich countries agreed that specified manufactured exports would have duty-free access to the markets of the rich countries, But Japan and the EEC members set quantitative ceilings beyond which imports of manufactured goods from the LDCs would no longer have preferential treatment. The United States urged that developing countries should put an end to the 'reverse' preferences that they grant to different rich countries.[21] Other rich countries specified that they would withdraw the preferences if domestic problems necessitated such action. On top of all these limitations on the utility of the scheme there is the further problem that there is no legal guarantee that the rich countries will in fact implement and continue the schemes that they have formulated. Hence, despite the fact that the GSP was incorporated into the strategy of the UN Second Development Decade, the poor countries justifiably have not been very enthusiastic about its impact on trading patterns. As a Yugoslav economist has commented:

'The System . . . contains no built-in guarantee and donors can shut off the carefully built export drives of an LDC. Exceptions [by the rich countries] have been taken in precisely those product

130

where LDCs enjoy comparative advantages and can compete effectively . . . Product coverage is not broad enough . . . Ceilings and quotas to be applied to certain donors [can] be utilised in a dangerous manner.'[22]

The GSP reflects the character of the organisation (i.e. UNCTAD) which was responsible for its inception. UNCTAD works by consensus, and resolutions passed at UNCTAD are not binding on those who cast a negative vote or express a reservation. Experienced UNCTAD diplomats know well that action can be expected on only those resolutions which have the unqualified support of the rich countries. Hence UNCTAD rarely leads to action. At the third UNCTAD conference (held in 1972 at Santiago) no decisions were taken which could lead to immediate or substantial changes in aid, trade or monetary matters. This does not mean that no progress whatever was made at Santiago. Two important resolutions were adopted: one on facilitating the transfer of 'development-oriented' technology to the poor countries, the other on adopting special measures for the *least* developed countries. At the fourth session held at Nairobi in 1976 rich and poor countries agreed to implement a series of reforms with respect to trade, aid and investment which may contribute significantly towards the building of a more equitable international economic order. Similarly, some progress was made towards giving the developing countries a greater voice in the IMF and in the Tokyo Round of GATT negotiations,[23] which commenced in 1975, but the resolutions adopted at international meetings like UNCTAD conferences were by no means unambiguous and they commit nobody to any specific action. The Santiago 'transfer of technology' resolution calls for the promotion of technology transfer from the rich to the poor countries. It also asks the rich to 'participate actively in the identification of restrictive business practices which affect the transfer of technology', but it does not specify the methods by which these aims are to be achieved. The resolution also is not entirely unambiguous about the position of the intergovernmental group that had previously been established to look into this question; hence it has not created any permanent machinery which can administer and co-ordinate the implementation of the resolution. The Santiago resolution on monetary reform was responsible for the creation of the 'Group of 20'. This has undoubtedly increased the bargaining power of the poor countries within the IMF (though this really came only with the shift of financial power to OPEC), but the resolution did not establish the terms of reference of this new 'Group of 20'. The poor countries were also unable to establish a link between the Special Drawing Rights (SDRs) of the IMF and international aid.[24]

The UNCTAD III resolution on special measures for the least developed countries did not establish a special fund out of which these countries could be helped. The least developed countries are specially poor countries with maximum lack of industries and literacy. Because of their relative remoteness they have not attracted a great deal of aid or foreign investment. They have suffered most acutely from the agricultural protectionist policies of the rich countries. The UNCTAD III resolution called for an extension of the GSP to products of special export interests to the least developed countries, but it remains to be seen how and to what extent this reconsideration is implemented. Moreover, the way in which the resolution defines a least developed country is itself rather unsatisfactory; e.g. large, densely populated countries like Bangladesh have been excluded from this category.[25] The resolution is also vague and unexplicit on the concessions that should be granted to the least developed countries within the regional groupings of which they are members. The twenty-five 'hard-core' least developed countries are (generally speaking) peripheral areas in the regions in which they are situated. Resources in the form of qualified labour as well as capital tend to move away from these countries. The more advanced countries within the region, which are themselves poor, will have to grant concessions to the least developed countries if the latter are to overcome their handicap. But such help can only be extended by the poor countries to the poorest ones if the international community actively supports such policies. Beyond a general recommendation that regional development banks should look into these problems, the Santiago resolution does not specify the way in which the international community should contribute towards the evolution of a regional policy that takes into account the requirements of the least developed countries.

The limited and disappointing results of the Santiago conference have created a great deal of disillusionment about UNCTAD. The 'Group of 77' (actually comprising ninety-six poor countries) and 'Group B' (consisting of the rich Western countries) have both become increasingly disheartened with the results that the periodic conference (held once every four years) produces. The rich countries believe that the demands of the poor are 'unbalanced' and 'unrealistic', while the poor countries view the stand taken by the rich as niggardly and overcautious. The rich and poor countries carry on a dialogue that tends to become purposeless and devoid of substance, and the gulf that divides them has not been very successfully negotiated at either the second UNCTAD conference (held at Delhi in 1968) or the third. The poor countries think that this is because the rich have strongly resisted major revisions in the pattern of international economic relations. Although the poor countries have a majority in UNCTAD, international economic organisations such as the World Bank, IMF and GATT are dominated by the rich countries. The facts that the decisions of UNCTAD are not legally binding and that implementation of these decisions requires a concensus have induced the developing countries to press for a strengthening of UNCTAD's position within the UN system. Simultaneously, the poor countries are also seeking increased representation in the World Bank, IMF and GATT. The Third World countries have sought to strengthen UNCTAD after the events of 1973. The limited rapprochement and reconciliation achieved between the developed and the developing countries at the Seventh Special Session of the UN General Assembly may well lead to an eventual redefinition of UNCTAD's global task after the Nairobi Conference of 1976.

Recent events have in no way reduced the importance of commodity agreements or other export stabilisation schemes. The developing countries seem to regard the rise in the price of primary commodities as a transient phenomenon. They seek to consolidate the gains they have made in the early 1970s by entering into commodity agreements and into international arrangements which link the price of primary commodities to the prices of manufactured exports of the LDCs. The proposal to establish such a link was first voiced in UNCTAD and was repeated at the UN Special Session on Raw Materials and Development, where the Declaration for the Establishment of a New International Economic Order called for a

'just and equitable relationship between the prices of raw materials, primary products, manufactured and semi-manufactured goods exported by the developing countries and the prices of . . . goods and equipment imported by them with the aim of bringing about sustained improvement in their unsatisfactory terms of trade and the expansion of the world economy'.[26]

In order to build such a link the resolution advocated the 'expeditious formulation of commodity agreements and the introduction of compensatory finance schemes to meet the needs of developing countries'.[27]

The developing countries, however, are in favour of schemes and agreements which do not infringe their national sovereignty. An overriding objective of the establishment of the New International Economic Order is to emphasise the importance of recognising the 'sovereign equality of states'. They are thus unlikely to agree to measures which involve the granting of discretionary control to the rich countries.

However, it is not impossible for reconciliation and rapprochement to be achieved on this issue. It is vitally important that the policies of confrontation and bilateral accommodation that have characterised rich–poor trading policies since the coming of the energy crisis should give way to generalised and universal schemes which seek to contribute to both world economic expansion and the development of the Third World. The Tokyo Round of GATT negotiations and the fourth UNCTAD conference provide an excellent opportunity for moving over from confrontation to co-operation in World trade.

APPENDIX TO CHAPTER 6

The Rate of Effective Protection in the LDCs

The concept of the effective rate of protection (ERP) has been briefly discussed in this chapter.[28] The ERP is usually calculated by the use of input/output coefficients. Effective protection is the protection that is accorded to a particular economic activity as a result of the protection of all the different stages of the manufacturing process. It is evident that protection might raise the prices of both the inputs and output of an industry. The ERP estimates the amount by which value added in a particular activity is raised by protection. A number of methods for measuring ERP have been given; Corden's method is the most frequently used.[29] It is given by the formula:

$$g_j = \frac{t_j - \sum_{i=1}^{n} a_{ij} t_i}{1 - \sum_{i=1}^{n} a_{ij}}$$

where
g_j = effective protective rate for activity j
a_{ij} = share of i in cost of j in absence of tariffs
t_i = tariff rate on i
t_j = tariff rate on j

Therefore the effective protection rate depends not only on the pro-

134

tection of industry j but also on the input coefficients and the level of protection of the inputs of industry j. The effective protection rate is the percentage change in value added per unit in industry j made possible by the existence of a protection structure relative to a 'no tariff' situation but with the same exchange rate.

It is evident that the concept of ERP is not without its ambiguities.[30] Economists have differed on the ways in which non-traded goods should be treated in measuring ERP for a particular activity. Doubt has also been expressed about the ERP as an indicator of the *attractiveness* of different industries from the point of view of the investors. 'Why should the percentage increase in value added be a measure of this? Some may suggest that the percentage by which net profits would be raised would be the right measure?'[31] It has also been argued that ERP should be measured relative to a 'realistic' or 'equilibrium' foreign exchange rate rather than the official exchange rates of the LDCs.

The debate on these issues has by no means proved conclusive and most of the refinements that have emerged from it seem to be too ambitious for incorporation into the actual empirical work that is undertaken on the basis of the data produced by the LDCs. Hence the ERP is still measured in a fairly straightforward, or even crude, way. Despite its shortcomings it represents the best available, relatively simple measure of the structure of protection of a country.

NOTES

1 I. M. D. Little, Scitvosky and Scott, *Industry and Trade in Developing Countries* (Paris, OECD Development Centre, 1970).
2 B. Balassa *et al.*, *The Structure of Protection in Developing Countries* (Baltimore, IBRD, 1971).
3 N. B. Chenery, 'Patterns of Industrial Growth', *American Economic Review* (May, 1960).
4 Balassa *et al.*, op. cit., pp. 49–70.
5 See Appendix to this chapter.
6 These are simple averages. In the case of Pakistan, for the net ERP of the primary-producing sector we have used the net ERP of the agricultural sector as the figure, because the net ERP for the primary-producing sector as a whole was not available.
7 Pakistan operated an Export Bonus Scheme from 1959 to 1971.
8 See S. R. Lewis, *Economic Policy and Industrial Growth in Pakistan* (London, George Allen & Unwin, 1969).
9 G. Winston, 'Capacity Utilization in Economic Development', *Economic Journal* (March 1971), pp. 36–58. See also A. Phillips, 'Measuring Industrial Capacity in Less Developed Countries', Discussion Paper No. 110

(Department of Economics, University of Pennsylvania, Philadelphia, 1969) and W. Hogan 'Capacity Creation and Utilization in Pakistan Manufacturing Industries', Economic Development Report No. 84 (Development Advisory Service, Harvard, mimeo, 1967).

10 See Little *et al.*, op. cit and Balassa *et., al.*, op. cit.

11 Figure is for 1966–67 .

12 The proportion is high for Thailand within ASPAC (68 per cent), and Paraguay within LAFTA (33 per cent). Figures are for the early 1970s.

13 Tony Killick, 'Commodity Agreements as International Aid', *Westminster Bank Review* (February 1967).

14 G. D. Gwyer, *Perennial Crop Supply Response: the Case of Tanzanian Sisal* (Wye College, London University, 1971).

15 The producer countries and consumer countries each have 50 per cent of the votes in this Council.

16 Secretary of State for Foreign and Commonwealth Affairs, *Fourth International Tin Agreement*, Cmnd. 4493 (London, HMSO).

17 Coffee stocks have in the past been used for price stabilisation, but many consumers consider that storage reduces the quality of coffee.

18 Secretary of State for Foreign and Commonwealth Affairs, *International Coffee Agreement 1968*, Treaty Series No. 103 (London, HMSO, 1969).

19 Those interested are referred to Schiavo-Campo and Singer, *Perspectives of Economic Development* (New York, Houghton Mifflin, 1970).

20 The United Kingdom was not a member of the EEC when agreement was reached within UNCTAD on the GSP. After the United Kingdom joined the EEC the UK proposals had to be merged and reconciled with the EEC preference scheme.

21 The Francophone African countries accorded preference to EEC products as part of the system of EEC association. But in the new Lomé Convention, which includes the African, Pacific and Caribbean Commonwealth countries, reverse preferences have been abandoned.

22 Gosovic, *UNCTAD: Conflict and Compromise* (Leiden, Sjhtoff, 1972), pp. 91–2.

23 See Chapter 6.

24 See Chapter 8.

25 Bangladesh, like India, is, however, included in the new priority category of the 'MSAs' – the most seriously affected countries — affected, that is, by the rise in oil and food prices.

26 *Monthly Chronicle*, New York, UN (May 1974), p. 68.

27 Op. cit., p. 72.

28 See p. 99.

29 W. M. Corden, 'The Structure of a Tariff System and the Effective Rate of Protection', *Journal of Political Economy* (June 1966).

30 For a thorough discussion see B. Balassa *et al., The Structure of Protection in Developing Countries* (Baltimore, IBRD, 1971), Appendix A, pp. 315–34.

31 I. M. D. Little, Scitovsky and Scott, *Industry and Trade in Developing Countries* (Paris, OECD Development Centre, 1970), p. 170.

PART THREE

AID

CHAPTER 7

Aid as an Agent of Development

7.1 AID, TRADE AND THE WIDENING GAP

A central aspect of international development that we ought perpetually to keep in mind is the fact that it can safely be predicted that the gap between the richer and poorer countries is bound to grow in both absolute and relative terms in the foreseeable future. In Chapter 1 were presented estimates (based on moderately optimistic assumptions about development in the poorer countries) of the extent to which the gap is likely to widen round about the turn of the century. The specialists may quibble about the exact magnitude of the different variables and their growth rates, but intellectual sophistry of this sort cannot conceal the hard fact that the average Indian, Pakistan or African will in the year 2000 have a much lower standard of living *in comparison* to the standard of living enjoyed by the average British, American or USSR citizen.

In the course of the next thirty years the gap between the rich and poor countries may widen by between three and four times, and the consequence both political and economic of this colossal growth in inequality are likely to be immense. Indeed, it goes without saying that the stability of the world order as we know it depends crucially on the way in which this problem of the ever-widening gap between nations is handled by the international community. Two-thirds of the world's population will not reconcile itself to a level of living that is permanently diminishing in comparison to the standards enjoyed by the privileged citizens of Northern America, Europe and the oil-rich countries. A crisis in international relations is almost inevitable if the rich countries complacently accept their lead and advantages as a fact of life. If the international economic system is incapable of providing the wherewithal for an effective reduction of inequality within the community of nations, the LDCs will feel justified in their attempts to destroy the political and economic system which perpetuates international inequalities.

A general realisation of the seriousness of the problem was recognised by the Report of the Commission on International Develop-

139

ment, headed by Lester B. Pearson.[1] The Commission was set up in order to study the various processes by which the poor and rich nations have co-operated in order to promote development in the former since the Second World War. It studied, in other words, the ways by which endeavours have been made to bridge the gap between the 'haves' and the 'have nots' in the international community. The commissioners undertook a comprehensive analysis of trade, aid and investment policies. The findings of the Commission are of importance to us, as are also the recommendations it made for the future.

The Pearson Commission noted that the development efforts of the LDCs as a group were more constrained by the conditions that determined the size of their balance-of-payments gap and aid bill than by the factors that affected the generation of their domestic surplus.

The availability of foreign assistance was, in the opinion of the Pearson Commission, an important factor influencing growth – this despite the fact that no obvious correlation exists, in a cross-sectional sense, between aid allocation and the growth rate. Aid constituted about 10 per cent of total investment and financed about 20 per cent of the exports of the LDCs. Aid was an important means for the provision of technical and managerial skills. An expansion in the aid effort would be beneficial for the LDCs.

The Pearson Commission recommended that:

(a) Aid allocation must be determined by the objective of enabling the poor countries to attain a growth rate of 6 per cent of their GNP in the 1970s. For a country growing at a 6 per cent rate would by 'the end of the century be able to participate in the international economy as self-reliant partners and to finance the investment and imports they need for continued rapid growth without foreign capital on concessional terms'.

(b) The international development organisations should undertake periodic reviews of aid utilisation by the LDCs, and future aid commitments must be based upon the abilities of specific countries to use the aid funds effectively.

(c) The total flow of aid and private investment should equal 1 per cent of the GNP of the developed countries. The 1 per cent target 'must be fully met by 1975 at the very latest'. There is a greater need for official assistance in the form of grants, soft-term loans, etc. Official aid must be raised to 0·7 per cent of the donor's GNP.

(d) An overhauling of aid administration procedures is necessary.

140

Tied aid should be phased out. The form in which aid is given should depend upon the requirements of the recipient.

(e) Multilateral aid must be raised to 20 per cent of total official development assistance by 1975. The multinational aid agencies should play a much more important role in aid administration in the future. This would involve a review of their practices and policies.

There can be little doubt that the Pearson Report laid primary emphasis on the aid effort. The 'widening gap' would continue to widen unless the developed nations substantially increased the volume of assistance that was being given to the poor nations. It was argued that, if adequate aid were forthcoming for the next forty to fifty years, most of the LDCs of today would be in a position to earn their keep, as it were, by about the year 2000. A number of LDCs would be in a position to compete in the international markets and would be able to buy the required imports from their own export earnings. In other words, the Pearson Commission assumed that the association between trade and aid is such that, if aid expansion takes place now, the earnings from trade will in the future be substitutable for aid receipts.

This view has been seriously questioned by a number of the economists who participated in the Columbia Conference on International Development held in 1970. The Conference looked in detail at the proposals put forward by the Pearson Commission, and from its discussion has emerged a wealth of new ideas, approaches and insights.

The majority opinion among the participants at the Conference seemed to specify that the Pearson Commission has mis-specified the trade–aid relationship. The Columbia Conference reasserted that the trade situation that confronts the poor countries is a bleak one. There was a general consensus of opinion that the proposals put forward by the Pearson Commission for reforming the international trade system and liberalising the markets for the exports of the LDCs were inadequate. Hence, given these policies, trade could not in general be expected to play a leading role in stimulating or sustaining development in the poor countries.

The aid proposals of the Pearson Commission were in general regarded as conservative. The Columbia Conference stressed that, even if a 6 per cent growth rate were attained, the gap between the rich and poor countries would be four times its present size by the year 2000. A 1 per cent aid target, though large in terms of present aid flows, would be totally inadequate to deal with an imbalance of this size. It was necessary for the whole attitude to the problem of international assistance to be fundamentally altered. The Columbia Commission argued for an aid target related to the income per capita in the LDCs; specifically, aid must not be less than $400 per person per annum in the LDCs by the year 2000. Aid should be related to specific social targets (e.g. better nutrition for children, health standards, education levels, etc.) and must be concentrated in the group of countries which have a per capita income of less than $300 per annum. It was felt that the LDCs which had a higher per capita income would benefit more from improvement of the trade environment than they would from aid allocations.

The Pearson Commission's recommendation that aid should be enough to finance a 6 per cent growth rate in the LDCs was also the subject of considerable criticism by the Columbia Conference. The Pearson Commission had postulated that aid allocation must primarily be linked to the objective of attaining 'self-sufficient' growth in the LDCs by the year 2000. Aid was hence viewed essentially as a temporary and self-liquidating process. The need for aid would diminish as the country developed and as 'normal' trade earnings on the one hand and domestic saving rates on the other expanded.

The Columbia Conference viewed with apprehension the suggestion that aid should be regarded merely as a means of achieving a 6 per cent growth rate in the LDCs and should cease when the LDCs became capable of financing and sustaining such a growth rate themselves. The gap between the rich and poor countries would increase to four times its present size if the LDCs grew at a 6 per cent rate from now till the year 2000. It is unrealistic to assume that the relative bargaining strength of the poor nations *vis-à-vis* the rich would have improved by that date. On the contrary, the international economy would then consist of countries which would, in relative terms, be four times as rich or four times as poor as they are now. It is impossible not to conclude that 'self-sustaining growth' has very little meaning if viewed in this context. Can trade in particular – and economic relations in general – among partners who are so widely different in their economic structure and performance, ever lead to the evolution of an international system of pricing and production that caters to the needs of the poor countries? If not, in what sense will the latter be independent of the stronger and richer nations?

A primary objective of aid allocation policy must be the reduction of the ever-widening international gap. Aid must not be seen as a temporary self-liquidating, stop-gap measure. Instead, it must be frankly recognised that aid, as we know it, ought to be the first step that has been taken towards the evolution of a progressive international taxation structure based on the principle: 'From each according to his ability; to each according to his need.' In other words, the fact must be faced that aid is a *permanent* feature of the process of international resource allocation. The extent to which it is distributed in accordance with the true principles of equity and efficiency reflects the contribution of the well-to-do members of the international community towards eliminating the imbalances and inequalities within the world economic system. Indeed, international assistance that is given without regard to the relative needs of the recipients is self-defeating, in that its contribution to the development of the recipient country is highly unlikely to be very fruitful. The contribution of the rich economies towards the development requirements of the poor nations will thus have to be geared to the development needs of the latter and not to the interests, both political and economic, of the rich countries themselves. This is a feature of central importance. If aid is to be used as an agent of development we will have to move towards the creation of an international institutional aid allocation mechanism which minimises the political control of the aid donors and allocates assistance strictly in accordance with development criteria. The sceptics say that it is foolish to think that such a system can be evolved: the richer nations could never be induced to put their national interests in the background. If this is true, it is inevitable that we are moving rapidly towards an international catastrophic holocaust in which civilisation as we know it may well be destroyed.

In the 1960s and 1970s there has been a renewed interest in the aid versus trade debate. Economists have tried to identify the extent to which aid and trade can supplement each other. There has now also been some concern with the effects of aid and trade restrictions.[2]

Quantitatively, aid is still very much the junior partner to trade. In recent years official assistance has been equivalent to about one-fifth of foreign exchange earned through merchandise exported by developing countries. A reduction of exports would therefore hit developing countries much more severely than a proportionate reduction of aid.[3] The lesser average quantitative role of aid does not, of course, imply a lesser marginal role. There is no *a priori* generalisation to be made concerning the relative worth of an extra dollar of aid versus that of an extra dollar earned through trade. Also, aggregate figures can be highly misleading in this case, for, while some countries obtain almost their entire foreign exchange through exports, others are highly dependent on external assistance. Aid programmes are not spread evenly across the board; rather, national programmes concentrate on a vey small number of countries, though different donor countries have different geographical areas of aid interest.

The availability of foreign exchange, or, more broadly, of foreign resources, can of course be increased by export expansion as well as by additional transfers in the form of aid. To this extent at least, trade and aid are exactly equivalent; both provide foreign resources. Once this level of generality is abandoned, however, serious arguments have been brought forward to support a preference of trade over aid or vice versa.[4]

On a theoretical level, while both trade and aid allow a country to avoid the need for the inefficient domestic production of necessary foreign inputs, aid also provides additional real resources. Aid would therefore seem preferable on this account. The argument, of course, implies that the opportunity cost of resources used in the production of additional exports is greater than zero; this will almost always be the case. However, opportunity costs may often be considerably lower than nominal costs if the resources used in export production are specific to it and/or if, for any reason, they would not actually be used unless exports were increased. Even with this qualification in mind, aid will increase *total* resources available to the country, while the contribution of trade will be limited to avoiding the income losses of transforming domestic into foreign resources.

Trade, on the other hand, gets the nod on the basis of another general consideration. Trade has traditionally been considered the engine of growth, in addition to having its classical welfare-increasing role. The competitive stimulus of expanded trade relations, the push to modernisation as the only path to industrial survival, the elimination of the grosser inefficiencies of import-substitution pushed to the limit, all have traditionally been viewed as powerful points in favour of the trade expansion route.

It has also been argued[5] that, even though the yield of investment of foreign aid may initially be greater than that of investment on additional exports or on the least inefficient import substitutes, the economic policies of developing countries (especially aversion to devaluation, combined with weak monetary and fiscal policies and with overambitious development plans) tend in time to push import substitution (financed through foreign aid) to the point where the yield of investing aid falls below that of investing on new exports, on expansion of traditional exports and on least inefficient import substitutes. While the conclusion is a valid one, the reasoning behind it

144

is rather misleading, mainly because the argument draws a developmental conclusion from what are essentially efficiency considerations. It is perfectly true that freely fluctuating foreign exchange rates, or frequent devaluation of fixed rates, would restore balance-of-payments equilibrium, but naturally they would do so partly by reducing imports. To the extent that substitutability of domestic for imported capital and intermediate goods is low, external balance is then reached at a high cost in terms of growth. In developing countries, and in the context of structural transformation needs, a large proportion of imports does not really carry a minus sign – as in conventional income-determination analysis – for without those imports the welfare loss is dwarfed by the possible impairment of future growth prospects. Equilibrium accompanied by stagnation is hardly a desirable solution. The foreign exchange constraint would indeed be alleviated by this strategy, not so much by increasing foreign exchange availability, but rather by the reduction of foreign exchange needs attendant upon slower growth.

At a practical level of discussion, several points have emerged concerning the relative desirability of trade and aid. At this level it is useful to make a distinction between the points of view of the developed and developing countries.[6] Some of the more relevant among the several possible arguments are the following:

1 Additional trade has the advantage that it does not add to developing countries' indebtedness; neither, however, does aid in the form of grants. Besides, some forms of trade (e.g. bilateral arrangements) do imply a kind of indebtedness, in the form of import obligations.

2 Additional trade has no strings attached to it, whereas aid normally is conditioned in some respect or another. However, some trade expansion may also have to be bought with political or economic concessions. From the developed country's viewpoint, conditionality is, of course, an advantage of aid, for it allows a degree of influence over the recipient country which can be used for either economic or political objectives, or both. Also, there may be an honest desire to influence the use of external resources for the recipient country's own benefit, in the belief that allocative decisions can be more efficiently made from the outside than if they are left to a presumably inefficient developing country's government. A special subadvantage (in reality of tremendous importance) for donor countries is the possibility offered by aid programmes, directly or indirectly, to promote the donor country's ideology. An increasing degree of pragmatism of donor countries

has, however, crept into the scene, and at the same time more and more developing countries are quite aware of the possibility of such ideological interference and have found ways to resist it.

3 From both the developed and developing countries' viewpoints, aid administration procedures are costly and time-consuming. Although improvements are possible, procedures are to some extent dependent on the very same motives which govern the granting and acceptance of aid in the first place. The results which an aid programme is supposed to achieve are so many and so complex that its administration is necessarily costly and complicated; it has to consider the donors' desires for channelling the aid in certain directions and for certain purposes, as well as the recipients' preoccupation with avoiding excessive interference with their economic policies.

4 An important advantage of aid over trade, from the developed countries' viewpoint, is the avoidance of direct losses to domestic producers. While the political capacity of the developed countries to give aid and alter its magnitude is limited by the *general* attitude of their citizens towards international development, their political capacity to grant trade concessions (in the sense of preferential treatment of the developing countries' exports or at least of removal of implicit discrimination against them) is limited, probably more severely, by the political strength of the domestic manufacturers who would stand to lose from such concessions. To paraphrase an old economic maxim: while aid costs everyone a little, trade preferences cost a few people a lot. Thus, while the general resistance to transferring budgetary funds to poor countries is the aggregate result of minimal individual economic losses, the particular resistance to granting trade concessions may be the very powerful one resulting from clear and present danger to the economic interests of a specific group.

5 Aid may be thought to be more or less uncertain than trade. Thus, the cost of aid to the developed countries is more clearly identifiable and measurable than the *total* cost of trade concessions. For the developing countries, depending on the circumstances, future aid inflows may be seen as more or less uncertain than future export earnings. On the other hand, the uncertainty attached to new export markets is undoubtedly an important factor limiting the willingness of the developing countries to seek increased foreign resources through export expansion. Also, satisfactory export performance may have the perverse result of reducing aid transfers to the country. Conversely, if export performance is a positive criterion for the granting of aid, the rewards of successful

146

export expansion would be reinforced by an increase in external assistance.

6 Finally, both the developed and developing countries may have a preference for earned income over handouts; in fact, they certainly do, but whether this general preference in practice plays a significant role is highly questionable, in the face of down-to-earth considerations.

The varity and complexity of arguments for and against trade or aid should make it clear at this point that any generalisation is at best very doubtful. It is sufficient to note the considerable differences in the attitudes of different countries, both developed and developing, towards aid programmes and trade concessions. At any rate, the conflict (which is only apparent) disappears if the more general question is formulated, i.e. the question of maximising the net real flow of external resources to the developing countries and the efficiency of their utilisation, while keeping the costs to the developed countries down to a politically acceptable minimum.

Neither 'Trade not Aid' then, nor 'Aid not Trade', but obviously 'Trade and Aid' is the answer; innumerable concrete circumstances will determine the proper weight of each, at different points in time. We fully concur with Pincus's conclusion on this point: 'There can be no clear-cut generalisation about the absolute merits of aid and trade. The viewpoint of each party and the conditions under which aid and trade are conducted will determine the preference of each.'[7]

The very distinction between trade and aid loses clarity and operational meaning if the interactions between the two are taken into consideration. (Linking aid to trade should not necessarily have the effect of obscuring the consequences of each, if some care is exercised to isolate conceptually the subsidy element from the commercial element.) In addition to being a useful concept for policy purposes, this link-up is inevitable; one would be hard put to visualise an international subsidy which did not have a significant influence on trade patterns between the parties involved, or a trade concession which did not contain an element of transfer. It would appear then that the proper question is how to link aid to trade in an efficient and politically realistic way. Again, concrete steps would have to be taken in the light of current conditions. A few general possibilities can, however, be briefly mentioned here.

One clear link of aid with trade is embodied in the various supplementary financing schemes (see Chapter 6). Another major step would be for aid to be given in the form of a subsidy on imports from developing countries greater than the tariff on those imports (i.e. a negative tariff). This is a more generalised version of the tariff preferences proposed by UNCTAD. It would be much more effective since the subsidy would give preference over the local producer as well as over the rival exporter from the competing developed countries, but for this very reason it would be politically more difficult. There may be some ground for very qualified optimism in this respect as, not only is there a parallel situation in the negative income tax proposal in the United States, which is enjoying increased acceptability, but also the damage which negative tariffs would imply for the larger producers in the developed countries (in the short run), given the modest possibilities for increased production of manufactured exportables by the developing countries, would be very modest. A negative tariff can be viewed as equivalent to an agreed partial devaluation of the currencies of the aid recipients, without their having to pay the penalties on import prices (i.e. as an internationally agreed dual exchange-rate system).

Apart from supplementary financing and from negative tariffs, aid can be used to stimulate trade. Among aid-financed projects, those with an export potential could be specially emphasised, technical assistance on export promotion could be given,[8] and donor countries could prevail upon their private firms establishing branches or subsidiaries in developing countries, or licensing production there, to permit exports of new production more freely. Also, aid could be given more on a regional basis and for multinational projects or groups of projects, thus encouraging the developing countries' trade with one another; this could be associated with the use of regional banks (e.g. the African and Asian Development Banks). Yet, one still feels that a policy by aid donors of using aid to help trade (i.e. the recipient's trade, not the donor's!) would be meaningless unless accompanied by a trade policy giving easier access to the donor's markets and reducing the current discrimination against processing and fabrication inherent in (and often concealed by) tariff structures. Only in this sense would aid be truly supplementary to trade.

We must also note that aid is of less value to the advanced LDCs. The oil-rich LDCs clearly have no need for aid; the intermediate LDCs (e.g. Argentina, Turkey and Spain) would benefit more from expanded export opportunities and foreign investment than from aid. But Chad, Niger, Laos and Bangladesh need aid desperately. However, even the poorest forty of the LDCs see aid as linked to a reform of the whole international trade and monetary system. This is clearly seen in the UN resolutions on the New International Economic Order.

148

7.2 AID DEFINED AND MEASURED: THE NATURE OF AID IN THE POSTWAR WORLD

Granted the importance of aid in international development, we may next turn to the problem of defining it in a precise way. What is meant by aid? Aid implies the idea of a gift, of assistance rendered, of unilateral transfer, of a *quid sine quo*. This means that not everything which results in a transfer of resources, and which is often loosely referred to as aid, is in fact included in our definition. For instance, private foreign investment, export credits, and public loans at commercial rates of interest do not represent aid, even though they may be useful to the recipient, since there is a *quid pro quo* – in fact, sometimes the *quo* is a lot bigger than the *quid*!

The fact that aid has become a global process in which all the richer countries are involved itself set in motion processes that led as a byproduct to a better definition of aid; the global nature of aid gave rise to the evolution of the concept of burden sharing among donors. Burden sharing means that the burden of aid should be shouldered by the various donor countries in some sort of agreed ratio related to their respective economic or financial aid-giving capacities. The attempt to work out agreed formulas for burden sharing immediately raised the question of what should or should not be counted as aid within the meaning of the agreed formula. Discussion on this question among the donors took place mainly in the Development Assistance Committee of the OECD. In the Pearson Report this led to a clear distinction between the total flow of financial resources from richer countries to poorer countries on the one hand, and public aid on the other hand, with separate specific targets for the two categories (1 per cent of GNP for total flows and 0·7 per cent of GNP for public aid). Even this distinction, however, was clearly in need of further subdivision, since public aid could be anything from a straight grant or gift to a loan at 5, 6 or 7 per cent interest payable in hard currency. This led to such further refinements as the definition of the grant element in aid and the evolution of agreed standards regarding the terms of loans within the DAC, including rate of interest, duration, grace periods, etc. The target of 0·7 per cent of GNP for public aid, if it were really implemented as well as accepted on paper, would amount to a considerable expansion; the present flow of public aid is little more than half of this target figure, and considerably less than half if the grant element alone is considered. The percentages thus obtained are further reduced if the Eastern donor countries of the Council for Mutual Economic Assistance (COMECON) as well as the Western donors of the OECD are included.

The idea of an international 'target' for aid to the LDCs in terms of the available resources of the richer or donor countries originally formed part of the proposals for the First UN Development Decade of the 1960s. The idea has historical roots further back into the 1950s. It had a counterpart in a similar 'target' of a 5 per cent growth rate for the national income of the LDCs or recipient countries themselves.

Neither of these targets was very clearly defined; nor was there any specific consistency model developed at the time to link those two targets. Both targets initially had little more than declamatory value; neither represented any binding or legal commitment. The unanimous acceptance of the 1 per cent target by the donor countries did not therefore amount to more than a statement of good intention to follow policies – presumably more direct policies in the case of public aid than in that of private investment – which would move total 'aid' (as defined for inclusion in the 1 per cent target) towards this target figure.

From the beginning it became clear that to have any 'potency of life' the 1 per cent target would require some kind of definition of 'aid'. A need arose to distinguish between the different forms of resource transfers to LDCs: grants, loans, private investment, etc.

The second form taken by the distinction between real aid and the flow of financial resources was the elaboration of a series of sub-targets, within the 1 per cent overall target, regarding the *terms* on which aid was to be given. Thus, in its 1965 Terms Recommendation, the OECD enjoined upon its member countries that at least 81 per cent of all public aid should be given at less than 3 per cent rate of interest, with a minimum loan duration of twenty-five years for 82 per cent of all loan commitments, and a weighted average grace period of 7 per cent or more (these targets are continually raised). The DAC annually calculates comparative 'terms performance' of its member countries.

In fact, these subtargets have become extremely complicated since various alternative combinations, indicating a certain 'softness' of the flow of public financial resources, are optionally given to the member countries.

While these subtargets defining a degree of softness and hence the presence of real aid also have a rather vague status and cannot be considered as more than a declaration of good intentions, they too have had a considerable effect in softening the terms of transfers of public capital to poorer countries. There is perhaps a tendency for this influence to be more marked in countries where there was in the first place an intention to increase real aid and to soften terms and perhaps less effect in bringing sinners into line. In that sense it is legitimate to question the real effectiveness of the subtargets.

The original target, 1 per cent of national income of donor countries, was subsequently raised to 1 per cent of GNP at market prices. This effectively amounted to raising the target by about 20 per cent. The question arises: why not maintain the old basis of national income and raise the 1 per cent target to, say, 1·25 per cent? Presumably the answer is the beautiful simplicity and symbolic value of 1 per cent. Just possibly it could also be argued that the GNP is conceptually preferable to net national income as a basis for determining aid-giving capacity, since the GNP measures resources which either could be channelled back into the replacement, maintenance and repair of capital used up in production – thus bringing us back to the lower national income figure – or else could be used for giving aid to poorer countries. This, however, is not a particularly convincing line of reasoning. It must be assumed that the replacement of their own domestic capital basis is considered by donor countries as a prior change on total resources and that the relative priorities of foreign aid in relation to other claims are only considered in respect of resources left over after replacing capital (i.e. in relation to national income). To this extent, it may have been more direct and honest to keep the national income basis and raise the target percentage instead. The raising of the target at the second UNCTAD conference (two-thirds of the way through the development decade) can perhaps be best considered as a recognition of the fact that, under the old accounting system of 1 per cent of national income, many more items had come to be included within the 1 per cent target than had been dreamed of by President Kennedy and his economic advisors (who had been thinking of real *aid*). Of course, if this was the motive, the changeover from 1 per cent of national income to 1 per cent of GNP was a very indirect and rough-and-ready way of dealing with this, as compared with the approach through the grant element or through subtargets relating to softness of aid.

The culmination of this effort to disentangle real aid from the flow of financial resources is the recommendation of the Pearson Commission to establish as a subtarget, within the 1 per cent overall target, 0·7 per cent of GNP in the flow of *public* (government) aid. This can, of course, be justified on two grounds: (a) it is only in connection with public capital transfers that the question of aid in the sense of a *quid* without a *quo* really arises; and (b) it is only *public* aid which it is more directly within the power and control of governments to determine. It is perhaps interesting to speculate that 0·7 per cent of GNP is not too different from 1 per cent of national income;

thus we are back to the old Kennedy idea that 1 per cent of national income should be given in real aid. On top of this there is now the implicit additional Pearson target of 0·3 per cent of GNP in terms of private investment, export credits, etc. This must remain largely non-operational since the flow of private investment is not really in the power of governments except very indirectly. (The Pearson Commission pointed out that this is only a minimum target, but this does not quite dispose of the doubt.)

It is obvious that a target without a firm date attached by which it is to be reached is essentially meaningless, even as a statement of good intentions. The Pearson Commission recommended that the new operational target of 0·7 per cent of GNP for public aid should be reached by 1975 or shortly thereafter, but in no case later than 1980, but even this range and formulation leaves a good deal of uncertainty.

This is not the place to discuss and develop upon the implications of meeting the 1 per cent target. One salient fact, however, stands out. During the 1960s the 1 per cent aid target was certainly not achieved, even if the total flow of financial resources from the rich countries to the LDCs as a group is taken into account. Nor was there any sign that the target would be achieved by the end of the 1970s. A number of economists have come up with this conclusion. We ourselves have tested a number of hypotheses suggested by the 1 per cent target. For example conformity with the 1 per cent target, in the incremental sense, would lead us to expect the growth rate of per capita GNP of the donor countries to be positively correlated with the percentage of GNP given in aid; i.e. we would expect those donor countries which grow fastest also to increase their aid fastest. However, the facts fail to show any kind of conformity with this hypothesis. The correlation of the growth rates of the sixteen donor countries of the DAC during the period 1960–74 with the percentage of GNP transferred to developing countries in 1974 turns out to be $r = +0·04$; i.e. r is as near zero as it can conceivably be. It must be concluded that the volume of resources transferred to developing countries by 1974 bore no relationship whatsoever to the growth rates of the GNP of donor countries during the preceding First Development Decade and half of the Second.

Thus, a definition of aid that is acceptable to most economists is one which dramatically shows up the inefficiencies of the existing concepts that underlie resource transfers to the LDCs. Resource transfers, the cost of which exceeds their contribution to the development process of the recipient country, cannot be classified as economic assistance. It is necessary that the donors restructure their aid administration set-up in order to provide the financial resources that are most needed and can be most effectively used by the poor country concerned.

7.3 AID ALLOCATION CRITERIA: THE THEORY

At least in a short- and medium-run sense aid allocation must be determined by the requirements of the recipient countries. Any resource transfer that takes place in order primarily to allow a donor country to meet some of its own economic or political needs (e.g. combating inflation, making profitable foreign investments, propping up an unpopular regime, etc.) is not economic aid. In other words, if aid is to have any economic meaning at all it must be related to the development process of the LDCs. The necessity for unilateral resource transfer from the rich to the poor countries has arisen because of the widening gap that separates these two groups of economies. The ultimate aim of economic assistance must be to bridge this gap.

As a result of the interest shown by economists in devising economic criteria for aid allocation, there is now available a theoretical framework based on the famous 'two-gap models' which has been extensively used by the development economists in order to project the aggregate requirements of both domestic saving and foreign capital of the LDCs. A number of LDCs have explicitly based their economic plans on projections that have been derived from the two-gap models.

A two-gap model in its simplest formulation assumes that there are two constraints on development: the availability of domestic saving and the availability of foreign capital. It is assumed that labour is in abundant supply and is (disguisedly?) unemployed, and that expansion in the capital input will automatically call forth the required labour. This assumption allows the theorists to characterise the economy they are studying by a Leonteiff Production Function. McKinnon has shown that *the same amount of foreign assistance will be more effective in a country that is faced with a balance-of-payments constraint rather than a savings constraint.*[9] It was thus usually held that aid should be allocated to those countries which demonstrated a capability to generate domestic (public or private) savings but were finding it increasingly difficult to meet their import needs.

The impact of aid upon development has led to the emergence of the 'two-gap model'. This arises from the dual nature of the aid resources transferred to the LDCs:

1 Aid adds to the total resources, or savings, of the LDC available for investment (at any rate it does so if it is assumed that aid resources go into investment, rather than consumption, in a 1 : 1 relationship).

2 In addition to adding to total resources and investment, aid specifically adds to the foreign exchange resources.

Strictly speaking, there is no reason why the analysis should remain limited to two gaps. It could be argued that some forms of aid, especially technical assistance, remove barriers other than foreign exchange or savings (e.g. availability of local skills). This could further enhance the contribution of aid to GNP growth beyond that which the simple neo-classical analysis would suggest.

The gap models have been subjected to extensive criticisms. It is pointed out that the gaps can be identified only in *ex ante* sense; *ex post* they have no significance. The size of the dominant gap depends crucially on the growth rate. A country may have a savings constraint at a higher growth rate but a balance-of-payments constraint at a lower growth rate, or vice versa. If savings or export earnings do not increase at the rate required by the target growth rate, the growth rate of income will itself fall short of the target and no resource gap will appear.

Moreover, it is difficult – some would argue impossible – to estimate with a reasonable degree of accuracy the existence of the dominant gap from historical data which reflect definitional identities, not behaviouristic patterns. The gap models have, however, served some very useful purposes. They have drawn attention to the fundamental problem of estimating the elasticity of factor substitution in the different production activities undertaken in the LDCs. This elasticity is neither zero nor unity. It varies from activity to activity, and the specific needs of the LDCs can be taken into account only within the context of an analytical framework that allows the planners to evaluate the changes that are taking place in the elasticity of factor substitution in the different economic activities as a result of development. The needs change as the input coefficients change in the interindustrial production matrix.[10]

The second UNCTAD conference tried to estimate the size of the resource gaps of a number of LDCs in 1968. It came to the conclusion that most of the LDCs either had a dominant trade gap or would generate one if the growth rate were raised to the Pearson Commission target of 6 per cent per annum. It was thus suggested that, if the criteria for foreign aid allocation were that implied by the gap analysis, there was considerable scope for expansion in the flows of resource transfer from the developed countries to the developing countries.

The gap analysis suggests one set of economic criteria that should be applied when aid is being apportioned among recipient nations. Other economic criteria have also been recommended, and some of the more important among them are:

1 To eliminate poverty in the poorest countries. This is identified as the 'welfare' objective of foreign aid.
2 To discriminate in favour of countries which have effective aid administration set-ups.
3 To discriminate in favour of countries where the *future* marginal efficiency of aid is highest.

These objectives are rarely consistently pursued in the aid programmes of any of the major aid donors. Partly, as a number of economists have pointed out, this is due to the multiplicity of the economic objectives that the donors of foreign aid have in mind. A given programme of foreign aid has to balance the 'development' objective against the 'welfare' objective. In a short-run sense it is certainly true that these objectives may be irreconcilable. The aid package that is finally decided upon reflects the compromise that has emerged when the aid administrators have sought to reconcile the different objectives.

If this is so, the operationally important question is: what weight have the donors applied to the various objectives in determining the mix of a given aid programme? An inability to quantify, if only in an approximate sense, the allocations that are made in response to specific criteria has reduced the usefulness of this type of approach. Moreover, analysis of this type is incapable of taking into cognisance the institutional and historical factors influencing aid allocation.

Furthermore, the criteria enumerated above are not 'value-free'. They require international comparisons based on how the donors view the policies being pursued by the recipients. Hence it may be questioned whether *any* objective criteria for aid allocation can ever be evolved. What is 'development' from the point of view of the recipients may not be 'development' from the point of view of the donors. Indeed, if, as the radicals among us maintain, aid is being given by the donors in order to attain their own economic interests and relentlessly to exploit the poor countries, it would be futile to expect to be able to explain aid allocation patterns by their effect on the development of the LDCs. However, such a view ignores the fundamental complementarity of the interests of the different components of the international economy. It is precisely because the economic interests of all the countries are, at least in a long-run sense, coincidental that we have advocated a transfer of resources from the rich to the poor countries and hence are justified in expecting the evolution of an aid rationale, as it were, that specifically takes into account the development needs of the LDCs. This means that there need be no ambiguity in the allocation criteria that *should* be used for aid distribution. The criteria should provide an index which measures the contribution of the rich countries towards the effective reduction of the widening gap between the rich and poor countries. The value judgments implied by aid allocation based on criteria of this sort reflect merely an extension of the concept of the welfare state from the national to the international level.

NOTES

1 L. B. Pearson, *Partners in Development*, Report of the Commission on International Development (New York, Washington and London, Praeger, 1969).

2 The rest of this section is based on H. W. Singer and S. Schiavo-Campo, *Perspectives of Economic Development* (New York, Houghton Mifflin, 1970).

3 This consideration partially underlies the rationale for supplementary financing; it is *prima facie* appealing to link the provision of aid to medium-term export earnings and movements and to use external assistance to help smooth the trade earnings cycle.

4 For thoughtful discussions of the subject see particularly the studies of Harry G. Johnson, *Economic Policies Toward Less Developed Countries* (Washington, Brookings Institution, 1967), pp. 55–60 and of John Pincus *Trade, Aid and Development* (New York, McGraw-Hill, 1967), pp. 41–8. Johnson treats the question on a somewhat more theoretical level, while Pincus looks at several practical aspects and makes the important distinction between the developed countries' motives and those of the developing countries.

5 Johnson, op. cit., pp. 58–60.

6 See Pincus, op. cit., pp. 41–8. The following partly parallels Pincus's discussion.

7 Pincus, op. cit., p. 184.

8 One very interesting and potentially promising step in this direction is the 1967 international agreement for GATT–UNCTAD co-operation in export promotion, which includes the setting up of direct technical assistance activities in this field.

9 R. I. McKinnon, 'Foreign Exchange Constraints in Economic Development and Effective Aid Allocation', *Economic Journal*, Vol. 74 (1964), pp. 388–409.

10 For a further discussion of this see Chapter 2.

CHAPTER 8

Forms of Aid

8.1 SCOPE OF AID

We have seen that the flow of resources to LDCs is at the same time wider and less wide than true aid. It is wider than aid because it includes a number of transactions which are strictly commercial and in which there is no presumption that there is a unilateral advantage to the recipient of the flows. These include private investment abroad, which by definition cannot be aid because it is strictly commercial.[1] They also include such things as export credits, or loans made by governments or international organisations (e.g. the World Bank), at more or less commercial rates of interest (e.g. 8 per cent per annum) without grace periods and repayable as a firm commitment in hard currency. Such a loan would not be called aid, the 'grant element' in the loan being zero or close to zero.

In recognition of this fact, the UN target has been subdivided to specify that at least 70 per cent of this total flow of resources must be aid, i.e. 0·7 per cent of GNP of the donor countries. Thus it would be more justified to speak of a '0·7 per cent aid target'. But even this concept of aid is still much too broad. Even if private and other obviously commercially-oriented transactions are ruled out, the remaining transactions, which are largely flows from non-commercial organisations (e.g. governments, the Rockefeller Foundation, Oxfam, personal charities, etc.), still include a great variety of forms of aid. The troubling point is that the true aid element in these various transactions is very different. At one extreme may be placed the government loan at 8 per cent repayable in hard currency which, as already mentioned, has a zero or negligible 'grant element'. At the other extreme may be placed the unconditional gift by a rich government or Oxfam to the government or people of an LDC without any obligation or strings attached; in this transaction the true aid element, or 'grant element', is close to 100 per cent.

Between these two extremes is a continuum of many forms of aid, too numerous to mention. There is the 'soft loan', e.g. a loan at 2½ per cent interest, repayable over a long period of thirty years, with an initial grace period[2] of seven years, possibly with a provision that repayment can be postponed if the recipient country is in difficulty, etc. Another type of intermediate transaction, neither fully commercial nor wholly aid, is a grant or gift which, however, can be used by the recipient only for the import of specified capital goods from the donor country. If the recipient country could otherwise have obtained these goods more cheaply or better elsewhere, or possibly even domestically, obviously part of the value of this gift in effect represents a subsidy to the capital goods producers of the donor country and that part should not be considered as aid to the recipient. In other words, if 'trade' and other commercial transactions can be defined as a *quid pro quo*, while 'aid' is defined as a *quid sine quo*, the difficulty is that in real life many transactions are somewhere in between: a *quid pro 'half a quo'*.

Economists and aid statisticians have not been at a loss in dealing with this particular difficulty. The answer has been to disaggregate these in-between transactions into two separate transactions: that part of the transaction which can be called 'fully commercial', and that part representing the 'grant element' which can be called 'fully aid'. For instance, in the case of the soft loan mentioned above, the present discounted value of the repayment obligation involved in this transaction can be calculated. If the total soft loan was £1 million while the present discounted value of the repayment obligation involved was £400,000, we would say that the 'grant element' in this transaction was 40 per cent; then £400,000 out of this £1 million would be counted as aid while the rest would be counted as a commercial flow.

Ingenious as this device of disaggregation and calculation of the grant element is, it still leaves a number of loopholes for measurement and definition. An obvious one is the selection of the poorer discount rate for the purpose of calculating the present discounted value. This can make a considerable difference in the case of long-term transactions. Another deficiency is the failure of the calculation of the grant element to take into account other restrictions attached to the use of the loan or grant. A loan or grant at the free disposal of the recipient to cover budget deficits or balance-of-payments deficits, or to support the general development plan of the country, is obviously much more valuable to the recipient than a similar loan or grant hedged around with very restrictive conditions, or perhaps limited to a project which would not be within the recipient's priority scheme without the loan or grant. It can be seen that the device of the grant element is more useful in measuring the cost of aid to the donor – and it was essentially developed for this purpose, especially for comparing the relative aid burden carried by different donors – than in measuring the value of aid to the recipient. For this purpose, in fact, an entirely different set of concepts and measurements would have to be developed.

There is another reason why even the non-commercial flow of resources – the 0·7 per cent UN aid target – is still too wide a definition of what should be called aid. A rich country will allocate resources to a poor country for a great variety of reasons. The purely commercial motive and purely humanitarian aid motive are only two possible motives among a variety of others. An obvious example is the military motive; you make grants or supply equipment free of charge or on soft terms to a military ally or a country which you expect to become either a military ally or an enemy of your enemy. It is non-commercial, but is it aid? The UN definition would exclude military aid, but in practice this is not easily disentangled from development aid. The Americans have the concept of 'military support aid'; this means that you strengthen an ally, not only by direct military aid, but also by economic aid which enables him to carry the recurrent cost of the economic burden of a larger military establishment than would otherwise be the case. Is this military aid or economic aid?

Then there is aid which is perhaps not strictly military but which is closely linked with diplomatic support. A rich country may give aid to a poor country in order to buy its vote at a crucial UN discussion, to keep a tottering government in power, to 'cement the Commonwealth ties' (in the case of the United Kingdom), to promote the teaching of the French language in Africa (in the case of France), to counteract Chinese or American influence (in the case of the USSR), or to keep Cuba isolated within Latin America (in the case of the United States). What of all this is true aid and what is not? In general, in these cases the underlying motive of the donor – honourable or dishonourable according to one's judgment – should not enter into the measurement. As long as the flow is non-commercial and meant to be devoted to development, it should be included as aid whatever the motive. Among the above examples, aid to promote the teaching of the French language in Francophone Africa would be only doubtfully called aid since the intended use is not clearly related to development (though this is arguable and shows that our definition of aid may call up the equally difficult problem of defining development). Military aid would be more clearly excluded because it is not considered as part of 'development', but even this is far from clear. The establishment of an aircraft industry in a LDC can be both a military proposition and a part of the industrialisation of the country;

159

swords can be beaten into ploughshares, and tractors and tanks have obvious similarities.

8.2 WIDER AID CONCEPTS

It is time now to look at the reverse side of the coin. We have previously said that true aid can be larger than is indicated by the flow of financial resources, even when this is limited to the unilateral flow and to the case of aid destined to development purposes only. The flow of financial resources and that part of it which is normally called aid is only a part – and a comparatively small part at that – of the total relations between rich and poor countries.

It follows that effective and true aid can be given by a rich country to a poor country by the rich country's opening its markets wider to exports from the LDC or by its offering imports to the LDC at a lower price. Vice versa, aid can be nullified by the rich countries' operating restrictive policies to limit exports from the LDCs, also by their worsening the terms of trade of the LDCs, lowering the prices obtained for their exports and/or raising the prices which they have to pay for their imports. Thus the reader of this book should realise that the matter discussed in this chapter under the heading of 'aid' should be seen in close relation to the matters previously discussed under the heading of 'trade'. Most LDCs, if given the choice, would prefer, not an expansion of aid, but rather trade concessions – e.g. the conclusion of international commodity agreements raising and stabilising the prices of major export commodities, or revisions of the tariff structure of the richer countries to enable them to export more, say, labour-intensive manufactures.

In addition to export proceeds, there are such non-aid relationships between the rich and poor countries as tourism, shipping, insurance, transference of technology and others. All these do not come under the heading of 'flows of financial resources', yet concessions in these fields could be as valuable – or even more valuable – to the LDCs as increased aid. It will be clear that the questions of aid performance of different donor countries, as published annually by the DAC of the OECD,[3] are a very doubtful exercise if taken by themselves. The behaviour of a rich country in relation to the LDCs must be seen in the round; to concentrate only on the small segment of it entitled 'flow of financial resources' can give a very misleading picture.

The extreme case of a trade concession is where a rich country sends its exports to the poor country free of charge. In this extreme case, the commercial element is so clearly non-existent and the aid element is so dominant that this type of 'trade' is always included in

160

aid, as the special form of commodity aid. The best-known type of commodity aid is food aid, such as has been given by the United States under the Food for Peace programme – more technically known as Public Law 480. On occasion, however, commodity aid has also consisted of other essential supplies. There is also a multi-lateral commodity aid programme: the UN World Food Programme, jointly administered by the United Nations and the FAO in Rome. The 1974 Rome Food Conference envisaged substantial expansion of this form of aid.

Commodity aid illustrates some of the difficulties of measuring and defining aid, particularly for the purpose of comparing the aid 'burden' carried by different donor countries. This problem is far from being theoretical, since a considerable share of the aid pro-gramme of the largest aid donor, the United States, consists of pre-cisely such commodity aid. How is such aid to be measured and valued? The United States, not unnaturally, measures the value of the aid at the artificially high domestic support price of the wheat, maize, rice etc. delivered under this programme, since this is the cost of buying up the food to the government agency[4] charged with securing this food for the US aid programme.

However, it could well be argued that this food should be valued at the world market price, which may be considerably lower. Or it could be argued that the food should be valued at what the world market price would be if this US surplus food were not artificially removed from the commercial market by being supplied under US aid programmes but were instead added to commercial supplies; that price would, of course, be hypothetical, but it could be a great deal lower again than the actual world market price. Going even further, it could be argued that the food is surplus to the require-ments of the US economy – i.e. is the result of policies designed to help American farmers, not to aid the LDCs – and therefore that its opportunity cost to the US is zero or close to zero. Any of these positions would be defensible and appropriate for measuring the value of the food aid for different purposes.

It is apparent that the apparent simplicity of valuing such aid immediately resolves into a great many complexities when the problem is more closely scrutinised. Nor is this the end of the complications. Quite often the food aid, while essentially a grant, is hedged around with certain conditions. For instance, the recipient country may be committed, out of the sales proceeds of the food delivered as food aid, to provide a certain proportion of local currency for the expenses of the US embassy or for scholarships under US programmes etc. Should this repayment be deducted

161

from the grant element? And if so, how should it be valued? Again, many different answers are possible depending on the purpose of the measurement.[5]

The problems of defining and measuring aid, which have been briefly illustrated above for the case of food aid, all have their equivalent for many other forms of aid. Even if the loan or grant is defined in terms of money, its real value to the recipient may be less than the normal cost to the donor, e.g. if the use of the money is tied to specific commodities, projects, sources of supply, etc. That important part of aid which appears as 'technical assistance', as distinct from 'financial aid', is by its very nature similar to commodity aid; the donor country provides an adviser, and the value of the aid is measured by the salary which the donor country pays to the adviser. Yet if the recipient country had been given a free grant of money to recruit its own consultants, it might have been able to obtain the necessary advice more cheaply from a different country or through a consulting service.

On other occasions there may be undervaluation of the technical assistance rather than overvaluation. For instance, if the United Kingdom makes a technical assistance grant in the form of a fellowship to enable a Kenyan to undertake graduate studies of economics or chemistry in a UK university, the value of the fellowship is measured – apart from living expenses – by fees which have to be paid to the university; however, these fees may be very much less than the true cost of the facilities to the UK taxpayer, university fees being heavily subsidised. Perhaps enough has been said to indicate that the question of measuring and valuing aid is not without its pitfalls, and that not too much should be read into the comparative data on the total flow of financial aid to the developing countries.

8.3 BILATERAL VERSUS MULTILATERAL AID

The distinction between bilateral and multilateral aid may at first seem clear, but like many other 'clear' distinctions it becomes blurred on subsequent analysis. The 'pure' case of bilateral aid is where one single donor, normally a donor government, deals directly with one single recipient, also normally a government. The 'pure' case of multilateral aid is represented by a global or world agency, normally part of the UN system, dealing directly with a recipient government or group of governments. However, there are many intermediate forms of aid between these extreme forms of bilateralism and multilateralism.

To begin with, much of such called bilateral aid is given in a multilateral framework. For instance, aid to India and many other

162

important countries is channelled through an aid 'consortium'. In *aid* this aid consortium all the donors or major donors are represented *consortium* and discuss the respective amounts of aid which they plan to extend to India in the coming year, the type of projects that each of them proposes to support, the amounts to be financed by hard loans, soft loans, grants, etc., and other aspects of their respective aid pro- *World* grammes. The consortium is chaired by the World Bank, which has *Bank* previously prepared an independent report on the aid requirements of India, Indian development policies, priority projects to be sup- ported, etc. The Indian government is, of course, also represented and submits its own report and estimates of aid requirements. The discussion in the aid consortium is then followed by a pledging con- ference, at which the various donors represented commit themselves to extend aid in the light of what the other donors in their turn are willing to pledge.

The aid recipients, as well as the aid donors, have shown an in- creasing preference for placing bilateral aid in such a multilateral framework. The advantages to both sides are fairly obvious, though some recipients may feel that this is a method where the donors have an opportunity of ganging up against them. Such bilateral aid comes within the statistical definition of 'bilateral', rather than under *consultative* 'multilateral', but this is clearly a matter of arbitary definition.

In other cases, in place of the aid consortium there is the 'consulta- tive group'. This is a somewhat weaker form of multilateral frame- work, lacking the pledging element or element of commitment of the aid consortium but otherwise proceeding in a very similar way. Recently the major donors, with their growing unwillingness to commit themselves, have accordingly developed a preference for consultative groups rather than consortia.

Closer to the multilateral end of the continuum there is aid ex- tended, not by global institutions (e.g. the World Bank or UN Development Programme), but by such institutions as the regional development banks (e.g. the Inter-American Development Bank, the Asian Development Bank, the African Development Bank and the Arab Development Bank) or subregional development banks (e.g. the East African Development Bank). Other institutions of a non- global nature extending multilateral aid include the European Development Fund in Brussels, which is the organ of the EEC. This kind of aid is usually included as multilateral even though its sources are less than worldwide.

The term 'bilateral' is applied more to the source of the aid than to the recipient; e.g. UK or US aid directed to the East African Community in Arusha, rather than to Kenya, Tanzania or Uganda separately, is still classified as bilateral, even though there is a multi-lateral recipient.

The percentage of total aid flowing through the multilateral channel is gradually increasing. For a number of reasons, by no means all involving glowing enthusiasm for international co-operation, donors as well as recipients are coming to prefer the multilateral channel. Smaller donors particularly (e.g. Sweden, Holland and Denmark prefer the multilateral channel because it enables them to avoid the heavy administrative overhead expenses of building up their own aid organisations, which would be a very heavy charge on a small aid programme.

One difference between multilateral aid and bilateral aid arises in the criteria for allocating aid among different recipients. In the case of bilateral aid, allocation is obviously heavily influenced by political considerations, historical links and commitments, diplomatic links, etc. Thus the bulk of UK aid goes to the Commonwealth and few remaining colonies, the bulk of French aid to Francophone African countries, the bulk of US aid to Latin American or strategically important countries along the periphery of the USSR and China, and the bulk of USSR aid to allies such as Syria, Iraq, Cuba and India. By contrast, the global multilateral aid sources (e.g. the World Bank and UN Development Programme) tend to spread their aid more or less evenly – widely but thinly – over all their member countries. There are strong pressures to do so. In the case of the UN Develop-ment Programme the wide and even distribution has been inevitable and is now in fact enshrined in 'indicative planning figures' for each country. In the case of the World Bank, such distribution is con-cealed by the apparent insistence on 'sound projects'.

In both the bilateral and multilateral programmes, the large countries tend to be discriminated against in the sense that their per capita aid tends to be lower than that of the smaller countries. In the early days of the International Development Association (IDA, the soft-financing agency of the World Bank in Washington) an attempt was made to rectify this by concentrating resources on such large countries as India and Pakistan which were obviously dis-criminated against, but this move ran into great political difficulties and had to be abandoned. Countries which have no special reason to concentrate aid for political reasons (e.g. Sweden and Canada) have an additional reason here for prefering the multilateral channel.

8.4 HARD VERSUS SOFT AID

The question of allocating aid among different countries, which has just been emphasised in relation to multilateral versus bilateral aid leads to another important distinction. Should aid be allocated according to some criterion of need or according to some criterion of capacity to use the aid effectively?[6] In some ways, of course, the answer must be 'both'. Some criterion of need must be involved since we limit aid to the poor countries presumably because the rich countries – in the West and Middle East – do not need aid. Similarly, we do not want to see aid wasted; we want to see it effectively used for the purpose for which it is given, even if these purposes are purely humanitarian. For example, if we give aid to help the victims of earthquakes or civil war, we do not want to see the aid money go into the pockets of civil servants or speculators.

The answer 'both' has still another meaning. The best type of aid is the aid which benefits the needy and at the same time makes them more capable and more effective in improving their own situation by their own efforts; in this way the criterion of need and effective use are ideally combined. Perhaps the best way of doing this is to channel aid into employment creation, to utilise the unemployed and under-employed manpower of the recipient country for productive investment (e.g. irrigation or rural roads) which creates a permanent basis for continuing development and additional employment. Unfortunately, the present rules of the aid game are very ill designed to have this ideal effect; employment involves largely local expenditures, whereas aid is largely geared to providing the import components of large-scale capital-intensive projects.

But when all this is said there does remain a real dilemma: whether to place aid where it is most needed, or whether to place it where it will lead to the most immediate increases in output. Even if, to the economists, this dilemma is more apparent than real (since the increase in output only constitutes real development if it benefits the lowest income groups of the LDCs), to the aid officials, whether multilateral or bilateral, the dilemma is real enough.[7]

And now for the third meaning of the answer 'both'. Both objectives, i.e. need and effective use, are legitimate aid criteria, but they require different forms of aid. Normally aid allocated on the criterion of need should be soft aid, without payment obligations. This is clear in the case of financing rural public works for the purpose of employment creation and in financing local expenditures generally. In the case of aid given on the criterion of effective use, hard terms can be justified in so far as the repayment can take place out of the increases in production, which will still leave the recipient better off if the terms of repayment are not exhorbitant. There is, however, a provision in the latter case, which is that repayment of aid involves a double sacrifice : (a) the real resources must be found and kept away from home investment, and (b) the foreign exchange needed for repayment must be found and kept away from imports or must be found by additional exports. Thus, aid on hard terms is only justified if the recipient is enabled by the aid both to produce the additional real resources needed and also to produce the additional foreign exchange resources needed, by expanding exports or replacing imports. There is thus a place for both hard and soft aid. It cannot be said that the present division of aid between these two forms corresponds very closely to a rational distinction of the kind just made, though things seem to be gradually moving in this direction.

In section 8.1 it was pointed out that aid should be defined as *quid sine quo*. This means that in the case of hard aid only the grant element should be counted as aid. But, of course, it does not mean that there is no place for hard aid in the aid picture. It is only when hard aid is mistakenly fully counted as aid and displaces soft aid that it becomes hypocritical to rely on it. Provided the true aid, or the grant element in aid, reaches agreed and acceptable targets and volumes, there is no reason not to have a rational policy whereby part of this grant element is embodied in soft aid and part of it in hard aid on repayable terms. In the past, however, hard aid was given without much consideration for the repayment burden and repayment capacity of the recipient. Partly as a result of this, the debt burden of developing countries has increased at an alarming rate and constitutes one of the major unsolved problems in relations between the rich and poor countries.

8.5 PROJECT AID AND PROGRAMME AID

Aid either may be tied to the execution of a specific development project (e.g. building a dam, setting up a cement factory or building a hospital) or may be given without such specific project tying (e.g. in the form of budgetary support, a credit line of free foreign exchange or supply of surplus food at the disposal of the government). The tying of aid to projects is only one possible form of tying; aid can also be tied to goods from the donor country, or to foreign exchange requirements (imports) as distinct from local currency expenditures. Normally, 'tied aid' or 'united aid' refers to the tying of aid money to the purchase of goods from the donor country, and it is in this sense that the term will be used in section 8.6. There is no necessary relationship between the tying of aid to projects and the tying of aid to goods from the donor country. The World Bank, for example, seems firmly wedded to the principle of project aid to what many critics believe an excessive degree; on the other hand, the Bank, as an international organisation, does not and obviously cannot tie its aid to buying goods from any particular donor country. By contrast, the United Kingdom may well give, say, India a loan not tied to any specific project but in the nature of a general line of credit for spare parts or raw materials, or it may give the loan even without restriction and yet tie the expenditure of this credit line to British goods only. It is therefore somewhat confusing to speak of tied and untied aid generally without specifying the nature of the tying referred to.

Is it justified to tie aid to specific projects? There are many arguments *for* answering this question positively or negatively. The main arguments for project aid include:

1 The donor country or agency has a better judgment of what is required than the recipient government would have if the expenditure of the money were left to its own judgment.
2 By tying aid to projects the donor makes certain that the recipient is forced to develop a proper project, properly prepared, studied, programmed and executed, while in the absence of such a tie the aid for lack of carefully prepared projects might not be spent for developmental purposes or would be wasted on hastily prepared projects.
3 By tying the aid to the project and doling the aid out as the project materialises and proceeds, the donor maintains some kind of leverage and control over the money which would be absent in the case of more general support.
4 Project aid makes it natural and easy for the donor to combine financial aid with the proper technical assistance in regard to a particular project, e.g. skilled consultants for feasibility studies, pilot schemes, training of staff for running the project and writing of proper specifications for the supplies needed.
5 There is the demonstration effect of good project preparation; if the recipient country is forced to develop effective projects in order to attract aid it will learn by doing the proper organisation for project appraisal, and project preparation is more likely to develop.

This is not an exhaustive list[8] and there are a number of arguments *against* tying aid to projects:

1 If the donor uses aid as a leverage to force his own idea of priorities upon the developing country, this violates national sovereignty.[2]

2 It may also be ineffective because a country will not be whole-hearted in supporting projects which do not reflect its own priorities.
3 It is somewhat arrogant of aid donors to believe that they know the priorities of development better than the government of the recipient country which is directly faced with the problems.
4 There is an element of illusion in project aid. If the recipient LDC is given money for project A which is in any case part of its own priorities, its own money will be released to carry out another project much lower down the priority list for which the money otherwise would not be available. Thus, while aid donors and recipients sit together to discuss the details of project A – the top priority project into which aid is supposed to go – in actual economic fact the aid serves to finance a quite different project, project X, which is not discussed or analysed and may not even be known to the aid donor or indentified by either side. Meanwhile, both the taxpayers of the donor country and the citizens of the LDC are cheated into believing that the aid goes into the priority dam or road, with ambassadors and prime ministers solemnly snipping ribbons, making speeches and inspecting labels: 'This factory/dam/road/etc. comes to you through the aid of the friendly people of the United States/the USSR/the United Kingdom/China/Sweden/etc.

This last point is known as the principle of 'fungibility' or switching'. By now, both aid donors and aid recipients generally are well aware of this principle. As a result, aid donors do not normally extend project aid without satisfying themselves that the total programme of the recipient country (including project X, the marginal project) is such that they can aid it with good conscience. The aid recipients, on their part, are often quite happy to accept project tying precisely because they know full well that in actual fact it may release money for quite different projects and enable them to enlarge their total development programme. For political reasons, or for some of the other reasons mentioned above, both sides may be quite happy to maintain the fiction involved in project aid.

The situation in fact may be further complicated. For example, if the aid finances only a small part of the aided project (e.g. the cost of imported machinery) whereas the recipient LDC is required from its own resources to find the major part of the cost, switching or fungibility operates in reverse. Instead of setting resources free to carry out project X, resources have to be withdawn from project X to cover the recipient's share in the cost of project A; in the aided

LDC the development pattern is in fact being distorted in the direction of the priorities of the donor country. This may be a good or bad thing, depending on where the superior wisdom resides. If a LDC really believes firmly in its own priorities, it should not accept aid for a project outside its priority scheme if that aid ties down its own resources; i.e. it should not accept aid unless that aid covers the local and recurrent expenses of the project as well as the direct cost of imports.

An economist's judgment at the present time would be that there is too much project aid and not enough programme aid. It is noteworthy that the great success story of international aid, the US Marshall Plan, was not tied to specific projects. If it is objected that the European beneficiaries of the Marshall Plan could be more trusted than the present LDCs to put their money into good projects, this is a judgment which it would be very arrogant to take for granted today. It ought to be assumed that by now the governments of many LDCs have learned enough about the development business to justify something more like the Marshall Plan treatment.

The whole concept of development as consisting of specific 'projects' of new investment was the product of a very limited type of thinking, in which development was identified with growth of production, and growth of production in turn was identified with new net investment combined with a certain capital/output ratio.[9] Experience has shown this view to be wrong, yet the prevailing aid practice of project aid has failed to adjust itself to evolving experience and insight. But life has developed its own adjustments. For instance, the aid consortia already mentioned provide not only bilateral aid in a multilateral framework but also 'project aid in a programme framework'. Even though the aid is given on a project basis, the aid consortium discusses the total programme of the countries to which project aid is extended. One cannot help feeling that there is a great deal of institutional inertia involved in the adherence to project aid, even more so in the case of the World Bank than for the bilateral aid programmes. The aid relationship would be healthier if more aid took the form of money placed at the disposal of the LDCs in general support of reasonable and agreed development plans. The developing countries' attempt to link aid with the creation of international liquidity may be seen, among other things, as an attempt to move away from project aid.

Other evolving compromises between project aid and programme aid are (a) the broadening of the concept of a project to include groups of related projects, in the end amounting to something close to a sectoral programme, and (b) the channelling of aid through intermediaries in the LDCs (e.g. national development banks) so that the aid can be redistributed over a multitude of smaller projects. This last arrangement helps to deal with what is perhaps the worst aspect of project aid, which is that it puts a premium on the single large project and, within that category, on projects which require a maximum of imported capital equipment. Both of these results of project aid are directly contrary to the real needs of developing countries, which require employment creation, labour-intensive technologies, a maximum of local procurement, and maximum dispersion and decentralisation of economic activities. In partial recognition of this, rules concerning local procurement in aided projects have been generally relaxed over the last few years. Many aid donors will now finance local procurement provided that local costs and quality are not grossly out of line with world market prices (for untied aid) or with prices prevailing in the donor country (for tied aid).

8.6 FORMS OF AID : TIED AND UNTIED AID

On our previous definition, tied aid is aid where the recipient, as a condition of the aid, is obliged to use the aid money to buy goods from the donor country only.

The main practical problems concerning this definition centre on the word 'only'. We have just seen that, increasingly, aid provides for the possibility of local procurement, often even with a preference price range for the local products; in other words, the aid is available either for the local products or for buying from the donor country. In still other cases, enlightened donors may make exceptions for other developing countries which they also want to aid. For example, the United States may give aid to Thailand for an irrigation project but permit the Thai government to order the water pumps from India where these pumps are made more cheaply or more suitably than in the United States. The reason for this exception from tying is that the United States also wants to help India. The minor question of definition arising is whether the aid to Thailand should still come under the category of tied aid, in view of the exception made for India (and possibly other developing countries). The major question is whether this should be counted entirely as aid to Thailand or whether part of it should be counted as aid to India, which it really represents. As is the case with aid definitions throughout, numerous practical difficulties and borderline cases exist.

Tied aid is less valuable to the recipient than untied aid. With untied aid, as with free foreign exchange, the recipient can buy the

170

most suitable product in the cheapest market, taking into account other relevant circumstances (e.g. suitability of the product, availability of installation, repair and maintenance services). In the limiting case where the products of the donor country in many cases are the cheapest and most suitable for the aided project or for the development needs of the recipient country, the tying of aid is both unnecessary and ineffective; on the other hand, it does not represent a burden on the recipient. Normally, however, there is a burden. How heavy this burden is will depend, among other factors, on the degree of project tying, on the range of goods which the donor country can offer and their prices relative to other sources of supply, and on the advantage which the firms of the donor country are willing and able to take of the fact that the tying of aid has placed them in a monopoly position as far as tendering for the aided projects is concerned.

Empirical data are scanty, but in view of the wide spread of project tying and other realistic circumstances the evidence seems to suggest that tied aid may be worth about 20 per cent[10] or so less to the recipient than untied aid.

To the economist, this loss of 20 per cent is sad and unnecessary. If the donor countries are put together, their total gain from tying aid to their own products must be precisely zero. If one donor country gains from tying, in the sense that its own firms obtain a larger share of the total imports of aided LDCs than would otherwise be the case, by definition other donor countries must lose. The only exception is if the LDCs use their untied aid to order goods either locally or from other LDCs which are not aid donors – but this exception is in any case desirable and already allowed for, to some extent at least, even in tied aid programmes. Broadly, it may be assumed that the advantages to individual aid donors from tying their aid are more or less cancelled out through the actions of other aid donors' tying *their* aid. Each aid donor hopes to gain by tying, but this turns out to be an illusion because *all* aid donors tie their aid. Meanwhile, though no aid donor gains, all aid recipients lose because the value of aid is to them depreciated by perhaps as much as 20 per cent. Looked at in this way, the wonder is why the donors could not have reached general agreement to untie all their aid.

In real life, however, the situation is somewhat more complicated. In the first place, some aid donors may in fact gain from tying their aid. This is the case either if the donor country's normal share in the imports of the LDCs is less than its share in total aid, or if the donor country gives more aid relatively than other donors, or if the aided projects relate to commodities in which the donor country is less than averagely competitive with other donors. Once such donors actually benefit by tying their aid, it becomes rational for other donors – which really would benefit from a general untying of aid – to tie *their* aid in turn as a defensive measure.

Secondly, it is possible, and in fact likely, that aid would be less acceptable to the producers, taxpayers, parliaments and other interest groups in donor countries if it were not visibly tied to their products. Tying creates a domestic lobby in favour of aid, including trade unions and workers who are interested in reducing unemployment in specific industries or specific parts of the country. While this argument in favour of tied aid may be partly a matter of lack of economic education and sophistication, it is none the less real. This means that, though the value of each dollar of tied aid may be 20 per cent less than that of each dollar of untied aid, the total *volume* of tied aid may be so much larger than it would be with entirely untied aid that in the end the aid recipients are better off with tied aid than with untied aid. In other words, some – possibly the bulk – of tied aid is additional aid, not an inferior substitute for untied aid.

All this helps to explain why in practice it is not so easy to reach an agreement on untying aid. Even so, there is tremendous scope for agreement among the donor countries to go a long way further towards the untying of aid, to nobody's loss and to the gain of the LDCs. Fortunately the donor countries realise this, and considerable efforts and some progress are being made within the framework of the DAC of the OECD.

It has already been mentioned that multilateral aid is usually untied aid. Even this is not entirely accurate. For instance, in the case of multilateral technical assistance under the UN Development Programme, a number of contributors make their contribution in tied currency which can only be used for buying equipment, hiring experts or using training facilities of the donor country. Similarly, in replenishing the resources of the IDA the United States, being in balance-of-payments trouble in the early seventies, made attempts to tie its contribution to the degree to which the IDA drew upon US resources of supply. It is a pity that even the multilateral programmes cannot be wholly untied.

The aid consortia and other forms of aid co-ordination can do a great deal to reduce the burden of aid tying on the recipients. For instance, by allocating to each donor those types of projects in which the donor is best equipped, in terms of price and suitability, to provide the relevant equipment and other inputs, the effective burden of tying is reduced. Even this method, however, cannot prevent the firms of each donor country from quoting higher prices for their products when tendering for aided projects, knowing that firms in other countries are not allowed to compete.

NOTES

1 In fact, where a very powerful multinational corporation backed by all the power of modern technology and market influence deals with the government and business units of small and poor LDCs, the presumption may well be the other way round, i.e. that the balance of advantage could lie with the source of the funds rather than the recipient.

2 This is a period during which the recipient does not have to make any amortisation payments and/or interest payments on the loan. The idea is that the project supported by the loan may take say seven years to bear fruit, and once this has happened the repayment is no longer a burden for the recipient.

3 The annual volumes published by the DAC of the OECD entitled *Development Assistance: Efforts and Policies of the Members of the Development Assistance Committee* are the primary source of information of development in the field of aid, and the data are remarkably up-to-date for official publications of this kind.

4 The Commodity Credit Corporation.

5 For further details see H. W. Singer, 'Local Currency Proceeds from Food Aid', *International Development, Growth and Change* (New York, McGraw-Hill, 1964). Ch. 8.

6 See also Chapter 7, sections 7.3 and 7.4.

7 The dilemma is by no means peculiar to external aid. It also faces any government in its internal development policy. For example, should an agricultural extension service or the introduction of new hybrid seeds (the 'Green Revolution') be geared towards the larger farmers who are more educated and more capable of increasing production quickly or towards the small farmers who need the rise in their living standards more than the larger farmers? In the absence of positive action to the contrary the normal experience is that the larger farmers have more effective access to the opportunities provided through agricultural extension, hybrid seeds and otherwise, and hence an increase in output and improvements in welfare, as immediate objectives, will require rather different policies and approaches.

8 For a further discussion see 'Project Aid and Programme Aid' in H. W. Singer and S. Schiavo-Campo, *Perspectives of Economic Development* (New York, Houghton Mifflin, 1970), pp. 248–56.

9 The clearest expression of this is the Harrod–Domar model of growth which dominated developing planning for a considerable time.

10 Reference has already been made in section 8.2 to the problem of measuring the volume of aid involved.

CHAPTER 9

Aid: Quantitative and Qualitative Aspects

9.1 THE VOLUME OF AID AND ITS DISTRIBUTION

In view of the vagueness of the 1 per cent target no useful purpose would be served by debating the point as to whether it was met in the 1960s and whether it is likely to be met during the present decade. It is much more meaningful to see if the prevalent trends and patterns of aid disbursement and allocation facilitate the achievement of the twin objectives implied by the 1 per cent target: of increased development assistance to the LDCs on the one hand, and of a fair 'burden of sharing' among the donor countries on the other.

Table 9.1 shows that total net development assistance increased from \$8,572·3 million in 1962 to \$24,429 million in 1973, an annual growth rate of about 18 per cent. However, if the OECD price deflator is used in order to calculate the value of the financial flow of resources of 1973 in terms of 1960, it is found that the overall growth rate is significantly reduced for this period. Official development assistance (ODA) grew at a rate of about 6 per cent, 'other financial flows' (which consist of official export credits, direct and equity investments by the official sector and portfolio investment in multinational agencies) were more than ten times as high in 1973 as they were ten years earlier, and private flows more than doubled themselves over this period.

Bilateral grants and loans still constitute the major proportion of ODA funds. However, 'bilateral grants and grant-like flows' have declined as a ratio of total ODA and also as a ratio of total net flows. In 1960 they constituted 78 per cent of total ODA and about 45 per cent of total net flows; by 1970 the former ratio had declined to 75 per cent and the latter to 28 per cent. The contribution to multilateral institutions had increased dramatically from \$534 million to \$2,252·7 million.

Development assistance was given in the form of food aid, technical assistance and financial grants usually used by the LDCs for the purchase of capital equipment, though financial loans accounted for

... to Developing Countries and Multilateral Agencies, 1963–73 ($ millions)

Countries	1963	1964	1965	1966	1967	1968	1969	1970[a]	1971[a]	1972[a]	1973[a]
Australia	96·9	118·8	144·5	150·5	193·7	205·5	232·1	394·5	530·2	445·3	354·1
Austria	5·9	21·3	47·3	49·2	47·9	73·7	80·7	96·1	93·1	111·6	144·6
Belgium	174·7	164·3	220·9	178·0	164·4	243·0	257·3	308·6	317·4	405·1	506·8
Canada	130·5	141·8	169·3	266·7	271·9	307·6	364·1	630·1	924·2	1,015·4	1,104·6
Denmark	10·5	31·8	15·2	21·3	24·8	83·2	151·0	85·6	138·3	120·0	195·0
France	1,242·0	1,360·4	1,299·4	1,319·7	1,341·3	1,720·3	1,710·0	1,834·6	1,623·5	2,082·1	2,800·1
West Germany	620·7	706·4	734·6	788·5	1,145·4	1,663·4	2,028·3	1,487·1	1,915·2	1,756·2	1,790·0
Italy	321·1	236·8	265·5	631·6	287·3	550·4	847·7	681·9	870·9	690·6	645·0
Japan	267·4	289·8	485·5	627·1	798·5	1,049·5	1,263·1	1,824·0	2,140·5	2,725·4	5,844·2
Netherlands	134·4	118·4	238·8	254·1	228·2	184·0	384·1	428·4	437·7	721·5	612·1
New Zealand	—	—	—	9·2	9·7	12·4	16·8	23·4	25·9	31·5	38·5
Norway	21·5	23·0	38·4	17·1	30·2	58·8	75·0	66·6	64·6	55·8	94·7
Portugal	51·1	61·9	30·5	39·7	79·4	48·1	97·6	70·8	147·0	222·4	236·5
Sweden	53·4	67·2	72·7	108·0	120·7	128·8	212·1	229·3	243·5	273·1	359·5
Switzerland	202·8	110·1	191·9	109·5	135·5	238·8	119·3	137·2	245·4	176·7	299·1
Utd. Kingdom	720·8	918·8	1,032·0	911·0	803·0	835·7	1,136·2	1,227·6	1,431·8	1,501·1	1,058·2
United States	4,518·6	5,274·4	5,333·2	4,920·1	5,769·5	6,017·5	4,825·0	6,210·7	6,888·0	7,574·0	8,346·0
Total DAC countries	8,572·3	9,645·2	10,319·7	10,401·3	11,451·4	13,420·7	13,800·4	15,736·5	18,037·2	19,907·8	24,429·0

[a] Including grants by private voluntary agencies.

Source: DAC, *Development Co-operation, 1974* (Paris, OECD, 1974) Appendix tables.

175

most of the capital assistance; the growth rate of expenditure on technical assistance exceeded the growth of food aid, loans, etc.[1]

Over the last decade and a half the United States has been by far the biggest donor. However, its contributions have declined consistently over the period; in the early 1960s its share amounted to almost half the total disbursement, but in the late 1960s and early 1970s the proportion shrunk to about one-third. The other main aid donors have been France, the United Kingdom, Japan and West Germany. The former two countries had extensive commitments to nations that were once a part of their empires. It is significant to note that, whereas aid from the ex-colonial powers showed a declining tendency, Japanese and West German assistance has tended to increase rapidly over the later period. Canadian aid also tended to increase significantly.

The major portion of aid from the United States has been in the form of ODA; France also has given about 50 per cent of its 'aid' through official channels. For the United Kingdom, West Germany and Japan the situation is radically different; the majority of the funds given by these countries has come from non-official sources, especially during the later part of the period. In the case of Japan particularly this is offset to some extent by the fact that in the later years the 'other official flows' in the form of official overseas investment, official export credit, etc. have been of considerable importance; e.g. in 1972, out of a total of \$5,844·2 million, Japan provided \$1,178·9 million as 'other official flows'.

Table 9.2 shows the aid contribution of the major donor countries expressed as a proportion of their GNP at market prices during 1963–73. Over the period as a whole, Belgium, France, the Netherlands and Switzerland provided more than 1 per cent of their GNP in the form of aid.[2] The average for all DAC countries over the decade was 0·79 per cent. The US average was below the group average at 0·68 per cent. Moreover, figures from the same source indicate that US aid as a proportion of GNP has tended to decline continually; it was 0·86 per cent in 1961, 0·82 per cent in 1964, but only 0·51 per cent in 1969 and 0·61 per cent in 1973. UK aid as a proportion of GNP fell slightly up to 1968, but the trend was reversed until 1971, since when it has fallen drastically. This ratio rose over the period in the case of Japan and fell in the case of France. It rose until 1969 for West Germany, since when it has fallen considerably.

The last column of Table 9.2 shows that no country in the period had an average value for its ratio of ODA/GNP exceeding the UN-determined 'critical minimum' figure of 0·75 per cent. The average value for this ratio for all DAC countries was 0·37 per cent over

Table 9.2   *Total Net Flow of Resources from DAC Countries in Relation to GNP and Net ODA in Relation to GNP, 1963–73*

	Net flow of Resources as % of GNP	ODA as % of GNP
Australia	0·78	0·53
Austria	0·48	0·10
Belgium	1·11	0·49
Canada	0·55	0·31
Denmark	0·52	0·28
France	1·23	0·72
West Germany	0·80	0·37
Italy	0·66	0·14
Japan	0·75	0·24
Netherlands	1·11	0·47
New Zealand	0·30[a]	0·22
Norway	0·47	0·26
Portugal	1·62	0·99
Sweden	0·55	0.32
Switzerland	0·96	0·12
UK	0·89	0·42
USA	0·68	0.39
Total DAC countries	0·79	0·37

[a] For the period 1966–73.

Source: DAC, *Development Co-operation, 1974* (Paris, OECD, 1974) Appendix tables.

the period; the US average was 0·39 per cent and the UK average roughly similar at 0·42 per cent. What is even more alarming is that the value of the ratio of ODA/GNP seems to be going down. Figures from the same source indicate that the combined DAC ratio declined from 0·51 per cent in 1960 to 0·30 per cent in 1970. The United States ratio rose from 0·53 per cent in 1960 to 0·59 per cent in 1963, since when it has been falling regularly, and was 0·23 per cent in 1973. The UK ratio has also been falling since 1964 (0·53 per cent) and in 1972 was 0·35 per cent. The French ratio has been declining continuously; it was an astonishing 1·38 per cent in 1960 but only 0·58 per cent ten years later.

Next we may turn to examine the terms and conditions on the basis of which assistance has been offered to the developing countries during the decade. Once again the OECD figures are the best.[3] Unfortunately, as the OECD document points out, the terms policies can only be assessed on the basis of aid commitments rather than actual aid disbursements. According to the OECD estimates Switzerland is the 'kindest' donor in terms of the maturity index and Sweden in terms of the grace period index, whereas the lowest (average) rate of interest on development assistance is that charged by Canada and Denmark. France is a particularly bad donor by all criteria. In 1973 the DAC average maturity period was 29·5 years, the average rate of interest 2·8 per cent and the average grace period 7·8 years. The grant element as a ratio of total ODA commitment was 89·9 per cent for the United States, 87·1 per cent for the United Kingdom, 91·2 per cent for France, 67·9 per cent for Japan and 83·1 per cent for West Germany in 1973; this ratio was much higher for the smaller donors.

An examination of the countries to which the major aid donors allocate loans[4] leads to the conclusion that the overwhelmingly important determinants of aid allocation by the larger donor countries are political considerations and colonial ties. There seems to be a significant correlation between the allocation of military assistance and of development aid in the case of the United States – hence its substantial contributions to South Korea, Turkey, Indonesia (after 1965) and Pakistan; a significant proportion of US aid to India can also be attributed to strategic factors. France and the United Kingdom have mainly been assisting nations that once were part of their colonial systems – hence French commitments to Algeria, Senegal, Morroco and the Cameroons and UK concern with the South Asian and East African countries. Similarly, Japan's obvious preference for South and South-East Asian regions may indicate the importance of geopolitical considerations. However, it would be rather superficial to assume away the problem of aid allocation by stating that it is determined entirely by political factors. The terms on which assistance has been extended to the poor countries has also been influenced to some extent by the economic conditions prevailing in these countries. This becomes obvious when it is realised that there is in fact a two-way relationship between political preferences and economic structure.[5] The nature of this relationship cannot, however, be specified with any degree of certainty given the existing state of social knowledge.

If the pattern of aid allocation among the LDCs is compared to some indicators of economic performance, the only thing that can be safely said is that there is a definite association between GNP per capita and the term structure of aid (measured by the proportion of funds included in the grant element out of total ODA). The ratio of grant element to ODA is low in the case of countries with GNP per capita greater than $450 and relatively high for countries with GNP per capita about $100. No clear association can be discerned between the level of indebtedness and the value of the ratio of grant element to ODA. Similarly, other measures of economic performance also do not adequately 'explain' – in a regression equation sense – the pattern of aid distribution on the one hand or the term structure of aid on the other.

In conclusion, we may again ask the questions we raised earlier. Has there been a substantial increase in the flow of resources from the rich countries to the poor? And has the sharing of the aid burden between the donor countries become more equitable?

The first question may be dealt with briefly. It is clear that there has been an increase in the volume of foreign assistance, but this increase has not, in general, been greater than the corresponding increase in the GNP; hence the aid/GNP rose from 0·76 per cent in 1963 to only 0·79 per cent in 1973. More alarmingly, the average ODA/GNP ratio for the DAC countries declined substantially over the period. In view of these trends the objective of increasing the annual flow of resources is certainly an ambitious one. The current economic crisis has further worsened aid expansion prospects. The major aid donor countries are under considerable economic stress. Inflation, soaring oil prices and threats of raw material scarcity have *all* contributed towards the development of a cautious international economic approach. At present, we are in the middle of a protracted bargaining session which seeks thoroughly to overhaul the international trade and monetary systems. Aid prospects are related closely to the success of these negotiations. A breakdown of the Tokyo Round will almost certainly lead to the adoption of recessionist begger-my-neighbour policies which will preclude an expansion of aid.

The oil-rich countries of the Third World have to some extent sought to offset the decline in assistance; they have sponsored aid programmes that are generous compared to the programmes of the major donors. However, the pattern of aid allocation by the new-rich countries leaves a lot to be desired. Aid allocation seems to be primarily influenced by their political and strategic considerations; indeed, foreign aid is explicitly employed as an instrument of economic warfare. It is thus the political stance of individual countries and not their economic condition which makes them eligible for favourable treatment by the new-rich. An expansion of the aid programme of the new-rich countries will have an optimum impact on the Third World only if such an expansion is accompanied by a revision of aid allocation policies.

Let us now turn to the second question identified above : what has been the change in the pattern of burden sharing by the donor

179

countries during this period? We have tested a number of hypotheses to determine the burden-sharing effect. The acceptance of the 1 per cent target has a number of implications. In statistical terms, by failing to relate the share of GNP expected to flow from individual donor countries to LDCs progressively to the varying levels of per capita GNP of the various donor countries, the UN target set up the share of GNP represented by financial flows to LDCs as a constant (i.e. 1 per cent) unrelated to per capita GNP. Thus if the target was effective over a certain period we would expect (a) that at the end of the period the correlation between per capita GNP and the share of GNP to LDCs would be zero, and (b) that over the course of the period this correlation coefficient would move in the direction of zero.

A simple test shows that neither of these expectations was in effect satisfied during the 1960s. The correlation in 1960 between per capita GNP and total flows as a percentage of GNP was $r = -0.21$, while in 1968 it was $r = -0.43$. It thus appears that the movement during the decade was in fact away from the hypothesis of zero correlation; the mild correlation at the beginning of the decade became, if anything, more pronounced (even though by itself it is statistically not clearly significant). Moreover, the sign of the increased correlation is negative. This means that there is a tendency for the relatively poorer OECD countries to transfer a relatively higher share of their GNP to the LDCs. The spirit, if not the letter, of the UN 1 per cent target presupposes some progressive rather than regressive relationship, in the sense that the richer OECD countries should find it easier to reach or maintain the 1 per cent target than the poorer OECD countries. Considering, therefore, that the total target was not fulfilled in 1968, we would have expected the richer OECD countries to improve on their performance, and vice versa for the poorer OECD countries.

Thus the first conclusion must be that there is no indication that the 1 per cent target has been effective. Overall average performance has moved away from the 1 per cent target; the poorer developed countries have tended to do better than the richer countries, and in this sense there is a negative rather than a positive link between transfer capacity and the share actually transferred; and, finally, the movement has been away rather than towards the establishment of the share transferred to LDCs as a constant, i.e. 1 per cent.

This simple test may be repeated separately for the two components of the total flow of financial resources to the LDCs, i.e. ODA on the one hand and private investment on the other. The results confirm those previously reached. The ODA/GNP ratio moved from a correlation of $r = -0.20$ with per capita income of donor countries in 1960 to a more pronounced negative correlation of $r = -0.39$ in 1968. Similarly, the correlation of private flows with per capita income of donor countries moved from $r = -0.02$ in 1960 to $r = -0.19$ in 1968. Hence the statement previously made concerning the apparent ineffectiveness of the 1 per cent target can also be made separately for the components of the total flow. It should be remembered, of course, that during the 1960s there were no explicit subtargets, corresponding to the 1 per cent target, separately for official aid or private investment. The 0·7 per cent target for official aid has been established for the 1970s, but performance during the 1960s does not give much encouragement that it will be effective. It is worth noting that private investment seems to come closer to being a constant fraction of GNP, unrelated to the level of per capita GNP, than is the case with official aid.

Another test which may be made is to correlate the growth rate of per capita GNP of the donor countries with the change in percentage of GNP transferred to the developing countries. From the point of view of relating donor capacity to the burden of resources transfer, this relationship would be expected to be positive; i.e. the most rapidly growing countries would tend to increase their share of GNP transferred to the LDCs more (or rather diminish it less) than would the less rapidly growing countries. As far as the specific 1 per cent target is concerned, a zero correlation would be expected, since the percentage of GNP transferred to LDCs is set up as a constant. This hypothesis is, in fact, much better satisfied than the first hypothesis. The correlation between growth per capita GNP and percentage of GNP is very close to zero for the sixteen DAC countries in the 1960s: $r = +0.10$ for total flows, $+0.04$ for official aid and $+0.04$ for private investment. The sign (for what it is worth) *is* positive, but the essential point is that the correlation is practically zero. There is thus little evidence that increased donor capacity resulted in an increased share of GNP given as aid. On the other hand, there was a rough incremental achievement of the target that additional transfers or aid should represent a flat rate tax on additional incomes.

The results of our two simple tests require some conciliation. On the one hand, the negative correlation between per capita income and share of GNP given in transfer and aid was intensified during the 1960s; on the other hand, there was a trace of a progressive (and certainly not negative) association between the incremental growth rate of per capita GNP and the burden of transfer and aid. The reconciliation of this apparent contradiction may be sought in the

181

well-known fact that during the 1960s the relatively poor OECD countries (specifically, of course, Japan and Italy) tended to have faster growth rates of GNP than the relatively richer countries (typically the United States and United Kingdom). It will be readily seen that this provides an explanation of why, during the First Development Decade of the 1960s, the faster growing countries tended to increase their aid faster, while at the same time in the overall picture the relatively poorer countries carried a heavier share of the total burden at the end of the decade than at the beginning. The growth rate of GNP per capita was positively correlated with the growth rate of the total flow of resources (as distinct from the percentage share of GNP of the total flow) to the mild degree of $r = +0.26$. Since it was the poorer countries which had the faster rate of growth, this helps to explain the results of our first test.

One third and final test may be made. If the concept of burden sharing among donors as symbolised by the existence and activities of the DAC, and as implicit in the 1 per cent target, were in fact operationally effective over a certain period, the differences among donor countries in the burden of transfer (as measured by percentage of GNP) would be expected to diminish over the period. This last hypothesis is clearly born out by the figures. The differences in the aid burden carried by the OECD donor countries – as measured by the dispersion of the percentages of transfer of resources to LDCs around the average – were in fact clearly reduced during the 1960s. The corresponding dispersion for total flows was 0·55 per cent of GNP in 1960, but fell to 0·30 per cent in 1969. For official aid the corresponding fall was from 0·48 per cent to 0·33 per cent, and for private investment from 0·38 per cent to 0·25 per cent.

Thus it may be concluded that the idea of burden sharing and measurement of comparative performance based on GNP shares was most effective during the First Development Decade in the sense of *equalising* the performance of donor countries; i.e. the donors carrying a big burden reduced their transfer and aid relatively to those donors carrying a smaller burden. In this sense, but in this sense only, the 1 per cent target was effective during the 1960s: not in reaching the target, not in any way in adjusting the distribution of aid to real capacity, but only in making the distribution of aid more 'equitable' (in the sense of more equal) among the different donor countries.

9.2 THE BURDEN OF AID: THE RECIPIENTS' DILEMMA

In our discussion of the implications of the 1 per cent target we talked a great deal of the equitable distribution of the burden of aid among the donor countries. Despite the obvious importance of this problem the concern that has been shown by development economists, multi-national agencies, public bodies and governments has been viewed with considerable cynicism by the poor countries – as if a transfer of about 0·05 per cent[6] of the GNP of a country like the United States can create unsurmountable balance-of-payments and other problems for the donor and jeopardise the future of the international economy, whereas the ever-widening gap between the rich and poor countries is an inevitable structural characteristic of the twentieth-century world economy which we shall have to live with! Such an attitude is also evidenced by the bland complacency with which the corresponding problems of the burden of aid to the poor countries is being treated by the 'development establishments' of the developed world. Indeed, until well into the 1960s the developed world never acknowledged that aid could constitute a burden to the recipient countries.

The economic impact of the aid burden to the developing countries can manifest itself in two forms. First, there is the problem of 'debt servicing'. Since most of the so-called aid to the LDCs is in the form of interest-bearing loans, the poor countries have perpetually to find the means to pay off the annual interest charges. Second, the 'aid' that is received by the LDCs is also usually tied to the donor countries in one form or another. Both of these 'aid costs' are becoming increasingly important and will have to be taken into account by those who consider a comprehensive reorganisation and reform of the whole international aid system imperative.

9.21 Debt Servicing

If debt-servicing payments were to be subtracted from the annual flow of financial resources from the rich to the poor countries over the last few years, the net real financial flows would be seen to be decreasing gradually. This tendency is the joint effect of an increase in the repayment and amortisation funds by the LDCs, unmatched by a corresponding increase in the inflow of financial resources in the form of either 'aid' or investment. Moreover, the rise in debt repayments has also not been matched by the growth in the export earnings of the LDCs. This is not very surprising. There was a time, not so long ago, when development was thought of as an instantaneous process: all that was needed was the money, and, given the money, productivity would rise in no time, enabling the borrower to repay without too much trouble. This has not happened; for development effort to be initiated at all it is necessary to make substantial investments in the socio-economic infrastructure (e.g. schools, hospitals and roads), and projects of this nature have long gestation periods. On the other hand, the loans contracted by the under-

183

developed countries in the postwar period were of short duration and were made available on relatively hard terms. The debt repayment capacity of the LDCs has therefore lagged behind their debt obligations. This poses a very important threat to the prospects of development in the poor countries. As Eugene Black, then President of the World Bank, remarked as early as 1961, 'the machinery of economic development could be overloaded with foreign debt until it sputtered to a halt amid half-built projects and mountains of discarded plan'.[7]

An UNCTAD study[8] in 1971 drew the attention of the world to the acuteness of this problem. This study tried to estimate the gross flow of aid into the LDCs that would be required merely to keep the net flows constant. Its projections are concerned only with reported debt. The total outflow of financial resources is, of course, much larger, for to debt repayments have to be added short-term capital outflows and the repatriated profits of foreign private companies.

The UNCTAD paper showed that, if the 1971 terms of lending were maintained, in order for the *net* inflow to remain at the 1965 level (at 1965 prices) the *gross* inflow of financial resources would have to rise to $17,500 million, as debt-servicing charges would themselves rise to $10,400 million by 1975. These debt charges would constitute about 23 per cent of the export earnings of the LDCs; in 1971 they constituted about 19 per cent. If *all* future lending from official sources were to be contracted on the terms given by the IDA (i.e. interest-free, with a nominal service charge, fifty years' maturity and ten years' grace period), the gross inflow of financial resources to the LDCs would still have to rise by about $14,000 million merely to keep the net inflow to the poor countries at the 1965 level. It is thus only through an increase in the grant element that the problem of the increased debt-servicing burden to the LDCs can be adequately tackled.

The developing world has found its debt problems considerably magnified by the increase in the price of raw materials and manufactured imports since the early 1970s. The Special Sessions of the UN General Assembly drew attention to the need for dealing with this problem effectively. Both the World Bank and the IMF in 1975 extended special assistance to the Third World countries most seriously affected by the crisis. It is to be hoped that following the 1976 meeting of UNCTAD further progress will be made towards reducing the debt burden of the poor countries. Attempts to deal with the debt problems of the developing countries should not – indeed cannot – be isolated from attempts at reforming the whole 'aid system' that has evolved since the end of the Second World War.

9.3 THE FUTURE OF AID: AID REFORM

It is impossible to forecast the future of aid over, say, the next twenty years or so with any degree of confidence. Too many political, economic and other factors are involved. Who, thirty years ago, could have predicted the rise and subsequent stagnation of foreign aid, and the various phases and transformations through which aid has gone?

What we can do instead is to discuss some of the ideas which seem hopeful and important and appear to have a reasonable chance of being implemented, and also to follow up some trends which are already visible. The total volume of aid proper would have to double in order to reach the UNCTAD target of 0·7 per cent of GNP, and then continue to expand in line with the expanding GNPs of the rich countries. It is difficult to believe that this will happen in the near future. The potentially largest aid donor, the United States, which on the GNP criterion ought to account for about half of total aid, is in a retrenchment mood which seems more than ephemeral and appears to extend to both the major political parties, though for different reasons. One can still expect, hopefully, countries like Japan and the EEC to expand their aid programmes rapidly, and perhaps also the USSR and other Eastern countries if a political detente between East and West is firmly established. But this does not seem to amount to anything like the combination of doubling the present level and putting the whole flow on a rising trend of 5 per cent per annum in real terms.

Compared with real aid, private investment in the LDCs as well as hard loans, export credits, etc. have held up remarkably well in recent years in circumstances which have appeared rather unfavourable. The ratio between aid and other financial flows to the LDCs has been far from the 7:3 ratio implied in the UNCTAD target (i.e. 0·7 per cent of GNP aid, 1 per cent of GNP total flow); it has been more the other way around. At any rate, the main growth dynamics seem to be in private investment, export credits and hard loans. There is nothing wrong with this, provided that the investments really help the LDCs and that the debt repayments do not become too burdensome. This last proviso suggests a possibly hopeful future development: why not let foreign investments, export credits, hard lending, etc. grow and redirect aid so as to reduce the debt burden of the LDCs? Various technical possibilities of doing this exist, ranging from generous debt rescheduling towards financial aid to LDCs related to their outflows in respect of profits and dividends of foreign investment.

185

The trend towards multilateral aid has already been mentioned. Such a multilateralisation can be helpful if it helps with the untying of aid. It is to be hoped that more progress will be made towards aid untying, and that aid increasingly will take the form of free foreign exchange placed at the disposal of the LDCs which are trusted by the donors to make effective use of this aid on the basis of mutually agreed policies and development plans. This would remove much of the friction from the aid relationship, particularly when combined with progressive multilateralisation.

A special step towards both multilateralisation and aid untying can be taken by forging the much discussed link between the SDRs of the IMF and aid to developing countries. The issue of the SDRs itself was a big step forward in the aid business, since it removed the balance-of-payments burden which donor countries pleaded both for reducing aid and for tying it. It was also directly helpful to LDCs because they themselves were allocated a certain share of the SDRs (though a minor share corresponding to their IMF quotas), contrary to the original intention. What is now under discussion is the possibility of allocating the major share of the rich countries (about 75 per cent of the SDRs) not directly to them but rather to aid agencies, perhaps the IDA and the regional development banks. This means that the rich countries would not *get* the SDRs as a matter of right, but would have to *earn* them by supplying aid goods to the LDCs. From the point of view of the rich countries, the aid would no longer be a burden because it would increase rather than diminish their foreign exchange reserves; in fact, it would be a *failure* to aid which would result in a depletion of foreign exchange reserves, because other countries would earn the SDRs. Such a link has a great deal to recommend it. It could become one of the social inventions which make the world go round, like money itself. The technicalities can be solved if the will to act exists. The link cannot be taken for granted, but the difficulties have been well explored and shown to be by no means insuperable.

The most serious objection is that the SDRs are primarily meant to increase international liquidity and prevent balance-of-payments crises, which is itself a major interest of the LDCs. The liquidity purpose suggests a distribution of SDRs among both the rich countries and LDCs which could – and normally would – be different from that suggested for aid purposes. The ideal solution would be to have separate SDRs for aid purposes, additional to the SDRs issued for liquidity – but this is too much to expect. In a second-best world, the link remains a desirable objective which would go far towards smoothing the way to more effective aid. The developing countries have continued to press for the adoption of the aid-SDR links at the 1974 and 1975 Sessions of the UN, as well as at UNCTAD IV.

Other new aid ideas under active discussion include special aid to be given to counteract unpredictable losses in the export earnings of the LDCs due to drops in the prices of commodities, sudden crop failures, political emergencies, etc. The principle of such aid has already been conceded and operational for some time,[9] but its broad application still has not produced substantive results. It has been the subject of extensive study, even more so than the link between SDRs and aid. Again the technicalities of implementing such 'compensatory aid' are not well established and await a political decision to go ahead wholeheartedly.

Another proposal which has withstood the test of prolonged discussion and study is the 'Horowitz Plan'. Essentially, this consists of using aid to reduce the interest rates which the LDCs would otherwise have to pay on money raised commercially in the capital markets of the world for the purpose of financing development. It is not difficult to show that aid money used in this way could have a considerable leverage or multiplier effect, compared with more traditional forms of aid. The Horowitz proposal belongs in the same general family of ideas as the one mentioned a little earlier, i.e. to use aid to relieve the LDCs of some of their debt burden arising from hard forms of development financing.

It would also be a great advance – and at no real cost to the donor countries – if aid commitments could be made on a longer than yearly basis, e.g. for five years, tying in with the LDCs' development plans, or preferably on a rolling basis for five years ahead. Such extension might require changes in legislative procedures in some donor countries, but this would be justified by the importance of this matter to the LDCs and for the sake of the more effective use of any aid actually given.

Yet another aid development which could perhaps have more leverage effect than any other, and which still largely awaits implementation, is the financing of research and related pilot development work on technical problems of special importance to developing countries. The tremendous technological capacity of the rich countries has as yet hardly been tapped as a contributor to the development of the poor countries. The present technical assistance programmes are only a faint taste of what could be done. Here also the problem has been much studied. For example, in 1971 the UN Advisory Committee for the Application of Science and Technology to Development drew up a World Plan of Action in which some forty to forty-five priority problems were identified, and concrete plans for the creation of a World Plan of Action fund or account were put forward.[10] The target suggested by the UN group and accepted by the Pearson Commission[11] was for the rich countries to devote 5 per cent of their public expenditures on research and development to the specific problems of developing countries. This would not be very expensive in terms of the sum of money involved, but it should result in major breakthroughs in development. It would also help to do away with the idea that aid should be defined as something which happens geographically within the developing countries. What happens within the rich countries can be just as important, or more important, for the future of the LDCs. Again there are some hopeful signs that, through the DAC of the OECD, the richer countries may begin to move in this direction. It would be desirable if a greatly strengthened UN Development Programme would backstop such an international effort by providing seed money, and it is unfortunate that at this very juncture the Programme has been tied down entirely to the method of 'country programming'. This prevents it from giving the kind of leadership with global problems that an international organisation ought to give.

More recently, a group of least developed and most seriously affected countries have been singled out by the United Nations and UNCTAD for special aid. This is a good development, provided that aid to the least developed countries is additional and does not result in discrimination against other poor countries. In general, though the Pearson Commission was wildly optimistic, and more diplomatic than honest, when it thought that aid could become unnecessary by 1990, there is an element of truth in saying that successful aid should become less and less burdensome to the donors. More and more of the LDCs will leave the category of recipients and enter the inter-mediate group, and more and more countries from the intermediate group will move up to become potential aid donors; in this sense the donor/recipient ratio should become increasingly favourable. The concentration of aid on the least developed countries could be the beginning of this process.

Finally, let us return to the thought that the future of aid may be determined essentially more by what the rich countries do within their own borders than by what they do within the LDCs. The hope is that, in future, aid will not be negated by restrictive trade policies or by obstacles to migration or, on the other hand, by a brain drain of the needed skills from the LDCs or by social policies which create antagonisms between interest groups in the richer countries and the development of the majority of mankind. Thus, it must be hoped that the aid donors will increasingly let their total action and total

188

policy be of one piece in giving more support to the LDCs: by giving adjustment assistance and retraining to workers displaced by imports from LDCs, by pursuing full employment policies at home, by developing SDRs and other rational methods of balance-of-payments adjustment, by giving some priority in their research and development to the technological problems of the LDCs, etc. It is aid-supporting *total* action which is needed rather than an increase in the volume of aid itself. But such a hope for the future depends on the deepening of the recognition that we are fellow-travellers on a precarious journey in the 'Spaceship Earth'. Perhaps our growing worries about the environment will produce such recognition. Without such a deeper recognition of our common fate, the environment could just as easily deal a death blow to aid as it would otherwise serve to give it a solid foundation.

NOTES

1 Statistics are taken from DAC, *Development Co-operation, 1974* (Paris, OECD, 1974).
2 Portugal may be excluded, for the vast majority of its 'aid' went to finance the work against the freedom fighters in Angola and Mozambique.
3 Figures taken from DAC, *Development Co-operation, 1974* (Paris, OECD, 1974), Appendix tables.
4 See *Development Co-operation Review* (Paris, OECD, December 1971).
5 Such a relationship is acknowledged by 'Free enterprise' and Marxist economists alike.
6 This is a very generous estimate of the grant element within the financial resources transfer to most LDCs.
7 'Address of the President of the World Bank to the Annual Meeting of the Fund Aid Bank, 19th September 1961', *International Financial News Survey* (29 September 1961).
8 UNCTAD, 'The Outback for Debt Service', TD/7/Supp. 5 (October 1971).
9 This scheme is operated through the IMF: the '5th quarter' i.e. an extra drawing facility of 25 per cent over and above a member country's full IMF quota.
10 *World Plan of Action for the Application of Science and Technology to Development* (New York, UN, 1971). Examples of priority problems include: drought-resistant crops, use of brackish water, control of bilharzia, labour-intensive construction methods, etc. Also see *Science and Technology for Development: Proposals for the Second Development Decade* (New York, UN, 1970).
11 L. B. Pearson, *Partners in Development*, Report of the Commission on International Development (New York, Washington and London, Praeger, 1969).

PART FOUR

INTERNATIONAL FACTOR MOVEMENTS

CHAPTER 10

The Multinational Corporation as an Agent of Investment and Technology Transfer to Developing Countries

One of the more important changes that have taken place in the thinking of development economists in the last few years has been the shift in the analysis of the effects of foreign investment on LDCs. Not so long ago the main stream of economic thinking directed attention on the foreign investor as a provider of capital. Nowadays we are much more concerned with the role that the foreign investor plays in the process of the transfer of technology from the rich metropolis to the poor periphery. In other words, the modern economist is principally worried about the *quality* of foreign investment, i.e. about the effect of a given unit of foreign investment on factor productivity. If (as has been argued throughout this book) the dependence of the poor countries on the rich is fundamentally technological in nature, an elimination of this dependence will require an international diffusion of technological knowledge. It is surely right, therefore, to concentrate on the role of the foreign firm as an agent of technology transfer to the LDCs.

10.1 COLONIAL PRIVATE INVESTMENT

Why is it that foreign private investment has never in the past been an important instrument of the transfer of technology to the LDCs, whereas in the now developed countries foreign private investment has played a very important role in the process of technology transfer? In order to understand this difference in impact let us look at the pattern of international investment in the heyday of colonialism.

In 1914 the stock of long-term international investment was equal to $44,000 million, of which $24,500 million was invested in Europe and the United States and $19,500 million in Latin American and Asian countries (Africa's share was very small). The major creditors were the United Kingdom, France and Germany; the major debtors were the United States (up to about 1900 when it became a creditor), Canada, Australia, New Zealand, South Africa, Argentina and India.[1]

Before 1914, portfolio investment in the form of bonds and debt investments was a much more important component of international financial flows than was direct foreign investment. The governments of the debtor countries borrowed heavily on the foreign capital market for the purpose of infrastructure investment and in order to protect the convertibility of their domestic currencies. In 1914 about 70 per cent of total UK and French long-term investment consisted of government and railway bonds[2] Despite the fact that the major international borrowers were the governments of the capital-importing countries, the lenders were invariably private individuals.

There were important variations in the pattern described above as far as the LDCs were concerned. It is generally acknowledged that the fundamental difference in the role of foreign investment in Europe and North America on the one hand, and the African, Asian and Latin American countries on the other, lay in the nature of the relationship between foreign and domestic investors. Foreign investors in Europe and North America were controlled by a national government that was prepared to tolerate foreign investment only to the extent that it served the economic interests of the borrowing country. The governments of the colonies, on the other hand, saw their primary responsibility as one of preserving the interests of the colonial power which was, in ninety-nine cases out of one hundred, the only foreign investor. The government of the borrowing country was the agent of the investing country and was entrusted with the task of contributing to the maintenance of the stability of the imperial system. This was the overriding objective, and commercial and economic interests were all subject to it. If the latter clashed with this supreme aim of imperial policy they had to give way. Investment was channelled to sectors that were linked to the economy of the investor country. Foreign investment, whether direct or portfolio or controlled by a number of intermediate devices (e.g. the managing agency system in India), was invariably directed to economic activities connected with the export trade of the borrowing economies. The socio-economic infrastructure, the complex of commercial institutions and the structure of production were all geared to increasing the export potential of the colony.

The consequences of such a pattern of development were twofold.

194

First, and most important, the economy found itself sharply divided into an 'advanced' sector and a 'backward' sector. The advanced sector was logically a periphery of the economic system of the investor country. The backward sector was linked to the advanced sector in a one-way relationship: it provided the latter with the labour force and/or raw materials it required but did not share in the gains that accrued to the advanced sector as a result of international trade.

Second, the advanced sector was advanced only in relation to the rural hinterland in the colony. It used a technology that changed little with the times and was primitive by Western standards. The investor in the advanced sector, whether foreign or domestic, was concerned with maximising export earnings, and this, given the commercial and economic policies of the mother country, could only be done by keeping down costs and maximising output. Local investors and entrepreneurs were in no position to improvise through imitation or innovation an indigenous technology that would allow for an increase in labour productivity. Such innovation has usually taken place behind high tariff walls when foreign investment has been used by the protectionist country to supplement the national development effort. Lacking governments which could develop such policies, it was inevitable that the colonial countries remained incapable of using foreign investment as a vehicle of technology transfer.

Both these characteristics – economic dualism and an inability to assimilate and adopt sophisticated and advanced technologies – have been, as it were, built into the structure of most underdeveloped economies. Economic theory, especially since the seminal work of Gunnar Myrdal,[3] has held that private investment within the colonial framework and the pattern of international trade that goes with it have been the prime factors that have led to the growth of this structural deformity in most LDCs. It is natural therefore that the poor countries have been rather wary of private investment in the recent past and have in general tried to control inflowing private capital, so as to use it in a way that is complementary to their achievement of long-run development targets.

10.2 MODERN FOREIGN PRIVATE INVESTMENT

After the Second World War most of the colonies attained political independence. Consequently the climate for foreign investment changed dramatically. Foreign private investment had now to deal with an environment in which the major preoccupation of the government was with the achievement of rapid and sustained development. The centre–periphery relationship which had been fostered by the previous colonial administration, and to which foreign private investors had – willingly or unwillingly – geared their trade, was now viewed with abhorrence. The management of the foreign enterprise in a newly independent LDC was faced with the challenge of reorienting its business so as to make it appear acceptable to the new government. The development of the multinational corporation has enabled foreign private enterprise to develop an adaptability that is nothing short of amazing. Barring a very few exceptions, underdeveloped countries have by and large eagerly sought for direct foreign investment and for collaboration with multinational corporations. Even the USSR and a number of Eastern European countries have tried to secure foreign participation in industrial development on a long-term basis. The spate of nationalisation that threatened to destroy the 'empire' of the large multinationals seems to have halted somewhat. The developing countries and the multinational companies, after an initial period of mutual distrust, suspicion and intolerance – intensified briefly in the aftermath of the events of October 1973 – are slowly grasping the fact that they cannot wish each other out of existence! Both the multinationals and the LDCs are relatively permanent units of economic activity in this second half of the twentieth century. They cannot afford either to ignore each other or to launch a full-scale war. They must work towards compromises in which each party *sees* that its basic interests are being promoted.

There is some evidence that compromises of this sort are gradually emerging. The most important evidence lies in the increasing volume of foreign private investment in the LDCs. Total foreign investment to the poor countries from the DAC members has increased from an annual average of $3,111 million in 1960 to $4,381 million in 1967 and again to $8,430 million in 1972;[4] there was thus an increase of more than 100 per cent over the period as a whole. Direct investment constituted more than half of total foreign investment. The period 1960–7 was distinctly different from the period following 1967 in terms of the behaviour of direct foreign investment. The growth rate of direct foreign private investment in the latter period was considerably higher than that in the former. Latin America has the biggest share of direct foreign investment (over $1,200 million in 1967–70); Asia and Africa each have about $750 million. Direct foreign investment tends to be concentrated in the relatively better-off LDCs which are better described as 'intermediate' economies, or in the OPEC countries. As the Report of the Columbia Conference on

International Economic Development pointed out, 'countries with per capita incomes of less than $100 attract not much more than 12 per cent of private investment . . . it is neither a major spur nor a major problem in the poorest lands'.[5] Similarly, the major portion of foreign investment has taken place in the petroleum industry. During the period 1960–70 investment in manufacturing industries has been concentrated in Latin America, which accounted for about 50 per cent of total direct foreign investment in manufacturing industries and for no less than 62 per cent of the total stock of private investment in the manufacturing industries.[6] Similarly, investment in the manufacturing enterprises of European 'intermediate' countries (e.g. Spain) has also been of considerable importance. All in all, direct investment in manufacturing has been growing fairly rapidly, investment in the petroleum industry has remained constant and investment in mining and agriculture has shown a tendency to decline during the 1960s and the early years of the present decade.

Portfolio lending increased sharply during the period 1960–7 but has declined subsequently. The main form of portfolio investment has been the purchase of bonds issued by the governments of the LDCs and by international development organisations (e.g. the World Bank, Asian Development Bank and Inter-American Bank). In the late 1960s and early 1970s they accounted for about 20–30 per cent of total world issues. The issues of the multilateral institutions constitute about 20 per cent of bond issues for investment in LDCs. Development bonds, however, accounted for no more than 5·8 per cent of total bond issues in the capital markets of the DAC member countries.

The third main element in private foreign investment is export credit. Export credit has been expanding rapidly, but this is by no means an unmixed blessing for it contributes to the debt burden of the LDCs. Export credit in recent years has been given on terms that are extremely tight and expensive.

This rapid survey of modern foreign private investment shows that the multinational corporation is the only private institution that has proved itself capable both of providing the relatively large sums which are required for investment in the developing countries and of devising ways and means that allow it to make use of the varied forms of investment opportunities offered by the governments of the LDCs. Hence a number of multinationals have ventured into Latin America, Asia and Africa. The question of the role that foreign investment can play in the development process of the LDCs can be answered only by analysing the nature of the relationship between the multinational corporations and underdeveloped countries.

197

10.3 Multinational Corporations and the LDCs

The multinational corporation is a comparatively recent phenomenon in the world of business and industry. Conventional economic theory has not been very useful in helping to form a correct appreciation of the behaviour of a typical multinational firm.[7] However, recent developments in the theory of the growth of the firm, especially work done by Professor Edith Penrose, have provided an analytical framework within which the operations of the multinational can be meaningfully studied.

The large multinational corporation has been likened to 'a large self-governing bureaucracy', mainly independent of the control of both its shareholders and financiers. Autonomy, however, does not imply omnipotence, as the firm is subject to pressure from many groups (e.g. the government of the home country, the government of the countries where it is investing, the press and international agencies). The large multinational cherishes its independence, and the business world sets great store by the ability of a firm to increase its growth rate on the one hand and its rate of self-financing on the other. Therefore, in the subsequent analysis it will be assumed that: (a) the overall objective of the typical multinational is to maximise long-run profits, and (b) the multinational also tends to maximise the rate of retention out of the earnings of the company over time.

The multinational corporation has to pursue these objectives on a worldwide basis, and this naturally leads to a number of special problems. First, multinationals have a 'dominant' nationality,[8] i.e. that of the parent company, regardless of the nationality of affiliates, licencees or junior partners. The dominant nationality is important because most of the share holders of the parent company are likely to share its nationality and because the foreign investment of a multinational is treated as the investment of the country in which the parent is incorporated. There will usually be a flow of funds from the firm as a whole to the citizens of the country of the parent company (as they are the main shareholders). This involves, among other things, a movement of funds away from the economies in which the subsidiaries of the multinational are operating. The dominant nationality of the multinational also determines to a large extent its use of personnel, equipment and technology. Firms tend to buy factor services and technical equipment from their own country, 'not necessarily because they are concerned with nationality as such but ... because they are accustomed to certain ways of doing things'.[9]

Second, the retained profits of the multinational corporation represent its savings, some of which may have arisen because the corporation has had monopoly power to influence prices in the markets of foreign countries. The reduction in consumption that has made this saving possible has been spread over a number of economies. The investment of retained income has been similarly spread. There is, of course, no correspondence in the geographic distribution of the savings and investments of the multinational.

All multinational corporations are integrated across national frontiers either horizontally, vertically or both. A high degree of integration inevitably introduces an important element of arbitrariness in allocating overhead costs to different operations and in setting the prices of the goods that pass from one subsidiary to another. Usually these price adjustments reflect the desire of the corporation to take advantage of tax differentials as between different areas in which it is operating. Generally speaking, multinationals are in a better position to avoid taxation in a given country than are national firms. With a high degree of vertical integration, a multinational has great scope for adjusting transfer prices. This is bound to affect the distribution of income within countries. The governments of the countries in which a multinational has made investments in one form or another are naturally concerned with the danger of the deterioration of the balance-of-payments position of their country as a consequence of the pricing policy of the corporation. Thus government trade, tariff, tax and economic policies are, in a sense, a constraint on the multinational, which is therefore inevitably involved in a process of protracted negotiations with the host governments. These negotiations determine the extent to which the corporation is allowed to pursue policies which would lead to a maximisation of profits and/or retained income.

The multinational corporation's behaviour can best be analysed in the context of an oligopolistic or duopolistic model. In a typical LDC economy, the multinational is in competition with the public sector and a few large national firms. Its course of action is circumscribed by the agreements with the local government which determine its area of operation. The following propositions, put forward by Rothschild as early as 1947, concerning the behaviour of oligopolistic producers, describe the pricing policy of the typical multinational: [10]

1 Price rigidity is an essential aspect of normal oligopolistic price strategy.
2 Oligopoly leads to a multitude of conditions surrounding the quoted price.

3 Under oligopoly the price tends to be the outcome of a variety of conflicting tendencies within the firm.

4 Price wars, while tending to occur infrequently, are a dominant feature of the oligopolistic situation. Preparation for them leads to the adoption of measures which are peculiar to oligopoly.

In other words, the rigidity of the price structure indicates that the multinational may forego short-run advantages if these endanger the overall security of its interests or investments in a given country.

The nature of the multinational corporation is the main determinant of the pattern of its investment in the developing countries. It contributes to the development process in order to maximise its gains by operating in an environment which gives it a chance to make a profit. A development process that is being sustained by organisations interested primarily in profit maximisation is organically different from a development process in which the public sector sets the pace. The former is likely to generate tendencies that accentuate income inequalities within the developing country. In particular, the employment problems of an LDC are likely to be increased as a consequence of large-scale investment by a typical multinational. The direct effect of the multinational's investment is largely confined to the employment of a small, elite, semi-skilled and highly skilled labour force, the members of which earn incomes that are substantially higher than the incomes of the domestic labour class. The indirect effect of direct foreign investment undertaken by the multinational depends upon the willingness and ability of domestic enterprises to adapt to the production and marketing techniques devised by the corporation and of the government of the LDC to tax the profits earned by it.

Nevertheless, much hope has been placed in the multinational corporation as an agent of development. It is the only world organisation that has to date demonstrated its ability to integrate vertically entire industries and to integrate horizontally economic activities over a very widely spread area. The multinational has been undergoing an unending metamorphosis in order to be able to exploit its own growth potential. The typical multinational is forever seeking new markets and devising new products. It possesses an internal organisational structure which is extremely flexible in that new production and marketing processes can be adopted and old ones discarded with a minimum of friction. Moreover, the financial strength and manoeuvring capability of the organisation allows its managers to develop a corporate strategy with a very long view and very wide horizon. It is inevitable therefore that the multinational will seek to integrate the world economy in order to take the fullest possible advantage of the potential of such an organisation.

What form will this integration take? And will it be a good or bad thing from the point of view of the developing countries? Here there is a sharp division between 'the Right' and 'the Left' among academic economists. The Right has come up with a theory of the 'withering away of the state', based ironically enough on work done by Professor Galbraith (who himself can hardly be called a 'Right' economist). Galbraith's thesis of the domination of the US economy by what he calls 'the technostructure' has been used by economists of the Right to argue that the multinational is the first truly international economic organisation that has evolved in human history.[11] The multinational will raise capital in those parts of the world where funds can be obtained cheaply, invest these funds where labour costs are low and thus tend to equalise factor incomes all over the world. The Left insists that such a transfer process will never occur, mainly because the integration that can take place under the multinational is unlikely to reduce international inequalities.[12]

If the multinational corporation is to be an important agent of development and if the type of integration that it aims at promoting is to contribute towards an elimination of international inequalities, surely its main impact must be on factor productivity in LDCs. The Right argues that an increase in factor productivity will be brought about by a gradual process of technology transfer from the developed to the developing countries. The Left disagrees with this position. This question is of the utmost importance, for the economic division of the world between the developed and underdeveloped countries is – as this book has argued throughout – determined primarily by the technological advancement of the former and technological backwardness of the latter. The unequal relationship between the 'north' and 'south' is characterised by the technological dependence of the latter on the former. If, and if alone, the multinational demonstrates an ability to reduce this dependence, it can be argued that it is capable of promoting international development. What is the potential of the multinational corporation as an agency for the transfer of technology to the LDCs?

10.4 THE MULTINATIONAL CORPORATION AS AN AGENT OF TECHNOLOGY TRANSFER[13]

Professor Vernon has argued that, for many years to come, developing economies will not be in a position to develop modern science-based industries. He has developed the now well-known technological gap theory of trade[14] which runs in terms of a product cycle. It is only in the second stage, i.e. perhaps many years after the commercialisation of a given innovation, that the developing economies can hope to start producing the commodity concerned. The increased emphasis on the production of capital-intensive and research-intensive goods in the developed countries may not be totally disadvantageous from the point of view of the developing economies. Ideally, the importing of technically superior goods should increase the technological potential and absorptive capacity of the developing economy.

The multinational corporation has been a source of technology transfer to the underdeveloped countries. Broadly speaking, the problems it has faced are related to certain institutional characteristics of underdeveloped economies. These are problems of adjusting the needs and demands of science-based industries to traditional industries, problems of the replacement of conventional techniques and patterns of production by new methods, problems of technological bottlenecks and problems of adequate social and economic responsiveness to rapid structural change.

Technology transfer takes place in many forms, the most usual being either direct investment or some form of co-operation between the multinational corporation and domestic enterprises. The following paragraphs discuss problems that arise when the transfer takes the forms of direct investment, joint ventures, licensing and management contracts and sales.

10.41 *Direct Investment*

The multinational corporation invests in underdeveloped countries with a view to taking advantage of expansion in demand as the economy of the country in question develops or to protecting its stake in the market which might be threatened by tariff barriers. Hakam's study of foreign firms operating in Nigeria,[15] Gordon and Grommers' study of US private investment in Brazil[16] and Micksell's study of US foreign investment as a whole[17] all lend support to the view that the desire to protect existing markets is perhaps the most important motivation for the setting up of subsidiaries by multinationals in the developing economies.

The emphasis on the 'market protection' hypothesis points to the conclusion that industrial investment in the developing countries is more likely to come from firms already involved in the market of the country concerned than from new investors. This is also to be expected because the insider has greater knowledge about the potentialities of a project within the economy and because the cost to him of investing may be less than to an outsider, due to the existence of a network of distribution and sales organisations under his control.

Having decided to invest in a developing economy, a multinational corporation has to tackle the important problem of how best to manage the local subsidiary unit that has been set up. In the developing economies, successful growth and production demand efficient top-quality management. The managers of the overseas subsidiary of the multinational face several special problems: the operating environment differs from that of the home country; the subsidiary is open to criticism from public opinion in the host country; often nationals with different, and possibly inferior, levels of technical training have to be employed; managers have to be locally recruited; and 'special' relations with the government of the host country have to be worked out. As a result of all these factors there is a tendency to 'leave at home potentially useful technical concepts and managerial techniques and practices. This is particularly so in the areas of labour management, production control, and procurement, which are generally under local supervision.'[18]

Thus direct investment by the multinational corporations tends to be restricted to a relatively small group of industries which either can easily be controlled from the metropolis or do not require rapid changes in production and marketing methods. The growth of both of these types of industries cannot be expected to contribute directly, to a significant extent, towards the diffusion of technical and scientific knowledge within the LDC.

10.42   *Joint Ventures*

Multinational corporations seek local collaboration for a wide range of reasons. The most important is the need for local intermediaries, who are necessary to cope with officialdom, to obtain licences and to get sympathetic interpretation of regulations. Mediation with local financiers is another incentive to collaboration, particularly for firms primarily interested in the sale of know-how and licences and for firms which wish to keep their own financial commitments to a minimum. Local partners also usually handle sales, labour relations and publicity. In developing economies, when partnerships take place there seems to be a rigid functional specialisation; the multinational deals mainly with technical operations, management, foreign supplies and finance, and the local partner plays the role of mediator and deals directly with the local market.

In general, developing economies have tended to prefer the purchase of licences and know-how to the establishment of joint ventures, and the establishment of joint ventures to the setting up of independent subsidiaries by the multinational corporation. Nevertheless, in 1963 US multinationals owned approximately 18,000 foreign affiliates in which they held over 25 per cent of the equity. The United Kingdom, France and Switzerland held 1,800, 800 and 700 foreign affiliates respectively.

There seems to be very definite preference on the part of multinational corporations for wholly owned affiliates. 'United States parent companies move towards a partnership only when they are pushed to do so.'[19] European companies share these tendencies.

There are many reasons why a multinational corporation should seek control of a foreign enterprise. Fundamental is the inherent logic of the process of efficient management, which demands effective centralisation and co-ordination of decision making. Furthermore, in developing areas especially there are likely to emerge situations in which the global strategy of a multinational may necessitate the adoption of policies or actions which may be detrimental to the interest of the domestic enterprise or public authority of the country concerned.

On the whole, joint ventures tend to work better in developed countries since the contracting partners are of equal bargaining strength and possess similar technical and managerial potential. The OPEC countries seem to be encouraging the growth of joint ventures and expecting these enterprises to contribute significantly towards technology transfer to the OPEC countries. When multinational corporations set up joint ventures in developing countries, the scope for misunderstanding, mistrust and suspicion is greater, as the junior partner is usually not in a position to assess the deal that the multinational offers it.

On the other hand, the junior partner is unable to contribute towards the evolution and development of a technology that would allow the corporation to make a better use of the resources of the LDCs. Hence joint ventures between multinational corporations and local enterprises also tend to be confined to industries that use the technology developed largely in the rich countries. Joint ventures have not proved to be better channels of technology transfer to the LDCs than the subsidiaries of the multinationals.

10.43 *Licensing*
Licensing an independent company to use the patents and trademarks of the multinational corporation is becoming an increasingly important source of technology transfer. Patents and know-how are

licensed much more frequently than trademarks. According to Behrman's study, 20 per cent of all licences issued were for patents, trademarks and know-how, and 49 per cent for patents only.[20]

About 85 per cent of all licences are given to firms in the developed countries. The licensing of independent companies is more important than the licensing of affiliates. According to returns from 207 US licensors during 1957 and 1959, they held 4,114 foreign licensing agreements, of which two-thirds were with independent companies. However, the subsidiaries and affiliates that were licensed accounted for 80 per cent of all affiliates of US multinational corporations. The reasons for licensing a subsidiary are usually financial or legal. If exchange restrictions favour the remission of royalties paid for know-how or patents rather than the remission of dividends, or if there is a tax advantage, the multinational may choose to licence or sell patents to its subsidiary.

The possibility of a profitable return on royalties is a major inducement for licensing. Non-royalty income in the form of dividends may also be sought. Trade restrictions and restrictions on currency remittance may also provide an important reason for licensing.

The multinational corporation issuing licences takes into account also a number of factors besides direct profitability; Behrman's study also showed that, for nearly 80 per cent of US companies, income from foreign licensing accounted for less than 2 per cent of total income. There is a tendency to take the standard royalty rate prevailing in the country. The general practice is to impose a percentage royalty (of 1–10 per cent) on the sales of the licensee.

Import controls have been a major stimulus to licensing. Licences may become relatively useless, however, if import policy does not permit the import of the equipment necessary to make the licence worthwhile.

The expansion of business at home and the drive worldwide to keep up with new developments are in themselves an important incentive for licensing, because the results of research in the developed countries thus become available for transfer abroad. Between countries of the developed world licensing has tended to increase significantly over the last few years. The relative sophistication of production techniques has a bearing on the decision of the multinational corporation whether to invest or to give licences to local subsidiaries or partners. Parent firms prefer to issue licences for goods with short product cycles (e.g. pharmaceuticals). In underdeveloped areas, licensing is generally easy for the multinational, since the technological gap between it and the licensee is great and (usually) offers no threat to the corporation's technological leadership. But for industries where research and development costs represent a high proportion of expenditure, the multinational usually prefers to make direct investment. Furthermore, in considering whether to enter into a licensing arrangement the technical absorptive capacity of the recipient firm is also a major factor.

The areas of conflict between the parent and recipient firms with respect to technology transfer involve pricing, ownership and long-run technological development. These factors are usually affected by competition among parent firms, the relative bargaining power of the contracting partners and the policy of the host governments. It is commonly the developing countries' view that the price of technology is too high. They prefer licensing to foreign control. On the other hand, multinational corporations usually prefer direct investment to licensing in LDCs; the desire to maintain the quality of the product is cited as one reason for this preference.

The main reason for the meagre use of licences by multinational corporations lies first of all in the inappropriateness for the LDCs of the technology used in the developed countries. Second, the weak financial position of firms in the poor countries has reduced their bargaining power *vis-à-vis* the multinationals. This factor, along with their limited technological absorptive capacity and low marketing and production capabilities, makes them reluctant to invest in new technology, embodied or disembodied. The multinationals, on the other hand, consider firms in the LDCs to be incapable of assimilating technical know-how and hence prefer direct investment to licensing.

10.44 *Management Contracts and Sales*

The shortage of skilled personnel is an important characteristic of developing countries. Most of the top-level managerial staff employed by, for example, US multinational corporations have to be imported from the United States. Where joint ventures are set up, the multinational has to supply most of the technical and managerial staff, since it is usually responsible for the technical side of the business. Know-how is purchased from the multinational if it holds a minority interest in a joint venture. Data on the extent of such purchases has been prepared by the US Patent, Trademark and Copyright Foundation. This in the early sixties shows that thirty-three out of sixty-six US multinationals provided managerial services to their partners and subsidiaries as part of a capital contribution or under a licence agreement; twenty-nine companies sold managerial and other technical services, but only to those foreign enterprises which were licensees under patent or know-how agreements or were partners. It is maintained that the total return on the sale of management services is low relative to the return on licensing. The 1957 census of the US Department of Commerce showed that management fees from subsidiaries of the US multinationals were low. Subsidiaries working in the developing regions (mainly Latin America) were usually treated preferentially. However, fees for management services from *non*-licensees were high.

Furthermore, technical assistance agreements are also made between multinational corporations and their subsidiaries in foreign countries or independent foreign firms. Payment is usually on a royalty basis, but sometimes fixed sums are stipulated. In some cases, know-how is built into a foreign plant constructed by the multinational but payment is extended over a longer period and may not take the form of royalties on net sales.

Technical assistance contracts usually accompany patent or trademark agreements. To use the patent, special knowledge may be required, and if the seller refuses to disclose all the necessary knowledge along with the patent the technical assistance agreement becomes indispensable. Special techniques, for example, may be necessary to maintain the quality of a product or to produce it efficiently. Technical assistance may take the form of a guarantee on the part of the multinational to inform the foreign firms of all developments in this product line.

Technical assistance programmes include product specifications and layouts, formulas, 'trade secrets', selling techniques and the training of technical personnel. In developing economies, such agreements – both technical and managerial – are indispensable if foreign participation is desired. Usually they are part of the overall policy of a multinational corporation when it is investing in or collaborating with firms in developing economies.

The most important constraint on the multinational corporation as an agent of technology transfer to the developing countries has been the nature and character of modern technology itself. Expenditure on scientific and technological research is made with a view to the requirements of the developed countries. Much of the new science and technology has little or nothing to contribute towards the solution of the problems of the LDCs. Some of it is positively harmful, not merely in a global sense (typified by the increasing pollution consequent to industrial and urban growth) but also in a specific sense; e.g. the development of a number of synthetics has been, at least in the short run, of very real disadvantage to the primary-producing LDCs. 'For the mass of humanity science has probably brought more trouble than gain.'[22]

Technological development that is of relevance to the LDCs can take place within a number of organisations: international bodies, government agencies (in both LDCs and developed countries), consultant firms and multinational corporations. The multinationals can conceivably contribute significantly towards the development of the relatively more sophisticated technologies (e.g. communications technology, agricultural technology and technology used by the pharmaceutical industry) in accordance with the requirements of the LDCs. A change in production methods and marketing techniques will be required. The multinationals produce with methods that take the fullest advantage of economies of scale, and such economies of scale are, of course, unattainable in the large majority of small LDCs. The multinationals will have to explore the possibility of producing for small markets. More importantly, they will have to grapple with the problem of devising a capital-saving technology that nevertheless is efficient; a labour-intensive technology that inhibited the growth of factor productivity would be self-defeating in purpose. There is some evidence to prove that modern 'best practice' production technology, usually thought of as capital-intensive, actually economises on all factors of production. Moreover, as labour skill increases in the LDCs, a sophisticated and relatively capital-intensive technology will be required. This points to the fact that the transfer of technology to the LDCs involves the creation of an international institutional structure which will arrange for the provision of a bundle of embodied and disembodied technology suitable for the resource potential of the developing country concerned and will alter with the changes in the quality and quantity of the factors of production in the LDC.

The multinational corporations, however, are likely to consider technological improvisions for the OPEC countries, which are expected to be significant constituents of the international markets of most multinationals. The other developing economies will, however, assume some importance in one particular area. The multinationals are, it appears, eager to allow the LDCs to participate in the international division of labour that characterises the 'high technology' industries; the manufacture of computer punch cards in South America is an example of this form of participation. A multinational may ship the many components of a manufactured product to a low-wage country for assembly and processing and re-export the half-finished product to the metropolitan countries. A large number of LDCs are seriously considering the establishment of 'enclaves' which the multinationals may use for activity of this sort.

Even if the short-run effects of such investment are beneficial in terms of income generation within the LDC, it seems unlikely that the process of technology transfer from the developed to the developing countries will be adequately modified as a consequence of investment in assimilating and processing plants by the multinational corporations. The technology employed in such ventures will invariably be of an unskilled labour-intensive type which tries to capitalise on the relatively lower labour costs prevalent in the LDC. The backward and forward linkage effects of such production processes are likely to be low within the LDC; these linkage effects are produced within the production structure of the multinational itself. Similarly, the nature of the technology used by the multinational in manufacturing for export also precludes the possibility that the 'learning' effect of such investment will be substantial. The multinational is simply not interested in a diffusion of skill within the LDC when it sets up a processing plant in a low-wage country, for it requires such skill further along the production line.[22] Furthermore, the development of manufacturing for export by multinationals tend to increase the technological and financial dependence of the LDCs on the rich countries. The 'export-processing enclave' is completely unintegrated with the rest of the economy of the LDC; it is totally integrated into the marketing and production structure of the multinational. The LDC which possesses this enclave is in an extremely weak bargaining position *vis-à-vis* the corporation, for the latter is its only buyer. Since activities of this sort are extraordinarily 'footloose', the multinational is forever threatening the poor country with shifting production. The LDC is at the mercy of the multinational, and plant location, product diversification, market allocation and choice of technique decisions cannot be made without the consent of the foreign firm. It is unthinkable that a large-scale diffusion of appropriate technical knowledge to the LDCs can take place when their governments are for all practical purposes powerless before the multinationals.

The multinational corporation and the government of a developing country find themselves at cross purposes rather frequently. The multinational is perhaps the only organisation that will in the near future be capable of generating massive flows of embodied and disembodied 'hardware' and 'software' technology to the LDCs. In a world where aid and technical assistance programmes are shrinking daily, the multinational will in all likelihood increase in importance as the agent of technology transfer to the developing countries. However, the quantity and quality of technology supplied by the multinational leaves a great deal to be desired. The form of international economic integration that the multinationals seem to be aiming for will not, at least in the short-run, lead to a closing of the gap between the rich and poor countries. It is of extreme importance that the state should not be allowed to 'wither away' in the LDCs but should actively seek to influence the decisions of the multinationals investing in its country. Only then can it be hoped that the latter will be induced to consider seriously the adaption of existing technologies and the creation of new technologies so as to meet the specific requirements of the LDCs. The next section looks at the relationship between the multinationals and the governments of the developing countries.

10.5 MULTINATIONAL CORPORATIONS AND THE GOVERNMENTS OF THE DEVELOPING COUNTRIES

The investment undertaken by the multinational corporation is principally determined by expectations of profitability. The multinational operates in a way that increases income inequalities, both by an increase in the share of profit in the gross national income and by the relatively higher wages it is willing to pay to its employees. It tends to adopt a capital-intensive technology and hence is unlikely to contribute towards a reduction of unemployment. It also increases sectorial inequalities, for multinationals only invest in relatively few types of economic activities. Foreign investment therefore tends to reinforce the dualistic characteristics of a less developed economy.

It is inevitable that the governments of the LDCs will make some attempts to deal with these problems. This does not imply that the multinational corporations will have no strong allies in the poor countries. The ruling elite of a poor country may deliberately support a 'growth now, equality later' programme and be shortsighted enough not to recognise the nature of the two-way relationship between growth and equality. It will then permit the multinational to pursue policies that will accentuate economic inequalities. Similarly, 'progressive' governments, and even organised trade unions (though their strength in the developing world is almost non-existent), will tend to support the multinational as far as its labour policy is concerned. The introduction of collective bargaining, minimum wages, expensive social welfare services, etc. by the multinationals will be regarded as highly desirable. This is one field where the interests of the 'efficiency conscious' multinational and the 'progressive' governments will seem to coincide. However, such policies tend to increase income inequalities within the LDC and therefore to deter the development of the economy. They induce the local enterprise either to use capital-intensive techniques, or to scale down production, thus increasing the multinational's monopolistic control. The net effect of the high wage policies of the multinationals is thus unlikely to be beneficial to the people of the LDC *as a whole*.

The multinational corporation is a 'profit-seeking animal' and, as Paul Streeten has reminded us,[23] very little is to be gained by trying to convert it into a public service. The most sensible thing to do is to try to offset the social and economic inequalities created as a consequence of foreign investment by government policies that aim at controlling the multinational and at inducing it to transfer an increasing proportion of its profits to the government. The government should then use this money to reduce income inequalities within the LDC.

But to what extent can the government of a small underdeveloped country realistically hope to influence the decisions of a multinational corporation that has a subsidiary on its soil? Frankly, the outlook is anything but promising. Multinationals have developed an organisational structure that allows them to confront and challenge the decisions of the strongest and most powerful governments in the West. The governments of the Asian and African 'soft states' can hope to have only very limited influence on their policies. The head office of the company is located in Europe or the United States, and it is there that the most important decisions are made. The LDC will find that it has only restricted legal power over the multinational. Moreover, the multinational, will be able to circumvent the monetary and fiscal measures undertaken by the government of the LDC – by adjusting the prices of its inputs and outputs at different stages of production, by converting profits into management salaries, by drawing on the head office and other subsidiaries for funds, and by a hundred other methods. All this, of course, creates serious problems of domestic resource allocation as well as balance-of-payments disequilibria. The rather frequent use of the technique of wholesale and outright nationalisation of foreign enterprises by LDCs reflects mainly an increasing frustration on their part as a result of their inability to control the multinationals. If private international investment is to be an agent of development in the future, the problem of increasing the bargaining power of the LDCs *vis-à-vis* the multinationals will have to be seriously tackled.

There is little doubt that a great deal can be gained (from the point of view of development) through an increase in the bargaining power of the LDCs. The experience of the OPEC countries is a case in point. The way in which the gains from a specific economic activity are shared between the LDC and multinational corporation is determined by the relative bargaining power of the two. An increase in the bargaining strength of the LDC, reflected in reduced concessions to the foreign firm, will not usually induce the latter to cut down investment. Assuming that the government of a LDC is 'development minded', an increase in its ability to negotiate with the multinational will enable it to use a greater proportion of the gains occurring as a result of foreign investment for the purpose of off-setting the imbalances created by the multinational within the economy.

An increase in the bargaining power of the LDC means, above all, an increase in its ability to tax the multinational corporation. Under conditions of bilateral monopoly (oligopoly), the difference between the maximum tax rate which the multinational will be willing to pay for a given quantum of investment, and the minimum tax rate at which this investment can be regarded as profitable to the LDC, is quite wide. The LDCs find it difficult to determine the taxable capacity of the multinational and the maximum tax rate that can be levied. Moreover, due to competition between the LDCs to attract foreign investment, the maximum feasible tax rate is constantly declining. It is necessary to increase the ability of the LDCs to tax foreign investors, for the simple reason that investment invariably creates economic and social imbalances within the host country.

It is therefore necessary that the government of the LDC is able to implement economic policies that control the activities of the multinational corporations. The multinational is one agent among many that have to be taken into account by development planners. A 'development-oriented' government of a developing country has to create an environment in which different economic interest groups co-operate and function in a way that is conducive to the development of the economy. The extent to which the government will be able to influence the different economic groups will depend on its own bargaining strength. International integration based on co-operation between national states, conscious of development needs, will be preferred by the developing countries to the international integration that would result from an uninhibited expansion of profit-motivated foreign private investment. A growth in the ability of the LDCs to co-ordinate the investment policies of the multi-nationals their own national development plan will facilitate international economic integration along a pattern that will avoid glaring economic and social imbalances and inequalities.

NOTES

1 The figures are from N. Bloomfield, *The Pattern of Fluctuation in International Investment before 1914*, Princeton Studies in International Finance, No. 21 (Princeton, 1968).

2 Bloomfield, op. cit., p. 4.

3 G. Myrdal, *Economic Theory and Underdeveloped Areas* (London, 1957).

4 Figures are from DAC, *Development Assistance, 1971* (Paris, OECD, December 1971), p. 89.

5 B. Ward *et el.*, *The Widening Gap* (New York, Columbia University Press, 1971), pp. 238–9.

6 See DAC, op. cit., p. 89.

7 For an excellent review of the state of knowledge in this field, see G. L. S. Shackle, *Expectation, Enterprise and Profit* (London, George Allen and Unwin, 1969).

8 The term 'the international firm' is a misnomer and may introduce a lot of unnecessary confusion, as it implies that the multinational corporation is in some sense a supranational institution.

9 E. Penrose, *The Large International Firm in Developing Countries* (London, CUP, 1968).

10 P. Rothschild, 'Prices Theory and Oligopoly', *Readings in Price Theory* (New York, American Economic Association, 1947).

11 For Professor Galbraith's description of the role of the technostructure, see J. C. Galbraith, *The New Industrial State* (Harmondsworth, Penguin, 1967). For a view of the Right, see C. Kindleberger, *American Business Abroad* (Yale and London, 1967) and H. G. Johnson, 'The Multinational Corporation as an Agency of Economic Development' in B. Ward *et al.*, op. cit., pp. 242–52.

12 The Left position ranges very widely. See, for example: P. Streeten, 'Costs and Benefits of Multinational Enterprises in LDCs' in Dunning (ed.), *The Multinational Enterprise* (London, George Allen and Unwin, 1971), pp. 240–59; S. L. Hymer, 'The Multinational Corporation and the Law of Uneven Development' in Bhagvati (ed.), *Economics and World Order* (New York, 1970); and R. Murray, 'The Internationalisation of Capital and the Nation State' in Dunning (ed.), op. cit., pp. 265–89.

13 This section has incorporated some part of H. W. Singer and J. A. Ansari, 'The Multinational Corporation as Agent of Technology Transfer', OECD CT/4861.

14 R. Vernon, 'International Investment and International Trade in the Product Cycle', *Quarterly Journal of Economics* (May 1960).

15 A. N. Hakam, 'The Motivation to Invest', *Nigerian Journal of Economic and Social Studies* (March 1960).

16 M. Gordon and J. Grommers, 'United States Manufacturing Investment in Brazil,' *Harvard Business Review* (1962).

17 R. Micksell, *US Private and Government Investment Abroad* (New York, 1962).

18 T. Skinner, 'Management of International Production', *Harvard Business Review* (October 1964).

19 N. Behrman. *Some Patterns in the Rise of the Multinational Enterprise* (Chappell Hill, 1969).

20 N. Behrman, 'Direct Private Foreign Investment' in Miksell, op. cit.
21 Charles Cooper, 'Science and Underdeveloped Countries' in *Problems of Science Policy* (Paris, OECD, 1968), p. 51.
22 Some learning effect is, however, likely to be felt; e.g. there may be an improvement in management quality. But the 'skill' effect is unlikely to be pronounced.
23 P. Streeten, op. cit., pp. 240–63.

CHAPTER 11

International Labour Movements

Development is growth plus change, and change inevitably also has a geographical dimension involving the movement of labour from one sector of the economy to another, from one area of a country to another and, indeed, from one country to another. Generally speaking, people tend to move from low-income areas to high-income areas, from stagnant areas to rapidly expanding areas and from areas of poor or intermittent employment opportunities to areas where employment is more certain or guaranteed by contract. The economic, social and political consequences of such movements are deep and complex. They are somewhat neglected in the general development literature because they do not fit in with the classical theory of comparative advantages and subsequent trade theories, which are generally based on the assumption of immobility of labour.

Within developing countries there is a rapid, and in some cases overwhelming, flow of people, particularly landless people and more educated younger people, from the countryside into the town, creating fearful employment problems and social pressures. However, in connection with the relations between rich and poor countries we are less interested in such internal movements of labour and more interested in movements across frontiers, especially in labour movements from poor countries to rich countries. Obviously, some problems are common to both internal and international migration. For example, the effect on the rural community from which the migrants are removed is *prima facie* similar whether the migrants go to another area in the same country or go abroad; however, differences may arise if the pattern of sending remittances home or returning home to help with the harvest, or fill other seasonal labour requirements, is different for the international migrants, as it may well be.

Traditionally, international labour movements, like internal labour movements, can be attributed either to 'push factors' (e.g. lack of employment, low incomes, poor living conditions, dispossession from land, lack of access to land) or to the 'pull factors' (e.g. better incomes obtainable abroad, the preference for urban or foreign modes of living (the 'bright lights of the city'), the attraction of television etc., the provision of social security in another country and the absence of social security at home). The 'better incomes obtainable abroad' may be imaginary rather than real for the individual migrant or even for the migrants as a whole. Similarly, the improved social security for the international migrant may also be imaginary rather than real. The migrant may remove himself from the natural social security provided by the extended family or village community to an environment where it is a case of 'every man for himself'. More recently, with rising unemployment in the European countries, it has become evident that the migrants will be the first victims of economic recessions and unemployment, especially if they suffer from racial discrimination or linguistic handicaps.

Very special problems arise where migrants are highly skilled and trained people and constitute the brain drain from poor countries to rich countries. It is this aspect that this chapter begins by discussing.

11.1 BRAIN DRAIN

It is certainly striking and paradoxical that there should be important movements of high-level manpower from poor LDCs, in which the proportion of such manpower in the total labour force is very low, to rich countries where this proportion is already high. (The paradox is further heightened by the fact that under aid and technical assistance programmes an opposite movement takes place; i.e. high-level experts are shifted from the rich to the poor countries.) The extent of this brain drain is not particularly large in terms of absolute numbers, when related to total population. It is, however, very large in relation to the small stock and small new flow of such high-level manpower in the LDCs. In certain special fields, it is even high in relation to the total number of professional people in the rich country of immigration; e.g. the number of doctors moving from such underdeveloped countries as India, Pakistan and Egypt to the United Kingdom is by no means an insignificant fraction of the total UK supply of doctors. The figures are also somewhat questionable since it is not easy to distinguish between permanent and temporary migrants. There is a flow back to the LDCs, and this plus the immigration of technical assistance personnel may well mean that the balance is still towards the LDCs, but we cannot be certain of this and even less so of the extent of the two opposing flows.

At first sight it seems clear that such a brain drain must be a bad thing, certainly for the LDCs, which are losing their best people,

216

trained at considerable expense, but also for the world as a whole. Surely their scarcity value and worth to the world are much higher in LDC than in a rich country already swarming with such qualified people. When the question is put in this way it becomes clear that the answer must be, as usual, 'it all depends'. It depends on what the high-level professional would have done in his own poor country compared with what he is doing in the rich country to which he has migrated. Cases where the brain drain is good for the LDC and/or good for the world readily come to mind:

1 The migrating professional may be unemployed in his own country. The education system of some LDCs throws out, in certain special fields, more qualified people than the labour market of that country can afford to employ. This is true even of groups such as engineers in India and professional people of all kinds in Egypt. It cannot be said, of course, that there is no real *need* for more engineers in India or more doctors in Egypt. Rather, what is lacking is the effective *demand* for such people, due to poverty, to policy failures in the LDC or, perhaps, to the excessive salary expectations of the qualified people. Whatever the reason, the fact remains that if the qualified migrant would be unemployed in his own country, the LDC is not losing anything by his migration.

2 In some countries, high-level scientists and technologists may be suspect and in opposition to their government, and their alternative to migration may be gaol or guerilla activities. Or to take the opposite case, these highly skilled people may be so scarce that they all end up as ministers or high-level officials, not making much use of their specific scientific training. It can be argued that in such cases the brain drain is not the right solution for the problem. The best solution would be to change the domestic policies and situations which prevent the proper use of these scarce and valuable people at home. The brain drain, however, still appears as a second-best solution, preferable to the existing alternative. The loss of professionals through a brain drain may also serve as a spur to the LDC to make more effective use of such people.

3 If a migrating scientist or research worker is more effectively employed in the rich country where all the external facilities exist (e.g. equipment, libraries and above all the company of other related scientists), the effectiveness of his work may be much enhanced and, if he continues to work on the same problems, his value to both his own country and the world may be greater as a result of the brain drain. If the migrant previously worked on problems of high value to the LDC (e.g. doing research on

217

bilharzia or on drought-resistant crop varieties), his more effective research on the same problems with all the facilities available in a rich country may lead to a significant breakthrough, which otherwise would have occurred later or not at all. In many cases, such basic research does not have to be done within the geographical boundaries of the LDC, despite that the field applications are nearly always done better under actual conditions in the LDC than under simulated conditions in the rich country (though there are important exceptions to this rule).

4 At the other extreme, if the scientist or research worker was, in any case, working on problems more relevant to the general progress of science, the LDC is not losing much by his migration – except perhaps his value as a teacher and the stimulation of his presence among his colleagues. Many scientists and research workers in LDCs seem as much or more interested in the same general problems as their colleagues in the rich countries, rather than interested in problems of direct relevance to LDCs. This may be due to the common training of scientists or to the intellectual dominance of rich countries which makes their problems seem more sophisticated and exciting than those of LDCs. As distinct from the external braindrain, this situation may be defined as an internal brain-drain; i.e. the scientist etc. has intellectually migrated to the rich country, even though physically he may remain in his own country.[1]

The loss to the LDC of qualified people must be assumed to be larger than the incomes and salaries of those involved. It must be assumed that a highly trained scientist, doctor or engineer who is properly and fully employed makes a contribution to national income which is a high multiple of his own salary. This is so because of the external economies which his qualification makes possible in the work of others than himself. For the same reason, the loss must also be assumed to be greater than the direct costs of his education and training. These qualified people are also normally in the higher income groups, and their contributions through taxation, direct or indirect, are normally greater than the degree to which they benefit from government expenditure on health, social security, etc. All these considerations add to the social loss of the LDC. Since the migrant presumably gains privately from emigration, there is here a *prima facie* case of a clash between private and social costs and benefits (at least where the qualified person is properly and fully employed in his own country).

From the world's point of view, it must be assumed that a doctor in India looking after the serious diseases of Indians is more valuably employed than he would be in a rich country where the number of doctors is sufficient to cater for all serious cases and the additions are used for more marginal health services. This, of course, would not apply if the Indian doctor was in fact working in Delhi looking after the marginal health needs of a rich expatriate clientele who could otherwise easily obtain services abroad. This example shows the difficulty of general conclusions on the effect of the brain drain.

It is not difficult to think of further reasons why the brain drain may help the LDC: the emigrant scientist may stimulate interest in the scientific community of the richer countries concerning the conditions and problems of his own country; he may help students from his own country training in the richer country; he may return to his country as a fully trained man; or he may send remittance back from his high income. But basically the general presumption surely must be that the movement of skill and knowledge from the poor to the rich countries is the opposite to what is desired. Surely the movement should be the other way round. The forces of science and technology and high human skills are already all too strongly centred in the rich countries, where almost 99 per cent of the world's research and development expenditures are concentrated. This research is nearly all devoted either to the general progress of science and technology or to the specific interests of rich countries, i.e. the development of sophisticated new products or of complex new ways of replacing simple labour by abundant and much more efficient capital. In these circumstances, the general progress of science itself becomes automatically identified with the interests of the rich countries. The poor countries, with 70 per cent of the world's population, account for only 1 per cent of the world's research and development expenditures. A brain drain is needed, but it must be a brain drain from the rich to the poor countries, i.e. a reversal of the present flow.

Such a *desirable* brain drain can be brought about by physical external movement, i.e. by sending equipment, experts, teachers, etc. to the LDCs to strengthen their indigenous scientific and technological capacity or by sending doctors, economists, architects or other skilled manpower in short supply. There is, however, a second method. Just as there is an 'invisible' brain drain *from* the LDCs, so there can be an 'invisible' brain drain *to* the LDCs. The scientists and professional skills of the rich countries need not physically move to the LDCs as long as they concern themselves with problems directly useful to the LDCs rather than with problems irrelevant or even harmful to them (e.g. replacing their natural raw materials with synthetics). In this way, aid can be given to the LDCs in an effective and cheap way and without any aid money actually leaving the developed country.

The UN Advisory Committee on Science and Technology has suggested the quantitative target of devoting a fixed percentage (5 per cent of all research and development expenditure of the rich countries) to problems of special relevance to developing countries. In itself, such a target, of course, represents merely a set of empty boxes. However, in the UN World Plan of Action for the Second Development Decade the UN Committee subsequently filled the empty boxes by specifying some thirty or so concrete problems on the solution of which they suggested that the specified target percentage of research and development expenditure should be spent. These problems include such things as: extension of the Green Revolution (i.e. high-yielding varieties) from wheat, maize and rice to millet, sorghum, tuber crops, etc.; further development of new sources of edible protein; application of modern technology to fishing and exploiting new kinds of fish; new research on pest control suitable for small farmers; the use of tropical hardwoods and fibres for pulp and paper production; tracing and development of ground water; development of salt-resistant plants or use of sea water or brackish water for irrigation; control of bilharzia; cyclone-warning systems; use of indigenous building materials; and production of nitrogen fertiliser from natural gas. Nobody can say that the target represents empty talk; the problems have been placed on the agenda of the world community in general and of the scientific community in particular. Fortunately there are already some signs (e.g. in OECD) that the challenge is being taken up.

The goals suggested by the UN Committee have now become part of the UN Strategy for the Second Development Decade, unanimously voted by the General Assembly. It is a pity that the United Kingdom, together with many other rich countries, has entered a specific reservation refusing to accept the 5 per cent target, on not particularly convincing grounds. At the same time, however, the UK government has indicated that it does intend to increase the appropriations of public research and development expenditures for problems of special interest to developing countries (and indeed already has taken some action in this direction). As long as there is a movement from the present figure (which is probably less than 1 per cent) towards the 5 per cent target, perhaps the precise quantitative figure is not so important. All the same, it is to be hoped that the UK government and the other governments concerned will reconsider their position. The United Kingdom is in a good position to give leadership in this area. A target of 5 per cent to cater for the needs of 70 per cent of mankind hardly seems overambitious.

Apart from concrete problems of the kind mentioned in the UN World Plan of Action, it is also to be wished that more attention will be given to the more general questions of designing equipment suitable for smaller-scale production, equipment that is simpler to handle and easier to maintain and repair, as well as of simpler product design. In this connection, the proposal of general research centres for the development of labour-intensive technology – either in the form of an international centre jointly financed by the rich countries directly or through the United Nations, or in the form of more specialised institutions for the development of labour-intensive technologies in different sectors – deserves special attention.

In spite of all the emphasis on what the rich countries can do within their own borders, as it were, the equally great importance of building up the indigenous scientific and technological capacity of developing countries must not be forgotten. The minimum required here is to enable the developing countries to know of the technologies available, to be knowledgable about sources of supply, to be able to judge the suitability of different technologies for their own needs, to be able to negotiate with all the carriers of technology whoever they are (e.g. patent and licence holders, contractors, foreign investors, multinational companies and management consultants) and to adapt whatever technologies are brought in to special local conditions. With these rather formidable requirements, so far beyond the capacity presently attained by all but a few of the developing countries, the choice of indigenous technology versus imported technology is completely false. A country must have indigenous capacity in order to be able to import technology advantageously. Over a long stretch of development, the two are complementary rather than alternatives. Only where indigenous capacity exists is a real choice possible in the case of specific concrete projects or industries.

For the sake of completeness a third type of brain drain should also be mentioned; this may be called the 'fundamental' brain drain. The human brain is entirely formed by a process of protein synthesis and is virtually complete at three or four years of age. Many or most children in developing countries suffer from protein insufficiency, which may prevent the full development of the brain and may result in lasting and irreversible mental retardation in the sense that the full brain potential of the individual affected fails to develop.[2]

With six out of seven children nowadays being born in the poor

221

countries, the loss to mankind as a whole of its potential supply of Newtons and Einsteins is incalculable. In any rational world the prevention of this type of brain drain, by providing young children with the proper protein, would be a top priority. All too often, when we talk about the brain drain we forget not only about the invisible drain but also about this even more fundamental drain which represents one of the basic obstacles to economic development.

Measures which the LDCs could take to reduce the brain drain – and which the rich countries could support by their own action – include an emphasis on training qualified people inside the LDCs rather than on sending them on fellowships abroad to the rich countries. The latter will always present a temptation to stay or to come back to renew links forged during training. At present, the rules of many technical assistance programmes rather absurdly make it possible to finance trainees for fellowships in the donor country, but not to finance their training in their own country even if there are training institutions with vacant places. As a second measure, developing countries could also be fully entitled to insist on 'bonding' their highly trained and qualified people, requiring them to work for some years in their own country – preferably in rural or otherwise undersupplied areas (e.g. doctors in rural areas) – before they are eligible for emigration to a rich country. The rich countries could assist in this by refusing to accept qualified people from LDCs until they had discharged their bonding obligations.

One particular danger of the brain drain lies in the high degree of income inequality which it enforces on the LDCs. The incomes of highly qualified people are usually a much higher multiple of the average living standard in the LDCs than in the rich countries; as a result, overall income inequalities are also much more marked in the LDCs. Attempts to reduce these inequalities, either directly or indirectly through taxation, tend to come up against the obstacle of free international mobility of qualified people, and their income levels are influenced by what they can get in the rich countries. This often prevents the kind of more egalitarian policies which developing countries should adopt to cope with their problems of poverty and unemployment.

11.2 MIGRATION OF LESS QUALIFIED LABOUR

Such movements have been traditional in Africa (e.g. migratory labour from Malawi moving to South Africa, Rhodesia or Zambia). Two more striking and more recent examples of such movement are the migration of labour from Mediterranean countries to Europe as 'guest workers' and from India, Pakistan and Jamaica to the United Kingdom in the postwar period. This is largely a result of the full-employment policies followed in the postwar period by the developed countries – yet another reminder[3] that some of the most effective forms of aid which rich countries can render to the LDCs is action within their own borders. Full employment at home may be more valuable in providing export earnings for the LDCs, as well as work for their surplus labour, than special preference or concessions.

The movement of less qualified labour, on balance, is probably an advantage to the LDC. Remittances from migrants and the accumulated savings of returning migrants are of considerable importance to many of the LDCs involved. Moreover, the additional skills and experience acquired in the rich country may be a valuable asset to the LDC when the migrants return.

This migration often relieves the pressures in the LDC arising from the rapid population increase, the rate of urbanisation, the cost of infrastructure and the need for additional employment opportunities.

At the same time, migration benefits the workers in the rich country in so far as it results in their upgrading. This, however, is contingent upon the maintenance of full employment; any lapse from this would arouse popular resentment against the migrant workers who 'take our jobs'.

The calculation of the cost and benefit to the LDC of labour migration is complicated and comes out differently for different countries and different types of labour, for it depends crucially on what the alternatives to migration are. It is possible that if labour were not able to migrate from the LDC to the capital and employment opportunities in the rich country, the capital and employment would move from the rich country to the cheaper labour in the LDC; this scenario might or might not be more favourable to the LDC, depending on the effectiveness of its policies towards investors and foreign capital. Moreover, migration might reduce the pressure on the government of the LDC to provide employment at home, making the economy vulnerable and ill-prepared to cope with sudden reductions or reversals in the flow of migration.

Again it is possible to think of action by the rich countries which would help to increase the benefits to the poor countries of such migration. For instance, the practice in the South African mines to pay Malawi workers a large bonus at the end of their labour contract, of perhaps three years, probably maximises the volume of savings brought back to Malawi. Also the rich countries could pay special attention to the training of migrant workers to prevent them from doing only the unskilled jobs which the workers of the rich countries were increasingly unwilling to take on. It would also help if the rich countries were less selective, accepting unskilled workers along with skilled and accepting wives, children and old relatives along with the workers themselves.

NOTES

1 Although he will almost inevitably spend a good deal of his time also physically abroad attending conferences, meetings or on study leave or scholarships.
2 This is, of course, further added to by the lack of educational facilities and general stimulation and by widespread physical illness.
3 The case of adjustment assistance has already been mentioned previously as falling within the same category.

Index

INDEX